Don't Cry, Ninotchka

May all, your
dreams come true.

Nina Treece

Nina Carmichael Treece

International Standard Book Number
Trade paperback: 978-1-7331308-1-3

Design and production:
Cohographics, Salem, Oregon
www.cohographics.com

Printed in the U.S.A.

Coho Publishing
www.cohopublishing.com

DEDICATION

I wrote this book for:
My sons—Barry, Brian, Donny, and David.
My grandchildren—Matthew, Nathan, and Brianna.
My great-grandsons—Kyler, Aiden, Clayton, and Maksim.
And the future generation to follow.

I dedicate this book to:
Mama and Papa.
Because of their bravery, we are all living in America.

My gratitude goes to:
My husband Ron,
For encouraging me throughout this entire writing project.

Contents

FOREWORD

The more I wrote, the lighter I felt

More than ten years ago, my grandson, Matt Carmichael, had asked me to write the story about my life.

At first all I could do was write down a single page of facts. I used a pencil and, when I read what I had written, erased most of it and started all over again. This went on for many months.

After I joined Pat Love's writing class, my writing improved. Later, I talked my friend Marilyn Cady into leading another writing group.

As I read my stories in class, people kept asking me for more details, and so my stories grew. Marilyn urged me to write down my feelings, which was hard for me to do. I felt that they were private and should not be shared. When she finally convinced me, I discovered that writing about the horrors and pain I had experienced was therapeutic.

And so, this became a story of survival, my search for courage, and things I had to do. As a teenage girl living in Germany I was not dreaming of romance. I was dreaming of America where food was abundant. As a grown-up, I had to work and take care of my children. Safety and security were top priorities in my life.

I want my family to know how very grateful my parents and I were to be allowed to come to America. I want them to appreciate America, and all the blessings, freedom and opportunities they have here.

I had no intention of publishing my story. But all the people in my writing class encouraged me to do so. Friends who edited my writing also told me that I should publish, some of them even insisted.

I am still not fully comfortable about strangers reading private family matters. For that reason, I have categorized the contents of this book. That way the readers can choose the stories that sound interesting to them.

Everything that I have written, to the best of my recollection, is the truth. All of the dates and times may not be exact, but I have tried hard to state the facts accurately. Some of my family members may have seen things differently because they witnessed it from a different perspective, but this is *My Story*, written in *My Words*, and this is how I experienced it.

An Immigrant's Tale and Plea

Nina Carmichael Treece, October 27, 2017

I was small and alone with no friends of my own,
I was afraid and I cried, but there was no room inside.
The shelter was full, the fence was not safe,
There was nowhere to hide, but I tried to be brave.
The bombs fell like rain and the world was insane.
Mama found me somehow, and she hugged me so tight.
The strength of her love made the world seem alright.

We lived in a country where there was no hope.
The children were cruel and I could not cope.
I prayed to my God, "Please let me die."
But He gave me strength and soothed my cry.
I dreamed of America, a land far away,
That would welcome us all, and we would go there someday.

We loved this new land, folks were friendly and kind,
We were happy and free, and all of one mind.
I gave birth to four sons.
But there was also great pain,
When my son passed away, God kept me sane.
We built a home on the river.
We worked hard, and were proud,
We were not afraid,
And we could speak out loud.
But America has changed, and I am dismayed!

I pray to our God,
"Please protect this land,
And help us humans to understand,
That we are all brothers and sisters, that You love us all,
And hold us all, in the palm of Your hand."

PART I
Russia, Poland, and America, 1942–1954

In 1939, Stalin signed a nonaggression pact with Germany. But in 1941 Hitler invaded Russia, and the 900-day siege of Leningrad began. Because of that, all of the Russian-Germans living in Russia and Ukraine became enemies of the Russian Government, and had to escape to avoid being sent to Siberia, or be killed.

During 1941, the rapid advance of the German Wehrmacht into the USSR saved some 350,000 Russian-Germans from deportation to Kazakhstan and Siberia. The vast majority of the people that had been spared from Stalin's ethnic cleansing in 1941 lived in Ukraine.

During 1942–1944, the German military evacuated most of these Russian-Germans westwards. *

We were part of that group of people fleeing Russia by covered wagon.

---

* *Inserts in italics are excerpts from: Germans from Russia Heritage Collection (GRHC) https://library.ndsu.edu/grhc/ with permission.*

Introduction

My full name is Nina Vladimirovna Dolgodusheva—(Lina) Streich—Nina Carmichael Treece.

I have lived in four countries, speak three languages, and have an accent in every one of them. When I speak Russian, I sound Czechoslovakian; in German I sound like an American; in English I sound like German, Russian, or a mix of both. My children shake their heads, and insist that I don't have an accent. I just sound like Mom.

After we arrived in America, I tried very hard to sound and be like an American. I even tried using slang, which confused everybody and made it even harder for people to understand me. But the accent has remained to this day, and gets worse every time I speak another language.

I was born 1938, in Rohalik, a small Ukrainian village, near Sulin, about 25 miles from Millerovo. My mother, Valentina Schivilowa, and my biological father, Vladimir (Volodka) Grigoryovich Dolgodushev, were both native Ukrainians.

My papa went to war in 1941 with the Russian Army to fight the invading Germans.

After he left, Mama and I lived with my papa's family. Mama was very unhappy. She said that her mother-in-law (my grandmother) and my papa's two sisters hated her and treated her like a slave. They also neglected me. When Mama came home from working in the fields, she would often find me outside, dirty, hungry and crying. She would clean and feed me. But after that, she did not have time for me because there was always work waiting for her.

I don't know why she did not go live with her mother, her two sisters, Shura and Froysa, or her brother Simon. I know that she worked in a coal mine before she married; maybe that's what was waiting for her there.

Mama got involved with Wilhelm Streich, a Russian-German. And in 1942, during World War II, they escaped from Russia and took me with them. Mama must have been desperate, to go on this dangerous journey with Wilhelm, and leave all of her family behind.

When I was a grown woman, Mama told me, "Nina, you don't know. You don't know how it was for me. I felt alone. No one was helping me, and I could not live like that."

I told her, "Mama don't cry. I'm glad that you left Russia and took me with you. I know that my life is so much better here in America."

But I did love and miss my real papa, and I know that he loved me too. I was told that when he came home from the war in 1945 and found Mama and me gone, he was heart-broken. He looked for us everywhere.

After a time, my papa remarried and had two more daughters. Raya was born in 1947, and another, Nina (named so, at my papa's insistence), was born in 1949. I did not know that I had two half-sisters until my Aunt Froysa came to America for a visit in 1978, and told me everything.

My half-sister Nina wrote to me in 1991, and told me, "Our father worked as a Grain Harvester/Combine Operator. He kept house himself because he liked to do it. He bought Raya and me presents and played with us no matter how tired he was. So, you can see he loved his children very much." She finished the letter with, "Sadly our father died, November 7th, 1951, of a heart attack."

The last time I saw my papa was before he went to war. I was only three years old, so I don't remember him consciously. But I do remember a woodstove made out of bricks. It was about 4 or 5 feet tall, with a large flat area on top, and enclosed by bricks on three sides. That made a wonderful, warm sleeping area during the very cold Russian winters. I have a vague memory of two strong arms holding me, then lifting me up and putting me into that warm place.

Another memory of my papa came much later.

In 2005, my husband and I traveled by train through Mexico, to the Copper Canyon. The canyon was impressive, but we really enjoyed seeing the villages, and how the rural Mexican people lived.

In one small village with its quaint little houses, and dirt packed narrow roads, I had a very strong feeling of déjà vu.

Walking through that village gave me the strangest feeling in the pit of my stomach. It was a mixture of sadness and longing which I cannot explain. But that village felt so familiar. I just knew that I had walked through that same kind of village in Ukraine, with my real papa, when I was a small child. But it felt like I was much taller, so I must have been sitting on my papa's shoulders.

In that moment I felt so close to him that I got very emotional and started to cry. I did not feel like I was in Mexico at all. I felt like I had come back home and was with my real papa at last!

*Papa, and Nina—
wearing his hat*

Escape from Russia, 1942

I was about four years old when we started our escape from Russia. The journey took two years. I only remember the last part of our journey.

Following are excerpts from the *Germans from Russia Heritage Collection* website. It gives a more detailed description of our "Long Trek" and our arrival in Poland. I have included this in my memoir so that my family, or whoever reads my story, can get a more detailed account of that time in history than I can provide.

Life, Fear and Death on the long Trek

German-Ukrainian groups who departed from Ukraine on foot or by wagon and were part of the "Long Trek" from 1942-1944, faced many challenges. Upon receiving the order to evacuate, they hurried to repair wagons and harnesses. With the specter of advancing Soviet troops seeking revenge on all Germans looming over them, the villagers' trepidation can only be imagined, especially when they saw long wagon trains from neighboring eastern communities already streaming past them. Amid that frenzy, they often could take with them only basic necessities, and some farm animals.

Sometimes refugee families had to share the few available wagons. Whenever possible, the children were placed in the heavily laden wagons and the adults proceeded on foot. At times the children had to walk alongside the wagons with the adults. On the roads, the caravans were quite exposed and vulnerable to the harsh natural elements. It is not hard to imagine the many inconveniences and difficulties involved for pregnant women, children, the sick, and the elderly.

Malnutrition and outright hunger remained a persistent problem. Occasionally, refugees had to set up makeshift shelters or find abandoned farms and barns in which to stay. Sometimes they even slept under the stars. Depending on the terrain, weather, and other factors, a typical day's journey on foot and by wagon covered between 5 to 15 miles, but sometimes more.

The winding wagon caravans stretched out for miles, slithering their way westward. Poor roads and steep hills presented hurdles along the route, not to mention the constant worry of not finding enough food, as well as fodder for the draft horses and livestock. Wagon caravans at times had to stop at villages for a number of days because of bad weather and other logistical problems. When wagons broke down, fellow refugees or other wagon trains would not necessarily stop to help repair a broken spoke or wheel. But there were random acts of kindness, as well as generous offerings of food and shelter. Sometimes refugees who wandered off the main routes during a pause in the journey in order to feed their livestock, gather firewood, or secure food, simply never returned, having been picked off by guerrillas.

Not least of all, the menacing shadow, the Soviet army always pursued the caravans, and at times refugees would hear the sound of distant guns on the fluid battlefront.

In the spring of 1944, some of the more unfortunate wagon caravans fell victim to intermittent Soviet attacks and even capture.

Our wagon train was one of those.

Our Journey, 1942–1944

Mama, was born in Sulin, Ukraine, her ancestors were Ukrainian. But because of the war between Russia and Germany, and her involvement with Wilhelm Streich, who was a German-Russian, she too, became an enemy of Russia and we had to escape or be sent to a Siberian *Gulag* (labor camp).

Wilhelm Streich was born in the Odessa region of Russia. His ancestors were German. They immigrated in the 1780s, when Catherine the Great offered free land to any Germans who settled in Russia. Thousands came; they were hard-working and smart. They prospered but many of them kept to themselves.

Stalin's ethnic cleansing, started in 1936, had killed or sent thousands of Odessa and Volga Germans to Siberia to work as slaves in the labor camps.

After Hitler invaded Russia in 1941, all of the remaining German settlers were considered enemies of Russia. Their homes were confiscated by the Russians, and they were killed or sent to Siberia.

Getting ready for the journey

Mama, Wilhelm, and I, joined a wagon train with other Odessa-Germans who were also escaping Russia. Our destination was Poland and then Germany. The German Army helped the Ukrainian-Germans to escape.

We had two covered wagons (somewhat like the covered wagons of the American pioneers) hitched together; they were pulled by four horses. The back wagon held most of our belongings and we lived in the front wagon.

There were three families in our group: Wilhelm, Mama and me, Mr. and Mrs. Klimusch (a very nice older couple), Gottfried and Anna Frank, and six-year-old son Viktor. There was not enough room for all of us in the wagons. To spare the horses, the adults (and sometimes Viktor and I) had to walk beside the wagons.

At the beginning of our journey, I cried for my real papa. Mama tried very hard to get me to call Wilhelm "Papa" because it was important for our safety. It took a long time, and many bribes, such as a new dress, before I finally gave in and called him Papa.

The wagon train varied in size as we moved with the flow of the war. Often, we saw abandoned farms; sometimes we stopped and lived there for a prolonged period of time to rest, gather food, repair our wagons, and rest our horses.

We left when we ran out of food, or when we were told by the German Army Patrol that the war front was getting close. We would then continue westward. We slept in or under our wagons or wherever we could find shelter.

We endured many hardships. Sanitation was either very poor, or nonexistent. I had my head shaved twice because of lice. I remember Mama and I de-lousing each other. I loved the intimacy we had during those times. I felt loved and wanted and close to my mama. It felt good to have Mama comb my hair, and then caress my head with her fingers while she looked for the remaining lice. In between de-lousing I scratched my head until it bled. So, my new papa shaved my head. Thankfully, the louse and bedbug infestations ended after we moved into our permanent home.

We scavenged for food or begged whenever we came close to a farm or a village. Sometimes the villagers took pity on us, but there were times when they chased us away. We were often hungry, and there was nothing to eat. I remember crying and begging, *"Mama, ya chotschu kuschat, poszalustwa dai meney kuschat."* (I am hungry, please give me something to eat).

She would say, "Ninotchka (an endearing, diminutive form for Nina) I don't have anything to give you. Just think of something else, or lie down and sleep for a while." I am certain that Mama often gave me part of her own ration of food.

—The memory of being hungry has stayed with me my entire life. To this day I cannot throw good food away. I know that even now there are hungry children in the world begging their mamas for food, and I can empathize with them. I know how they feel.

The Russian winters were brutal. Frostbite was a common occurrence. At times my legs got so cold that my mama would bind them together like a mummy. Because of that cold weather, I have had circulation problems throughout my life.

We were always in danger of losing our lives, either from bombings, whenever the war front got close, or from Bandits who roamed the land.

When someone became ill, most of the time there were no doctors or medics available. Occasionally a German

Army Ambulance would come along. Otherwise, all we could do was use home remedies and hope and pray that those remedies worked.

We saw the aftermath of Russian bomb attacks, dead and dying people along the road, as well as dead horses and broken wagons. Some people were missing arms or legs. They were in such agony that they begged for death.

Thankfully, I have forgotten most of the horrors, but one incident is still very clear in my mind. This happened towards the end of our journey, when I was about six years old.

All of the able-bodied men, including my new papa, Gottfried, and Mr. Klimush, were called away to help the German army dig trenches. The women were very upset because they knew that the men were going into danger. They worried about what would happen to them and their children if the men did not return. Some of the women, including my mama, couldn't even speak German.

A while after the men left, my mama became ill. I don't know what was wrong with her. I just know that an ambulance came by, and they insisted that she go with them. Mama did not want to leave me, so the ambulance driver promised to stay right in front of our wagon. However, after a short time, the ambulance went farther on ahead, and I was left without my mama. I was afraid, and kept crying for her to come back. To distract me, Mrs. Frank let me wear my new dress.

Soon after the Ambulance left with my mama, we heard airplanes approaching. The wagon train came to a halt, and everyone ran for cover. Most of the people ran into an old barn, which was near the road.

I refused to leave without my mama. Anna Frank and Mrs. Klimush tried very hard to get me to come with them, but I kept kicking and screaming. So, after a while they gave up and left me in the wagon. When I heard a loud explosion, I got scared and climbed off the wagon, but I hurried too much and tore my new dress. I was so upset about tearing my dress, that for a moment I forgot about the bombs.

Then I realized that I was on the wrong side of the road. The barn, where all of the people were hiding, was across the road. I tried to get around the wagons, but the horses and wagons were too close together.

I crawled under our wagon to get across. I barely got past the outside wagon wheel, when a bomb exploded nearby, which spooked the horses, and they all started running. I had come very close to getting trampled.

I tried to get into the barn where the people were hiding, but it was full, and they told me, "Go away." I stood there for a while, not knowing where to go. Then I saw people huddled against a fence, so I ran over there and found a spot where I could cling to the fence. I was alone and scared. I cried for my mama and begged her to come back to me.

I prayed: "I promise I will be good; I will do what you tell me. I will be quiet when you tell me and not even sneeze too loud. I will stop crying for my real papa, and I will call "the man" Papa. Please just come back to me."

Meanwhile, when the bombs started falling, my mama realized that the ambulance was no longer in front of our wagon. She pleaded for the driver to go back, but he refused. So, she started back on foot. When a plane came too close, she got into a trench with the German soldiers. In between the bombs falling, she continued to run.

Somehow, she found me still huddled against the fence.

I was so happy to see my mama! I told her about the promises I had made, and that I was sorry for tearing my new dress, but she was not angry.

She just kept hugging me and saying, "*Ninotchka, ne plakay, ne plakay, Ninotchka.*" (Ninotchka don't cry, don't cry, Ninotchka).

She kept shushing me and saying, "*Usyo budit charascho.*" (Everything will be fine).

When the bombing stopped, Mrs. Klimush, Anna Frank and Victor found us. They told us that our wagons were on the other side of a very large field. We saw people running in that direction, and we joined them.

But then, we heard the Russian airplanes approaching again. There was nowhere to hide this time, so we just kept on running. The bombs were falling all around us. The noise of the bombs exploding and people screaming was deafening. I could smell smoke, saw overturned wagons, big holes in the ground, and dead people all around us. A man was lying in a pool of blood, with his leg blown off. He was yelling, "*Bitte, bitte, schiess mich!*" (Please, please, kill me!) I stopped and stared at him, until Mama pulled me away. She held my hand more tightly, and we continued to run.

Even now, when I close my eyes and think back to that time, I can hear the exploding bombs, and how shrapnel sounds. It is a high, shrill sound, unlike any other I have ever heard. I am amazed that we survived that Hell. When I see movie scenes of bombings, I have flashbacks, my memories come back, and I tremble. I see myself running through that field, and I cry for that terrified little girl, trying to survive in a world gone mad.

It seemed like the bombing went on for an eternity, but eventually it stopped. Many people were dead or injured. Thankfully, none of the people from our wagon were killed. We found our wagons undisturbed, and our horses alive. We continued on our way to Poland with the remaining wagon train.

Not long after that bombing incident, my "new papa" and the other men returned from helping the German army dig trenches. We were thankful and glad to see them.

We had a big celebration. The men had brought a sheep back with them, and they roasted it on an open fire. It had been a long time since we'd had meat, and the smell of that meat roasting was agonizing. My mouth was watering. I could hardly wait for the meat to be done.

There was plenty of meat for everyone, and we were happy. Somebody started playing an accordion and we were all singing and dancing. In that moment hunger and the war seemed very far away. Soon after the men got back, we continued on our journey, and within a short time we arrived in Poland.

World War II History: Poland

The city of Lodz (Litzmannstadt) by mid 1944 contained the last major Jewish ghetto in all of Europe; only the Warsaw ghetto had been larger before the Nazis liquidated it just a year earlier. As the EWZ (Immigration Main Office), processed the final waves of the Ukrainian German flood, SS (Special Action) deported nearly all of the remaining 74,000 Jews to Auschwitz's gas chambers. More than 200,000 Jews had lived in the Lodz ghetto as of 1942.

By the end of the war, over 3 million Polish Jews were dead, with only 50,000 to 70,000 surviving. Between 1941 and 1945, Nazis established six extermination camps in Poland. An estimated 3.5 million Jews were killed. Other victims were gypsies and Soviet prisoners of war.

Arrival and processing in Lodz (Litzmannstadt), Poland

From January 1940 until January 1945, the Polish city of Lodz (Litzmannstadt) served as the EWZ headquarters. The EWZ stood for: Einwanderungszentralstelle (Immigration Main Office), as the Third Reich's "Ellis Island," the EWZ at Lodz functioned as the central distribution point, welfare office, and archival repository for all ethnic Germans from across Europe, above all the occupied eastern territories.

In Lodz, all new arrivals first took a bath or shower for "delousing," soon followed by screening, registration and ultimately final resettlement. The EWZ consisted of various departments, such as administration, planning, accounts and registration, health and nationality matters.

Extensive registration procedures were involved with the EWZ. Usually 6 to 9 staff members conducted each screening session, which normally lasted 3 to 4 hours. Over time, as workloads increased, the session was

Litzmannstadt (Lodz) Ghetto Entrance

extended to six hours, then two days. Though families were always processed together, all individuals aged 15 and over were registered separately.

EWZ processed each family at a total of eight stations.

*At the **first station**, a policeman scrutinized the family's papers and added any missing forms. The **second station** prepared identification papers and compiled all personal information. After a photographing session at **station three**, the family proceeded to **station four**, at which all property matters were settled. The amount of property left behind was ascertained, and the resettlers were issued receipts stating how much and what type of compensation they were to receive.*

The primary EWZ form included sections to fill in one's name, age, place of origin, date of entry, and two photos (full face and profile). Each individual file also established an applicant's German background through so-called "national passport" (Volkstumausweis) or "resettler status form," which often had been issued to ethnic Germans during the Nazi occupation of the East in 1942. In addition, the "family form" identified the ethnic backgrounds of an applicant's parents, spouse, and children. Family histories were extensive, sometimes going back as far as four generations to prove German ancestry.

*The **fifth station**, was the most important. Designated as the physical examination station, it in fact performed racial examinations. The examiners had instructions to be discreet, since Himmler wanted the resettlers to think that these inspections were medical, not racial.*

*At **station six**, a family's political status faced scrutiny from the SS security police services. Interestingly, most of*

*the refugee cases from the eastern territories, including
the Soviet Union, passed these political examinations,
unlike the majority of Volksdeutsche from the West.
Perhaps the SS factored in the more repressive and
extreme features of political life under Stalinism.
Indeed, the EWZ records give us a better sense of the
extent of persecution during the Stalinist era. Many
Soviet German especially during the worst periods of
state persecution in 1930, 1937 and 1938, fell victim to
Stalin's collectivization drives and mass political purges.*

Station seven *decided a refugee's occupation and final
placement. In consideration of racial and political
factors, this stage determined whether a family was
assigned to work in agriculture, industry, or other trades.*

The **eighth and final station** *consisted of a review
panel that evaluated all the examination results in
order to establish a family's classification, upon which
it provided refugees with identification cards and
documentation. Lumens' careful examination of Lodz
indicates two fundamental categories prevailing among
the refugees: "O-cases (Ost), those selected as colonists in
the East, and the A cases (Altreich), those designated to
remain in the Reich. The primary consideration for both
was racial quality.*

*According to Marion Wheeler's findings, the EWZ, by
the beginning of 1944, had registered about 771,000
ethnic Germans from all parts of Europe with most
coming from the USSR. Out of that total number, the SS
resettled roughly 403,000 into Eastern occupied areas
(O cases) more than 70,000 received jobs in Germany
proper (A cases), and about 18,000 were not permitted to
resettle at all.*

Poland, 1944–1945

We arrived in Poland in 1944, about two years after we had left Ukraine. Poland was still occupied by the German Army.

We lived in Litzmannstadt with many other Russian-German refugees. The town had a very large Jewish ghetto, and a nearby extermination camp. It was also a "people sorting area," similar to Ellis Island. But evil.

The Nazis decided who lived and who died, who was sent back to where they came from, who stayed in Poland as a slave worker, and who could go to Germany. Race and ethnic purity were major deciding factors. The Nazis decided how useful a person was to the Reich. My new papa had helped the German army dig trenches during our "Trek." He was also helping the Nazi's while we were in Poland, which made him a useful man. Mama and I were light skinned, so we were racially acceptable.

Although I do not remember seeing the extermination camp, I do remember the stench.

One day when I was playing outside with my friends, I noticed a terrible odor. "What is that smell?" I asked.

A boy waved his hand, and said, "Oh, it's nothing. They are just burning Jews."

"What are Jews?" I asked.

"They are very bad people."

"What did they do?"

"I don't know, but my dad says they are really bad."

"But why are they burning them?"

"To make soap."

"Soap? You are a liar. Nobody burns people to make soap."

"Oh yes they do. My dad saw it with his own eyes."

I got upset and ran into the house, screaming, "Mama, a boy said that they are burning Jews. What are Jews, and why are they burning them?"

Mama said, "Nina be quiet!"

I continued, "But Mama, if they are people, why are they burning them?"

Mama got very angry and yelled, "I said be quiet."

She came at me, shaking a big butcher knife that she was holding. I got scared and hid under the kitchen table.

I have relived that moment many times. I was afraid because I thought that my mama was going to kill me with that knife. That's why I remember it so vividly.

Many years later, I found out that the boy was telling the truth. The Nazis were burning Jews. They were also burning anybody that was rebellious, or spoke out against them. My mama was not trying to kill me with that knife; she just had to shut me up because we were living among Nazis, and we had to be careful of what we said and did. There were too many displaced people, and the Nazis were eager to eliminate as many people as they could. Someone told me recently that the Nazis did make soap out of the ashes that remained in the Extermination Chambers and chimneys. The soot was ideal for soap making. They just had to add a bit more fat and some lye.

I don't have many memories of Poland, which seems strange because we lived there for several months. I had started school in Poland, so I was old enough to remember. I do recall that it was a German school, and that's where I learned how to read and write. I had no difficulties with the language because my new papa had taught me how to speak German during our Trek.

It was important that I knew German, as I was supposed to be my new papa's biological child. I remember my parents drilling me over and over, "You must speak German and tell everybody that your new papa is your Papa." They even bribed me with a new dress so that I would cooperate.

Mama frightened me when she told me, "If anybody finds out that Papa is not your real papa, we will have to go back to the war place."

After our arrival in Poland, I understood how important those instructions were. I saw some of my friends crying as they were leaving; one of my friends came to say goodbye and told me, "We have to go back to where the war is."

We both cried and hugged each other. I was sorry to lose my friend, and afraid that this might happen to us as well.

Another reason for my memory block is that our living conditions were horrible. We had to live in our covered wagon until we were "sorted." Then, when the Nazis decided that we could stay, we were crowded together with many other refugees. I did what I was told, because I did not want to go back to where the bombs were falling.

Because of our cramped quarters, I had to go to the hospital when I caught the measles, and stay there until I was no longer contagious.

When I found out that Mama and Papa were going to leave me at the hospital, I got hysterical. I remembered the time I was left on the wagon when the bombs were falling, and I did not want to be left alone again. I kept pleading with them not to leave me. I was so afraid that they would not come back.

They told me that they couldn't stay, and promised that they would be back. Then they walked away while I was screaming hysterically.

I cried every day for my mama. Day after day passed, and Mama did not come.

When she finally returned to take me home, I was overjoyed to see her.

I can still see that hospital. It is an old building with tall windows that open onto narrow balconies. I'm looking outside at a big open area, I see Mama and Papa walking away, and leaving me alone in a very scary place. I am calling for my mama, but she keeps on walking away. All my life, I have had a phobia about living alone.

The picture below was taken in Poland, (front, L to R: Nina, Mama, and new papa.) I was told that the others in the picture are: my new papa's brother, his wife, their son, and two daughters. They were not on the wagon train with us. I don't know how we found them or how long we were together. I do know that we never saw them again, after we left Poland.

In January of 1945, the German Army retreated from Poland, and we were transported by cattle car trains to the western part of Germany.

Scheinfeldt

Scheinfeldt was a small village in the western part of Germany; I don't remember seeing any signs of bombings there. I do remember an overturned railway train and spilled brown sugar, and the excitement it caused. The kids and adults grabbed any container they could, ran to the mound of sugar, filled up their containers, their pockets and mouths with as much sugar as they could, before the authorities chased them away. What a great treat that was.

An old nunnery had been converted to house refugees. We lived in a very large room with 20 families or more. There were rows of bunk beds side-by-side, all around the room. The mattresses consisted of burlap bags, filled with straw. The adults slept in the lower bunks, surrounded by blankets for privacy.

We had a lot of fun making up games and tossing stuff back and forth. One day, someone found some condoms which we inflated and tossed around. I thought they were great balloons and couldn't understand why the parents got mad and took our balloons away.

We were no longer suffering from extreme hunger. Most of the time we were given dark bread and milk in the mornings, and a thin soup and more dark bread later in the day. But we always wanted more to eat.

One of the older boys found out that cans of milk were delivered early each morning. The next morning, while it was still dark, some of us kids snuck out of bed and waited for the milkman. That morning, we had our fill of milk. We did not think of the consequences and how much trouble we would get into. Hunger is a powerful motivator. I don't remember our punishment, but I do remember how good that milk tasted.

My brother, Bill, was born at the nunnery in Scheinfeldt, in March of 1945. My parents were very happy to have a boy; especially Papa. He was very proud to have a son.

We lived in Scheinfeldt for just a few months. After that we were transported farther west, by train, to Kitzingen am Main, a small German town.

Gottfried and Anna Frank, and their son Viktor, were also sent to Kitzingen. About six years later the Frank's moved to America. They had relatives in America who sponsored them.

The older couple, Mr. and Mrs. Klimush who were also with us on the wagon train, went to live in Unter-Rimbach, a very small village in Germany, not far from Kitzingen. (When I was old enough, I rode my bicycle to visit them in their tiny gingerbread house. That is where I learned to hunt for wild mushrooms).

Hitler killed himself on April 30, 1945. One week later the war was over.

Excerpts from Heritage Collection, cont.:

After the war, Germany was divided into four sections: American, British, French and Russian.

In May 1945, Germany was in chaos. Observers reported that the destruction of some of the larger cities had to be seen to be believed. For example, 66% of the houses in Cologne were destroyed, and in Düsseldorf, 93% were uninhabitall. The economy was at a standstill, and no central government remained to implement instructions issued by the Allies. Millions of people were homeless, or attempting to return to homes that no longer existed. They included German civilians evacuated from the cities, or trying to escape from the fighting, in both

Eastern and Western fronts. Former forced laborers from across Europe (known as 'Displaced Persons' or 'DPs') and ethnic Germans expelled from Czechoslovakia, or from former German Eastern territories now ceded to Poland. There were hundreds of thousands of Germans on foot, trekking in all directions ... as if an ant-heap had suddenly been disturbed.

The food situation in occupied Germany was initially very dire. By the spring of 1946, the official ration for the American zone was probably as little as 700 calories per day. But that was more than the other sectors received.

Some occupation soldiers took advantage of the desperate food situation by exploiting their ample supply of food and cigarettes (the currency of the black market) to get to the local German girls, as what became known: "frau bait'. The Allied soldiers were ordered not to fraternize with the German people because they were the enemy. Some soldiers who felt the girls were the enemy, used them for sex nevertheless. The German people verbally abused women who dated Allied soldiers and called them 'Allied whores'.

During the 1945 battle for Berlin, and in the immediate postwar period, approximately one in three Berlin women were raped by Allied troops-mostly from the Red Army—while 10,000 women in Berlin died from sexual assault. Many women committed suicide after the rape, some forced to do so by their fathers because of their "dishonor," while others were shot and killed by their husbands for consenting to sexual relations with Allied soldiers.

By late 1945, shortly after the war, Communist authorities had captured or reclaimed most Soviet citizens of German nationality who fled during the conflict.

Even in the Western occupation zones, Allied officials ended up returning about 25,000 or one quarter of their 100,000 refugees to Soviet officials, in accordance with Allied agreements at Yalta and Potsdam (unofficially called "Operation Keel Haul"). These transfer policies not only applied to ethnic Germans from the USSR, but to all Soviet citizens of any nationality found in occupied Germany and the liberated countries of Central and Eastern Europe, including POWs, slave laborers, and others.

I lived in constant fear that our family would also be sent back to "where the bombs were falling."

Kitzingen and River House, 1945–1948

K itzingen was a picturesque, medium sized, town in Unterfranken on the river Main, and located between Würzburg and Frankfurt. That was our final German destination.

Kitzingen am Main, Kaiserstrasse

Upon arrival, we saw signs of the war. Burned and demolished buildings and bombed out ruins. But, most of the rubble had already been removed, and people were starting to rebuild.

We were glad to be located in the American sector. Besides getting more food rations, we felt that we had more protection, and a better chance of going to America. We also discovered that the American soldiers were very friendly, especially to us kids. Sometimes, they would even give us a candy bar to share.

The authorities crowded as many of us 'Displaced Persons' as they could into large rooms of old buildings, in the middle of town, until they could find permanent housing for us.

I only remember one incident while we lived there. I was close to seven years old, and I had a loose front tooth. My mama tied a string around the tooth, as she had done with all of my previous loose teeth, and I kept pulling on it to get the tooth out. I felt like everyone in that crowded room was watching me. Mr. Frank told me that the string was loose, and that he would fix it. I did not trust him, but he promised me that he would not pull out my tooth, so I let him touch it. I felt a little tug, and then he said that the string was fixed. When I touched the place where the tooth had been, I realized that it was gone. I was shocked. Mr. Frank had promised that he would not pull out my tooth. When they saw the look on my face, everybody started laughing, which made me cry. My crying made them laugh even louder. I felt betrayed and humiliated, but nobody bothered to console me, and there was nowhere to hide. I remember that awful feeling of being humiliated to this day. Strange that something, seemingly so small, can stay with a person all their life.

I was glad when we finally moved into our first real home. It was an abandoned warehouse located near a bridge that crossed the river Main.

The building had been divided into living quarters for refugees like us. There was a lower level with its own entrance, a main level, and an attic. We lived on the main level with three other families. We had a medium-sized room which held my parent's bed, my bed, a small table and four chairs. My baby brother, Bill, slept in a box at the foot of my parents' bed. Across a narrow hallway was a very small, windowless room which we used for storage and bathing. That is also where Papa made his moonshine vodka. I don't remember where the toilet was located, or where we got our water, but I am sure that the water and toilet would have been shared by everyone in the building.

We did our cooking on a wood stove in an area which was part of the main hallway. We shared that stove with the families on our floor, and the lady who lived in the attic.

I enjoyed visiting that lady because she was very kind. She was nice to me, and praised me whenever I did something for her. I was not used to being praised, and I loved how it made me feel. I would have done anything she asked, just to keep feeling that way. I visited her every chance I could. She let me help with the ironing and mending, and other household chores, and I loved doing them with her. Then one day when I went up to see her, the lady was gone. I asked my parents and other people in the building, but nobody knew where she was. I never did find out what happened to her. I missed her very much, and felt abandoned.

Our living quarters were small, but our room had a large window with a view of the River Main, beyond the railroad tracks. The room was bright and cheerful, and we were grateful that we finally had a private place we could call home.

To the right of the entrance of our building, was an open space. Beyond that, was a building that was a mess hall for the American military. That is also where they did their cooking.

One day when I was playing nearby, a friendly soldier called me to come to the window, when I did, he threw a piece of meat out to me. I was thrilled. I thanked him profusely and ran home to Mama. Her eyes got big when she saw the meat, and asked, "Where did you get that?"

I proudly told her. From that time on, I patrolled that area every day. I was always happy when I found food, especially meat. Sometimes the meat had some maggots on it, but I brushed them off, and took the meat home anyway. Mama would wash it and cook it thoroughly, so that it was safe to eat, and it tasted wonderful. Sometimes, I would just find food scraps, but I would dig through them, and salvage whatever I could. I always tried hard to find something so that Mama would be proud of me.

I learned from early childhood, that if you are hungry enough, you will eat anything that is edible and be grateful for it.

Germany was overrun by refugees. Even though the war was over and our section was occupied by the Americans, we lived in fear of being deported back to Russia. The German government did not know what to do with so many refugees, so they got rid of as many as they could, on any pretext that they could come up with.

For example: a nine-year-old boy that I knew, stole a jar of jam from a German family's basement. He was a good boy. He only took that jam because he was craving anything sweet. But the German family reported him to the police, and he and his whole family were sent back to Russia. I don't know if that was the only reason that the family was sent back. I just know that I missed my friend. It had scared me that they sent him back to the "war place," so I tried very hard to be good.

I think that one of the reasons we were not sent back to Russia, was because Papa was strong and a hard worker. The Germans needed him to re-build the bombed-out homes and buildings.

In spite of our fear of deportation, Papa often broke the law by making his moonshine vodka and selling it to the American GI's and to his friends.

One day, when Papa was cooking his brew, the *Polizei* came to the house. They were questioning people about a theft that happened at a nearby lumberyard. We heard them talking to the people in the first room, and knew it would not be long before they came to our door.

We had to hurry and tear down the distilling equipment in our little room. We managed to hide the equipment but, we could not get rid of the big pot of fermented stew, which was boiling on the woodstove.

Bill and I in the river house yard, dressed in our church clothes, about 1948

The police asked, "What is in the pot?"

Mama spoke up and said, "I am making soap."

It is true that she made soap out of rancid fat and lye, but the stuff in that pot contained potato peels, fruit scraps and sugar, and it smelled like old fermented fruit.

I was petrified. I knew that the police would never believe Mama's story. We'd been caught, and now we would be sent back to Russia, just like that boy I knew.

Then I saw the policemen look at each other and grin. One of the men said to Mama, "This will be a very interesting smelling soap." And with that, they laughed and moved on. I realized then, that not all of the *Polizei* were bad, and maybe I did not have to be so afraid all the time.

Oh, and Papa? After the *Polizei* left, he reassembled his distillery and kept on making his vodka.

Sometimes when Papa and his drinking buddies got together, he would show me off to his friends. He would fill a small glass with vodka, and tell me to drink it. As I drank the vodka, I would turn the glass slowly, without pausing, until it was empty. Everybody clapped, and Papa would look so proud. That is the only time I remember Papa looking at me with pride.

Papa continued making his moonshine until he died, at age 94

River House Memories

We lived in the River house for over two years.

About half a mile across the river from our house was a large pond, which was the town's swimming hole. That's where I learned to swim. An older man was always there, holding some of the girls as they practiced their swim strokes. He seemed very nice, and came over to help me as well. The first time his hand brushed against my private parts, I felt uncomfortable, but I let it go, thinking it was just an accident and that his hand must have slipped. But when it happened the second time, and his hand stayed there, I told him, "No, I can swim by myself," and pushed him away. He left me alone after that, and I learned to swim on my own.

One day, as I was standing in our room looking across the river, I got a bright idea: instead of walking across the bridge to the swimming hole, which was a long way around, I could just swim across the river. That would make the trip much shorter and quicker.

The problem was, I was not a good swimmer, and did not know about river currents. (The River Main is one of the largest rivers in Germany. On the surface, the river looks smooth and calm, but underneath, the current is very powerful).

Without thinking this through, I put on my swimsuit, ran down to the river and jumped in. I was about halfway across when my strength gave out. I was caught up in the powerful current, and struggling to keep my head above water. But the river was much too strong. I was being swept down river. Soon my arms felt like lead. I just couldn't lift them anymore. My head went under water again and again. My strength was gone, and I was drowning. I prayed to God." Please God I want to live, please give me strength."

Suddenly, I felt something grabbing me on both sides, and pulling me above water.

A young couple, who were swimming downriver, saw me struggling and came to my rescue. I held onto them for dear life, and they helped me get back to shore. After they made sure that I was all right, they continued swimming down the river. I never knew who they were, but I like to think that they were my guardian angels!

My rescue was a miracle. It was very seldom that people swam down the Main River. The chance of someone being there just when I needed them was most unlikely.

Another memory: Papa was mad at Mama. He was yelling at her, and slapped her. I started crying and ran out of the house (I had learned early on to disappear whenever Papa got mad). I got scared whenever I saw him hit her, and my heart always hurt for my mama. I ran down to the river and cried.

A while later when I came back, I saw Papa and our neighbor, Mr. Schmidt, fighting in the yard. They were yelling, and hitting each other. I felt sick to my stomach when I heard the men's grunts and saw those terrible blows. I was afraid that Papa or Mr. Schmidt would be killed.

I was already living in fear of being sent back to where the bombs were falling. If Papa died, what would Mama and I do? We were in a foreign country without family. How could we survive? Seeing them, stirred up all those feelings.

When the men heard my screams, and saw how upset I was, they stopped fighting.

I ran into the house to check on my mama. She stopped crying when she saw me, and assured me that everything would be all right. She didn't look like she was hurt, she just had a big red spot on her cheek. As so many times before, she said, "Don't cry Ninotchka." But it took a long time for me to calm down.

That was a dumb fight anyway, as most fights are. Papa was just jealous of Mama and Mr. Schmidt; which was ridiculous.

I also have this memory: I carried lunch to Papa's job, when he worked on a construction site. While I was waiting for him to notice me, I saw him climbing up a ladder, with a tall load of bricks, in a carrier, strapped to his back. Even at my age, I could see what a strenuous job that was. All of Papa's jobs were hard. I saw how exhausted he was when he got home, but I never heard him complain. His work provided a roof over our heads and food for our table, and we were grateful that he had a job.

Ration Card

From the time I could read and write, I had to do all of the translating and paperwork for my parents.

Papa could not read or write because his parents had died when he was very young, and his uncle raised him. He was not allowed to go to school because he was needed to work on the farm. Mama could read and write Russian, but not German.

So, after I learned how to read, they depended on me to do all their translating. I was always needed whenever they had important transactions to conduct. This made me grow up fast because I was aware of their burdens.

One of my jobs was picking up our monthly food ration card at the *Rathaus* (courthouse). That was a lot of responsibility for an eight-year-old.

One day after I picked up the ration card, I accidentally dropped it. As soon as I realized it, I turned around and looked for it, but just that quickly, the ration card was gone.

I was horrified! How could I have been so careless? I had lost a whole month's worth of food that my family depended on. I was sure that without that card, my family would starve.

This happened in the town square near the *Rathaus*, which was full of people. Any one of them could have picked up the card. I kept retracing my steps over and over. After a while I knew that the search was futile; the card was not there. But I didn't know what else to do; I just couldn't go home without the card!

My despair grew with every step. My crying became louder and more pitiful. I was so afraid. Where are we going to get food? I could not face Mama and Papa, so I kept on walking and praying, "Dear God please help me, please help me," over and over.

After what seemed like hours, I knew that I had to give up searching. When I realized that all hope was gone, I fell to my knees, and my crying turned into mournful wails.

Suddenly, a woman came up to me and asked, "Why are you crying?"

In a shaky voice I said, "I lost our ration card. My family is very poor, and without that card we will starve."

She stared at me for a while. Then, she quickly pulled the ration card out of her purse and gave it to me. When I saw that card, I could not believe my eyes. I thought that she was an angel, and this was the most wonderful miracle in the world. I was so relieved, I started sobbing. I jumped up and hugged the lady, and thanked her again and again.

I never told my parents what had happened that day. I did not want them to be mad at me for being careless.

After that scare, I made sure that the ration card was always tucked away safely.

Bullying

Is there a difference between bullying and discrimination? Having experienced both, I think there is. When I was bullied, I felt intimidated and weak. Discrimination went deeper. I felt like something was wrong with me, and that I was a lesser human being.

When we arrived in Germany in 1945, the Germans made it very obvious that we were not wanted, just by the way they looked at us. Some of the people made it very clear, by yelling at us, "*Ruskies* go home".

In retrospect, I understand why the Germans didn't want us there. They too went through the horrors of war. They lost that war, and their lives were in chaos. They did not have enough food or housing for many of their own people, so they resented having to share what little they had with the refugees and wanted them gone.

But as a child I did not see that. I only knew how I was feeling. I felt very alone. My parents were overwhelmed and did not have time for me. I had no friends and no one to talk to.

When I started school in Kitzingen, they put me in the first grade, then they transferred me to the second grade. Nobody told me that I was transferred because scholastically I belonged in the second grade. The transfer made me feel even more insecure because I believed that they didn't want me in their school. In spite of that, I walked two miles to school, five days a week, snow, rain, or shine.

Before class started, we had to stand, raise our right hand and say, 'Heil Hitler.' This seemed very strange to me. After all, the war was over, so why were they still hailing Hitler? (Eventually, they stopped doing that).

The teachers were very strict. If a child misbehaved, that child was called to the front of the class and told to hold out their hands palms up. Then the teacher would whack him/her across their palms with a ruler. I remember receiving that punishment once or twice, but I don't remember what I did to deserve it. The teachers liked me because I was a good student. Learning was easy for me. All I had to do was read the material two or three times, and I had it memorized. German spelling was also easy (much easier than

English) with a few exceptions, if you could pronounce the German word correctly, you could spell it.

The teachers treated me well enough, but the children wanted nothing to do with me. Some looked at me like I was dirt, while others laughed at the clothes I wore. Many of them yelled at me to go back where I came from, but most of them just shunned me.

I tried to be nice. I even changed my name to Lina, which is a German name. (It was changed back to Nina when we came to America). Nothing I did made a difference. The German kids just wanted me to disappear.

We belonged to the Lutheran church, and I went to church every Sunday. There, I learned that God loves all of the little children. I liked going to church; nobody bullied me and I felt comfortable. Later when I was 14, I was confirmed in the church.

One day, when I was about eight years old, the bullying at school was especially bad. I felt so lonely and unwanted; I cried all the way home to the river house. When I opened the door to our room, I saw that Papa was hitting my mama again.

I ran out of the house to my refuge place, in the corner of the veranda, behind some boxes. I was sobbing, and shaking all over. I felt afraid, alone and desperate. I didn't know what to do. I just wanted to die.

Then I remembered Father Brennan's words: "God loves little children. Heaven is a wonderful place. If you truly believe in God, He will answer your prayer, and when you die, you will go to heaven." So, I prayed. "Please dear God take me to your heaven, I don't have anyone here that loves me, or wants me. Mama said that my real papa is dead. I know that he loves me, please let me come to heaven so I can be with my real papa."

I was sure that God could tell that I really wanted to die, and that he would grant me my wish. I closed my eyes and waited. A long time passed and nothing happened. Slowly my hurt turned to anger.

"Okay God. You don't want me either. So, I'll show You, and I'll show them. I will live and I will be better than any of them. And someday everybody will be proud of me."

—That was a life changing moment for me! "I'll Show Them" became my mantra and my strength.

Many times, I have thought back to that prayer. I realize that in that moment I became a survivor. I fought back when I could, and I endured what I had to endure, because I knew that someday I would grow up, and then "I will show them!"

A week or two later, when I walked into the schoolyard, I saw a group of children and heard them shouting. When I got closer, I saw that one of the bullies was picking on a boy half his size, and the other children encouraging him. I knew that boy, he was a refugee like me. The bully was pushing the little boy and yelling, "Go home. We don't want you here. We hate you. Get out of here."

Suddenly, I just snapped. All the anger that I had pent up exploded. I pushed myself into the circle and started screaming. I don't remember all the words, I just remember shouting, "Leave him alone."

The big bully turned and came at me. I was ready for a fight. When he pushed me, I swung and kept on hitting him until a teacher pulled me off. It was only then that I noticed, the bully had a bloody nose and was crying.

The teacher took us both to the principal's office. I don't remember my punishment, but I didn't care. I felt that I had done the right thing. I had fought for that boy, and I decided that I would fight for myself from that time on. Later that little boy thanked me, and we became friends.

Eventually, the bullies left me alone, and I started to enjoy school.

After we moved from the River house to *Schützenplatz*, I met other refugee children and made more friends. I even became friendly with some of the German girls; but I was not welcomed into most of their homes.

I had two changes of clothes that Mama had sewn for me, which I wore only to school. I also received some hand-me-downs from the church. Many of the girls in school had beautiful clothes, and I always felt like a ragamuffin.

We all wore a rucksack, which held our lunch, our books, and our homework. We also tied a chalkboard to the rucksack. Paper was precious, because there was a shortage, so we used the chalkboard instead of paper whenever possible.

—To this day, I use paper sparingly. Even though we have a drawer full of writing pads, I write on the bottom part of a pad, tear it off, and save the top for the next time. Much of the time I also use the flip side of the paper, instead of discarding it.

German School System

Children started school at age six, School days were Monday through Friday, from 8 AM to 4 PM, and summer vacation lasted six weeks. From the first grade to the fourth, we were taught the basics: reading, writing and math. Those subjects were drilled into us. At the end of each year there was a test. The children who did not pass, had to repeat the grade, or go to a "special" class.

After the fourth and fifth grade, children were evaluated. Depending on the child's grades, the teacher and parents decided whether the child should remain in the *Volksschule*—which was grades one through eight—or go to *Oberschule*, where for the next four years, the child would prepare for college. I wanted to go to *Oberschule*, and my teachers tried very hard to talk Papa into letting me go, at the end of the fourth grade, and again at the end of the fifth grade, but he would not allow it. He wanted me to finish school as soon as possible and go to work because we needed the money.

In the *Volkschule*, after the fourth grade, we were taught penmanship, history and geography. The last two years we could also take a foreign language class. I chose English. The teachers talked me into taking *Esperanto* as well because that was supposed to become the world language. (Obviously it never did, and I don't remember even one word of it).

After the fifth grade, classes were separated by gender. The boys were taught carpentry, mechanics, and other manly things. Girls learned cooking, sewing, knitting, crocheting, darning and mending, as well as typing and shorthand. Since I did not have a typewriter on which to practice, I chose shorthand (a lot of good that did me). We could also take music lessons.

Someone lent me a guitar so that I could take lessons. We had to copy the notes from the sheet music for every song we learned. It was tedious, but it was a good way to memorize the notes. I had copied several sheets of music, and was beginning to enjoy playing the guitar. My brother Bill got mad at me about something, and tore up all of my sheet music. I was furious, I did not want to copy all of that music again, so I gave up taking lessons.

One of the things I really enjoyed was acting because I could make believe that I was someone other than myself and lived in a different world. Our school performed several plays; mainly from Grimm's Fairy Tales, and I usually played supporting roles. In those days, it was easy for me to memorize my lines and acting came to me naturally.

The German school prepared children well for the real world. We worked hard at learning our lessons and doing our homework. Excuses were rarely allowed. We learned to obey our teachers and to respect our elders. We also learned things that would be useful in life after we graduated. (I have been told that, in those days, the same could be said about the schools in America).

Those who graduated after the eighth grade could go to business school or a trade school. We could also go to work in an office, or as an apprentice in a business. Of course, some kids went to work full time on their parents' farm.

I went to business school at night, and took a course in accounting. However, after I became an apprentice at Wachter's Butcher Shop, where the work was hard and hours were long, I gave up school after the first semester.

We grew up with such strong gender bias, my girlfriends and I talked about our future in terms of marrying a smart and successful man. We hoped that our husband would make enough money and we could stay at home; keep a clean house and take care of our children. We never talked about a serious career of our own.

Schützenplatz, 1948–1954

About three years after the War ended, we moved across town, from our room on the river, to a place called *Schützenplatz*. It was located on the outskirts of Kitzingen, past the railroad tracks. German soldiers had lived and trained there during the war. The area was isolated, and carved into a hill accessible only by a narrow road. Next to the road was a path that went further up to a *Gasthaus*.

After the war ended, the Germans converted the area into a *Siedlung* (settlement) for World War II Displaced Persons like us.

At the end of the narrow road, was a small one room guardhouse, where a husband and wife lived. Beyond that was a flat open area with six barracks arranged in a semicircle. Each barrack was divided into eight rooms. One or two rooms in each barrack was assigned per family.

There were six outhouses, three at each end of the barracks. In the center of the complex was a wash house with cold running water. That was the only water source for all of the barracks. Inside the wash house, was a fire pit. Built on top of it was a big cement tub where we washed and boiled our clothes. We scrubbed our clothes on a washboard with homemade soap, and boiling took the place of bleach. There were clotheslines inside and outside of the wash house. Even when it was freezing cold, we hung our clothes out to dry, brought them in while still frozen and let them finish drying in our rooms.

Our barracks

About 100 feet from the wash house was a garbage dump. A 10-foot square area, with cement walls on three sides. The garbage was hauled away on a regular basis. There was not much smell from the garbage because we did not throw away any food scraps, we ate everything that was edible. All smelly things were dumped into the outhouses.

The area around the barracks was kept clean at all times; that was a matter of pride.

All the people living in *Schützenplatz* were poor refugees. I assume that the reason my parents moved there was because I was too old to be sleeping in the same room with them, and that must have been the only apartment with two rooms, that they could afford to rent.

Our two rooms measured about 12 × 12 and 10 × 10 ft. (size may be exaggerated). We had one window and one light bulb in each room. The barracks were built for temporary use, so they were single wall, constructed of wooden boards with no insulation in the attic, walls or floors.

My parents and my three-year-old brother, Bill, slept in the back room. I slept in the front room, which was also our living room, kitchen, eating, and bathing area.

In the left corner of the front room was our kitchen area, a small wooden counter for food preparation, with a wash basin and a fresh water bucket on top. Under the counter we kept our eating and cooking utensils, and what little food we had. Next was our wood cooking stove. In the opposite corner was my narrow bed with a straw mattress. To the left under the window, was a table and four chairs; above, on a corner shelf, was our radio. A storage cupboard stood at the foot of my bed. In the corner was a covered slop bucket. There was just enough open space in the middle of the room for our weekly bath. In the back room was my parents' and brother's bed, a storage closet, and two chairs.

We had to use our wood cooking stove year-round. This made the small room very hot in the summer. Some of the time we just ate cold food. In the coldest part of the winter the stove kept us warm, as long as it was constantly stoked. But we had to be careful, and not use too much firewood and coal, or we would run out. So, we wore several layers of clothes, and wrapped ourselves in blankets. Thankfully the winters in Kitzingen were not too severe.

Saturday was bath day. Mama got out the washtub and hung up a blanket for privacy. We took our turns bathing. Brother Bill and I bathed in the same water. He went first, I hated that because I suspected that he peed in the bathwater. Naturally, he always denied it.

We did not have refrigeration. We didn't really need any, because we had nothing to refrigerate. Everything fresh was eaten or preserved before it could go bad.

Our main staple was potatoes, which we gleaned whenever we could. Mama would fix potatoes every way imaginable. Most of the time we had fried potatoes with onions and a little *Speck* (pork back). We also gleaned wheat, which we then took to the Miller to be ground into flour. Mama baked our own bread and rolls, and we used pork fat for topping. She also made noodles, which we ate mixed with hot milk.

Sometimes Mama made *Perishky*, a yeast dough filled with mashed potatoes, and fried onions, then baked. After we came to America, Mama filled the dough with hamburger and sauerkraut. It became the family's favorite, and I continued making *Perishky* after Mama died (see recipe in Addendum).

Of course, we had *Borscht*, a Russian soup which Mama cooked. She used whatever we had. Most of the time she made it with a soup bone, a scrap of meat, or *Speck*. She added onions, potatoes, tomatoes and cabbage or sauerkraut. Sometimes she put in carrots, and yes, sometimes she used beets.

In the Spring, she made a "green borscht." Instead of cabbage, she used *Sauerampfen* which is a sour tasting weed that I picked from a field across the river. Instead of meat, she used boiled, sliced eggs. If we had sour cream, we added that to the borscht. Mama told me that in Ukraine, green borscht was cooked in the spring because by then the preserved meat, the sauerkraut, and most of the root vegetables were gone.

Foods that I craved were meat and oranges. At school I sometimes saw girls eating an orange; oh, how I would envy them. I would stare at them; my mouth would fill with saliva and I would pretend that it was juice from an orange.

Sometimes when it was raining and my friend, Alice, and I had nowhere else to go (we seldom went to each other's apartment because there was no privacy, and we felt like we were in the way) we would stand inside the entrance of our barrack, with the entry door open, and talk. At times, a girl that lived in our barrack would come out and join us. Sometimes she would bring out a sausage, made of horse meat, and eat it in front of us. When she felt generous, she would give us a small bite. That sausage tasted so good. I would hold it in my mouth and barely chew, to prolong that taste as long as possible.

I could not understand why Papa did not allow horse meat in the house, it was cheaper, and we could have bought it more often. Did he not know how good it tasted? But I didn't dare tell him, because I didn't know what he would do if he found out that I had eaten horse meat. I had overheard Papa telling Mama that some of the neighbors were eating dogs and cats, and they were both disgusted at that.

I never had any pets, and neither did any of the people I knew, so I did not understand why they were so disgusted, until much later.

We had no shopping malls in Kitzingen, only specialty stores like a *Metzgerei* (butcher shop), a *Bäckerei* (bakery), and a grocery store. I remember carrying a milk can to the grocery store to have it filled with milk; and buying other necessary items like potatoes, onions, and flour when the gleaning was poor or nonexistent. About once a week, if we had enough money, I would go across the street to the *Metzgerei* and buy a little piece of meat, or soup bones. Sometimes, I also bought beer or vodka for Papa. In Germany children were allowed to buy alcohol. I never heard of any problems with kids abusing alcohol. Maybe it's because it was not a forbidden fruit?

There was a clothing and furniture store, but we seldom bought clothes. Most of our clothes were either handmade, or hand-me-downs. We mended our clothes and darned our socks to get as much wear out of them as possible. Our furniture was either handmade or bought second hand.

We never went shopping just for the fun of it because there was no point in looking at things we could not afford.

In spite of our poor living conditions Mama made sure that everything was always *sauber* (clean). At least once a week I got down on my knees with a scrub brush, and hot soapy water. I scrubbed the wooden floorboards in our living area and the common hallway until they were spotless. Mama said many times, "Just because we are poor, we don't have to be dirty."

Papa fenced in a small area behind our barrack, and built a little shed where he repaired shoes. That's how he earned a little extra money. At times we raised a chicken or two, and when they stopped laying eggs, we ate the chickens.

The *Gasthaus* on the hill had a bar which was a very popular hangout with the American GI's from the nearby US Military Base. We could hear American music playing almost every night. I would fall asleep listening to the latest American songs, Jambalaya was my favorite. As I listened, I would dream of the day we would be allowed to go to America.

We had applied for a Visa to America shortly after we arrived in Germany. There was a long list of people ahead of us, so we knew that it would take a long time before they would grant us an interview. But knowing that we had a chance for a better life, gave us hope, when there was despair.

Several children about my age lived in *Schützenplatz* so I was no longer lonely. We played the usual games like, hopscotch, jump rope, or hide-and-go-seek. While we played, we forgot that we were poor. We were just children, like all the other children of the world.

We were glad that we had a roof over our heads, and happy when we had something good to eat. Our focus was on basic survival. But we did have hope of living in America.

Many years later, my brother Bill told me a story that he had remembered of the time we lived in *Schützenplatz*.

He said, "One day, something fell from the sky and landed in the open area behind the wash-house. All of us kids were afraid and would not go near it because we thought it was a bomb. You were the only one that was not afraid. You went right over to the object, examined it, and told us that it was not a bomb. Later, we found out that it was a weather balloon." I don't remember that incident. But I am not surprised that I was unafraid. I knew what a bomb sounded like and what it did; it exploded and killed people. That thing was just lying there, so there was no reason to be afraid it.

Health Issues

I don't remember if we had any serious health issues during our escape from Russia. Except for the time Mama was taken away by ambulance, just before the bombing attack. To this day, I don't know why they took her, but when she returned, she seemed to be in good health.

While we were living in Poland, I caught the measles, and had to go to the hospital. I assume the reason for my confinement was, that we lived in very crowded conditions, and they needed to contain the virus.

I do recall having a tooth extraction while we were living in Germany. I was about ten years old when I got an infected molar; not just a loose front tooth which I usually pulled out myself. This time I had to go to a dentist, and Mama came with me. The dentist told us that the tooth had to come out. He did not give me anything for pain, instead he strapped down my wrists. Then he brought out a vicious looking instrument and started yanking my tooth, while I was screaming. He pulled and pulled, but the tooth did not budge. Next, he put his knee on my chest and twisted, and the tooth finally came out. After we left the dentist's office, Mama told me that I had embarrassed her because they could hear me screaming in the waiting room.

When I was about 11 years old, I woke up with stomach pains and nausea, which continued all morning. Finally, Mama told me to walk to Dr. Hubschman's office which was about a mile away.

The doctor told me, "Your appendix is infected and you need surgery." He asked if I could walk to the hospital, which was about half a mile away, I told him that I could.

He said, "I will call the hospital, and they will take good care of you when you get there."

After I left his office, I didn't know what to do. I couldn't just go to the hospital without telling Mama, and I couldn't call her, because we didn't have a telephone (nobody in our settlement had a phone).

I walked back home and told Mama what the doctor had told me. She said, "Ninotchka, I cannot go with you, but Papa and I will get there as soon as we can."

I had to stop along the way to the hospital a few times, because my stomach was hurting, and I had to throw up.

(Looking back, I can't believe that I had walked four miles with an appendix that was ready to burst).

At the hospital, after a quick examination, they took me into surgery immediately.

When I woke up, I was very thirsty because I had nothing to drink all day. (They did not use an I.V.) I kept begging for water, but the nurses said that I couldn't have anything to drink because that would make me nauseated. I don't know whether I was delirious, or just angry. I kept pulling at my incision until they tied my wrists to the bed.

To this day I have a large scar, and a deep indentation on the right side of my abdomen. I don't know whether it's because I pulled a stitch loose, or because the doctor was in a hurry and did a sloppy job.

I was glad to see Mama and Papa when they came to the hospital that evening. Mama got the nurses to give me a drink of water, and they untied my wrists.

I had to stay in the hospital for a few days until I was well enough to walk home.

After that, we all stayed reasonably healthy while living in Germany, and for a long time after we came to America.

Following is a story that, Maria, a lady in our pinochle group told us.

—She said, "I was born in Germany, the middle child of six. We were very poor. My father never made much money, and my mother was in poor health. When Father went to war in 1941, we really struggled to survive.

One of my saddest memories is the day my youngest brother got sick and died in the hospital.

My mother was ill, so my oldest brother and I had to take my baby brother's body home in a handcart. I was about ten years old, and my brother was only a few years older.

We cried all the way home. The next day we buried my brother in a pauper's cemetery."

Hearing her sad story, reminded me that many German people were also very poor, and suffered greatly; before, during, and after the war.

Adventures

I loved to read, but our school did not have a lending library, and there were not many free books available. Sometimes I would find a book, or someone would give me one, and I would read it again and again. My favorites were adventure stories

Mama felt that reading was a waste of time, and always found work for me to do whenever she caught me, so I had to hide it from her. Sometimes at night I hid under the covers and read with a flashlight, or I would sneak off to where Mama couldn't find me, and read as long as I could stay away.

I don't remember ever having a doll or any other toy. For my birthday and Christmas, I usually received candy and fruit, and fabric that Mama would make into something for me to wear. Most of the children in our barracks did not have store-bought toys, so we used our imagination and made our own toys and games.

There was a large wooded area just above our barracks. That's where I played "Tarzan" with some of the neighbor kids. We would climb trees, try to swing from branch to branch and pretend to hunt for "wild beasts."

I found a small clearing in the middle of some bramble bushes, and that became my secret hideaway. I planted wild-flowers, ferns and moss and decorated my den with pretty rocks. I went to that clearing when I wanted to be alone, to read, dream, or cry. That little clearing was my refuge. One day, when I went to hide, I discovered that somebody had found my hideaway and destroyed all of my beautiful things. I could not understand why anybody would do that. After that, I no longer felt safe there, and I never went back.

I had four 'best' girlfriends: Rosemarie was my sports friend. Ellen, was my story writing, drawing, and cave hunting friend. Alice, was my dress up and walk around town friend, and Ingrid, was my adventure friend.

Ellen and I loved exploring caves and underground tunnels. Whenever we found a hole in the ground, we had to see where it led. Sometimes, we took Ingrid along.

We were exploring one of those tunnels, and had just crawled through a very narrow opening, when suddenly the tunnel collapsed behind us. We couldn't believe what had happened. We stood there in shock until the dust settled. Then we started digging in the mound of rocks and dirt, but as we were digging more rocks kept falling down. Soon we knew that there was no hope of getting out that way, and we started to panic.

After a while we calmed down a little and realized that we had to find another opening. We did not know where the tunnel led, or if there was another way out. As we were walking, we noticed several smaller passageways leading off to the right and left, which was scary, because we could easily get lost if we made the wrong turn. All we could do was keep walking and hope that we were going in the right direction.

Another worry was how long the battery in our flashlight would last. We had a couple of candles, but they were just little stubs. The further we went, the more the possibility of total darkness became a real threat. Ellen and I managed to keep our fear mostly to ourselves, but Ingrid kept whining and crying and asking dumb questions like, "How much longer before we get out?" and "What if we can't get out?" I felt like strangling her just to get her to be quiet.

Finally, after what seemed like an eternity, we saw a light. We were thrilled. We practically ran toward that light. When we got closer, we were very happy to see that the opening was big enough for us to crawl out. What a relief!

You would think that this would cure us of our underground obsession, but oh no, we continued. None of the caves and tunnels we found lead anywhere interesting. They were dug out bomb shelters or escape tunnels. But we kept hoping that someday we would find "a big treasure."

When we found a cave entrance near the school, and saw that the iron gate was open, we just couldn't resist. We walked a long way into the tunnel, only to discover that it was someone's wine cellar. What a disappointment. By the time we got back to the gate, it was locked. We yelled for a long time before somebody heard us, and let us out. When we saw the lady's astonished face, we quickly apologized and then ran as fast as we could.

Someone must have been watching over us, because we never got seriously hurt.

Mushroom hunting became my lifelong favorite hobby. It began when I was 12 years old. That summer, shortly before school started, I rode my bicycle to visit Mr. and Mrs. Klimush. They lived in a small village about 15 kilometers from my home in Kitzingen. Their home was a tiny, gingerbread style, house which Mr. Klimush had built. The house had only one room, and one bed. We all slept in the same bed with my head at their feet and my feet at their heads.

Mrs. Klimush took me to a nearby forest and taught me where to hunt for mushrooms, and which ones were safe to eat. I loved being in the forest. It was so beautiful and peaceful. I got so excited when I saw a yellow Chanterelle mushroom near a fern or next to an old stump. Or when I found a *Steinpilz*, a German word for "rock mushroom" because it looks like a rock. We know them as King Boletus. They have a reddish-brown cap with a sponge underneath, and a fat stem. They are bigger and meatier than the Chanterelles. They also have a very different flavor and texture.

I stayed with Mr. and Mrs. Klimush for one week and went mushroom hunting every day. Mrs. Klimush fried them with a little butter and onions. She also cooked some potatoes and we would have a delicious feast.

I could hardly wait to go back the next summer. Once again, I had a wonderful time hunting for mushrooms. The following year I turned fourteen and had to go to work as an apprentice in Wachter's Butcher Shop. I had to work six and-a-half days a week with no vacation time. So, I never returned to Mr. and Mrs. Klimush.

Believe it or not: there was a "witch" living in one of the barracks. People would go to her to cure things like warts and with other problems. I had three warts on my fingers. At first, they were just a nuisance, but when they got bigger,

Mama told me to go see the witch and she would get rid of them.

The witch lit some candles, then she got some *Speck* (pork back), and rubbed it on my warts. While she was doing that, she mumbled words that I could not understand. After that, she gave me the *Speck* and told me to bury it by the River. She said, "When the *Speck* gets rotten, your warts will disappear." Sure enough, about two weeks later, my warts were gone.

I had big freckles on my face, and I hated them. I wondered if the witch could get rid of those as well. When I asked her, she said, "Of course I can."

She told me to take off my undershirt. Then she turned the shirt inside out, and rubbed my face with the front of that shirt. Next, she rubbed my chest with the same part. All the while she was mumbling incantations. When she was done, she said, "You must repeat what I did, every night, and tell your freckles to transfer to your chest."

I thought, "Well, I have nothing to lose, she got rid of my warts, so I might as well try this." I followed her instructions, and slowly, I noticed freckles appearing on my chest.

After about a month, I got tired of the nightly ritual, but by then almost all my freckles had transferred from my face to my chest.

Winters in Germany

I was about ten years old, when one of the German girls from school asked me to go ice-skating with her. I told her that I didn't have any skates, but she said that I could use hers. I was pleased that she had asked me to go, and told her that I would meet her at that pond by the river. When I asked Mama, she told me that the ice was not strong enough and forbade me to go.

We did not have a telephone, so I had to go down to the pond and tell the girl what my mama had said. She convinced me, however, that the ice was strong enough, and talked me into putting on her skates just to try them out.

I just couldn't resist. I put on the skates, and got on the ice, but I couldn't keep my balance. When I fell, the ice broke, and I plunged into the icy water. I was not in danger of drowning because I was in shallow water, but I got totally soaked. It was a very cold day, and a long way home. I knew that I would be in trouble when I got home.

The girl suggested that we go to her house. It was closer, we could dry my clothes there, and Mama would never know that I had disobeyed her. That's what we did, and Mama never found out. But I got punished enough by having to walk what seemed like ten Kilometers in freezing weather while wearing soaking wet clothes. It's a wonder that I didn't get sick.

We had a lot of fun sledding on several hills nearby. We used anything that would slide down, and then we wore ourselves out climbing back up the hill. Our favorite was a path that went up to the *Gasthaus*. It was steep, winding and narrow, dangerous enough to break our necks; so naturally we had to try and test our luck. Thankfully, our guardian angels were watching over us. We had a few tumbles, and some bumps and bruises, but our necks remained attached. Winters in Kitzingen were not very severe, but we usually had enough snow to have fun for maybe two months or more.

I was in my 50s when I finally learned how to ski. I am very glad that I did. After I met Ute, a German war bride, and an excellent skier, she and I skied every mountain in Oregon.

But our favorite was Timberline on Tuesdays, because the ski lift tickets were cheap that day. We would start when they opened, take a short lunch break, and continue until they closed the lifts. Skiing down a groomed slope is such a thrill and the views from the tops of Mt. Bachelor, Mt. Hood, and Hoodoo are breathtaking.

Many times, when I am in a stressful situation, like in a dentist's chair, I close my eyes, my mind escapes my body and I am skiing down one of the mountains.

Babysitting

I was about 12 years old when Mr. and Mrs. Frank, who were good friends of my parents, asked me to babysit their three children. My parents gave their permission, but told me not to stay out too late. I told this to Mrs. Frank, and she promised that they would be home early.

It got dark, and they had not come home. As the hours passed, I got more and more anxious. We lived more than a mile away, and neither the Franks, nor we, had a telephone. I could not leave the children alone, so I had no choice but to wait for their return.

By the time the Franks finally got home, it was close to midnight. Mrs. Frank apologized for being late, and said that she would explain everything to my parents the next day. She paid me and I left for home.

There was a partial moon, so I had enough light to see where I was going. All went well, until I got close to home.

Our barracks were near a popular *Gasthaus*, and soldiers would often be gathered at the bottom of our road, which was narrow and lined with bushes and trees. All the way home I kept thinking about that narrow lane, and I was afraid that I would meet some drunk soldier there.

Sure enough, after I came out of the railroad tunnel and turned slightly to the left, my worst fear came true. I saw a soldier on the right edge of the lane with his back turned towards me. I assumed that he was urinating, a common practice in our area. Even during daylight hours men would just turn their backs and urinate into bushes or against a wall.

I only had a moment to decide: do I continue up the lane or do I wait? Not knowing how long the man would be there, and not wanting to remain in that dark tunnel, I decided to take a chance and try to sneak by him while his back was turned. But just when I thought that I had gotten past him, the soldier turned and tried to grab me. Fortunately, he was very drunk and had a hard time keeping his balance, which gave me a chance to get away. I ran as fast as I could with him stumbling after me.

By the time I got to our door, my heart was pounding and my hands were shaking. I was glad that our door was unlocked; I quickly got inside and locked it. I was very relieved to be safely home. But soon I found out that I was not safe after all.

As I was taking off my coat, Mama and Papa came out of their bedroom and started yelling at me. They were furious that I had gotten home so late. I tried to tell them that I could not come home any earlier, because the Franks had stayed out too late, and that Mrs. Frank told me that she would explain everything in the morning. But they would not listen.

Mama slapped me several times. Then Papa sprinkled salt on the floor, and made me kneel on it. They made sure that I stayed on my knees, by checking on me periodically. My knees were burning and my back was sore, and it seemed like forever before I was allowed to go to bed.

The next day Mrs. Frank came by and apologized about keeping me out so late. She made it clear that I was not at fault. But my parents never acknowledged that I had no control of the situation, and that I could not have come home any sooner. I have never forgotten the unfairness of that punishment. I was sure that my parents hated me.

But then, an incident happened that proved just how much Mama cared for me:

Grape Picking

My friend Alice and I, and three other kids from the barracks, were hiking near a vineyard when we noticed some grapes on the vines. There were just a few bunches here and there so we assumed that they were left-overs from the harvest. We were having fun, hunting for grapes and eating the ones we found.

Then we saw a policeman coming up the hill. We were afraid of the police, so we automatically ran and hid. Alice and I hid in some nearby bushes, and two of the other kids ran away. But the policeman caught one of the boys. We could see from our hiding place that the boy was talking to the policeman, pointing in the direction where we lived, and probably telling him our names.

The policeman got to our door before I got home, and told my mama what had happened. Mama told him, "No, you make mistake, my daughter not steal grapes, I pick grapes, not my daughter."

The policeman knew that she was not telling the truth, but Mama kept repeating the same thing over and over. Finally, he gave up and went away.

Alice and I put off going home as long as we could because we knew we'd be in big trouble. When I finally got home, I saw that Mama was very upset, but I was surprised that she was not really angry with me. She told me that the *Polizei* had been to our house. I told her, "Mama, we did not know that we were doing something wrong. We thought that the grapes were leftovers." She told me that it was all right, and that she had taken the blame.

She said, "Nina, listen to me. I told the *Polizei* that I was the one in the vineyard picking grapes. I do not want you to have a *Polizei* record, that will ruin your life. I do this to protect you. Now you must promise. Do not say that you were in the vineyard." I promised her, and told her again that I was sorry.

I found out the next day that the policeman had reported the incident to our school. When I was called to the principal's office. He asked me, "Did you steal grapes yesterday?" I didn't answer for a long time. I didn't think that we had been stealing; also, I was thinking about what my mama had said, and I was afraid.

Finally, I said, "No, I did not steal any grapes."

He continued to interrogate me, but I kept telling him the same thing. He said that he knew that I was lying. But I kept quiet and he let me go. I felt terrible. Not only because everybody knew that I had lied, but also because the other kids got punished and I did not. So, of course, they were all mad at me.

I would rather have taken the punishment, but I was afraid that if I had told the truth, Mama would have been in trouble for lying to the police, and that I would have a criminal record, just like Mama said. Thankfully, nothing came of it and we never heard anything more about it.

However, I have never forgotten that incident. My mama's willingness to sacrifice herself as she did, proved to me without a doubt just how much she cared for me and my future.

Another memory:

I can't remember getting new shoes all the while we lived in Germany. My shoes were always hand-me-downs. Sometimes, they were too big, and Mama stuffed papers in the toes of the shoes, or they were too tight and hurt my feet, and Mama would wear them until they stretched out. Mama's feet were longer and wider than mine. Obviously, the shoes must have hurt her even more than they hurt me, but she wore them anyway. She told me that she didn't want my feet to be ruined by shoes that were too tight. Because of her, I have never had bunions, and my feet are not deformed in any way.

Again, my tears come, as I remember my mama's love.

Gleaning

Getting enough food to eat was always a worry from the earliest time I can remember. While on the wagon train, throughout the war years, and after the war, hunger or the fear of hunger was always with us.

Papa took whatever job he could find (which was always hard labor). His last job in Germany was as a kitchen helper at the U.S. military base. That was a great job because sometimes he would bring home leftover food.

One time he brought home a large container of scrambled eggs, made from powdered eggs. Mama told me that I could eat all I wanted, and that's what I did. I ate so much that I got sick. For the longest time after that I couldn't even look at a scrambled egg.

Mama and I would go to nearby fields, and glean anything that was edible. Somehow Mama found out when a farmer had finished harvesting, and we would try to be one of the first ones to get to that field. We would dig for things like potatoes, onions, beets, and carrots with a tool that Papa had made. Of course, we couldn't dig up the whole field, so we looked for an undisturbed strip of ground, and dug there. We also picked up any leftover spears of wheat, and took them to the mill to be ground into flour.

Most of the time we did not find a lot of leftovers because the farmers were very efficient. Plus, there were other gleaners competing with us. It was backbreaking work, but I didn't mind. To me it was a treasure hunt, and when I found something I was thrilled. Digging up a potato or a carrot was like finding gold.

We cooked and heated with a wood stove. Papa had built a hand cart which Mama and I took to the forest to gather any dead branches we could find. Also, several days a week I would go to the railroad tracks where the locomotives dumped the ashes, and sift for any leftover pieces of coal. I always found at least a few pieces to take home.

At a nearby shooting range, I dug up lead bullets that had been left after target practice. Then we sold the bullets for a few *Pfennig* a handful.

One day, Papa brought home two American soldiers who spoke German. They told us that in America a lot of food was left out in the fields after harvesting. They also said that fruit fell off the trees and nobody picked it up, it just laid there and rotted. Also, people threw perfectly good things into the garbage.

I could not believe what I was hearing. My eyes got big and my heart started racing. I burst out, "Mama, Papa, when we get to America, we will be rich!"

Imagine, a 15-year-old girl's dream: getting rich meant finding a lot of leftover food, and picking up peoples' throwaways in America.

L to R: Mama, Papa, brother Bill, Nina, and Papa's GI friend

—When we finally got to America, we did not have to glean to have enough food to eat. Also, we could afford to buy nice second-hand clothing. We worked hard, and were frugal, but we were never hungry, and we had everything that we needed.

But the most amazing thing was, about a year after coming to America, Mama and Papa were able to buy their first house.

Hitchhiking

I was about 13 years old when Hilda a friend of my parents, married an Englishman and moved to England. She left her nine-year-old daughter Nadia alone in Germany. Nadia had polio and was in the hospital in Würzburg. She was in a full body cast and had to wear it for several more months. Hilda asked my parents to look after Nadia, until she could join her in England. She sent money for toys and treats, and took care of our travel expenses.

At first Mama and I took the train from Kitzingen to Würzburg every other Sunday to visit Nadia. But after a while it became my responsibility. I didn't really mind. Nadia was a sweet girl, and was always happy to see me. I felt sorry for her because she was lonely, and missed her mother. I was her only visitor.

My parents decided that the train fare was a waste of money, so they bought me a bicycle. Würzburg was about 15 miles from Kitzingen, but to me it seemed like 50 miles. I had to ride my bike on a very busy highway, and I hated that, especially in bad weather.

One Sunday I got a bright idea. Why not hitchhike to the hospital? Of course, I did not tell my parents about my plan. I left my bicycle at a friend's house and walked to the highway. I got lucky because a nice older couple picked me up and drove me right to the hospital entrance. I thought to myself, well that was easy. Why didn't I think of that sooner?

Coming back was not so easy. I walked to the highway, and stuck out my thumb. Several cars stopped, but they were all American soldiers, and I knew better than to get into a car with any of "them." My hope was that another older couple or a woman would stop. But that didn't happen, and it was getting late. Finally, an older man stopped. After making sure that he wasn't wearing a uniform, and that he spoke fluent German, I got into his car. He was nice, and made me feel comfortable.

About ten miles later, he turned off the main Highway, and drove into a wooded area. I was confused, but not really frightened because he was a very nice man, and he made me feel very safe. When he stopped the car, I got out willingly. He said that he wanted to show me something interesting, so I walked into the woods with him.

Suddenly, he put his arms around me, and tried to kiss me. That's when I realized I was in danger. I told myself to stay calm. I pulled my head back, looked him in the eyes and said, "You can kiss me on the cheek, but not on my mouth. Only my husband can kiss me on the lips, after we get married."

The man stopped, and looked at me for the longest time. He must have recognized that I was still a child, and very naive. He shook his head and smiled. He let go of me, and we walked back to his car. He continued talking as though nothing had happened. Then dropped me off at the exit near my home.

I don't know what saved me that day, or on six other occasions, when men tried to touch me inappropriately. I was able to get out of each situation, without physical harm (but I have never forgotten them). Was that luck, or were my Guardian Angels watching over me?

After that close call, I stopped hitchhiking to the hospital, and went back to riding my bicycle. I still hated that ride, so a while later I came up with another idea. If there were two of us, hitchhiking would be less dangerous. I talked my friend Alice into hitchhiking with me. The first few times it was easy, and we got safe rides to the hospital and back.

However, one day on the way back from Würzburg, we just could not get a good ride. A couple of cars stopped but they were GIs, and we waved them away. We were told often that the American soldiers were dangerous, and any girl that would be seen with them was a harlot.

We waited for a long time, finally a car stopped, but again they were GIs. There were two of them, and they were wearing dress uniforms with lots of shiny buttons and emblems. I assumed that they were officers. Surely, we would be safe with them. Besides, it was getting late and we didn't have much choice. After some debate, Alice and I agreed to get into the backseat of their car. At first, all went well. Our communications were limited, but I spoke a little English, and they spoke a little German, so we managed to talk about basic things.

When we got to Kitzingen, I asked them to stop and let us out, but they insisted that this was not Kitzingen, and kept on driving. We begged them to stop several times, but they acted like they didn't hear us. They said that all they wanted was to have dinner with us. They knew a nice little *Gasthaus* just a few miles ahead, and they promised that they would take us home right after dinner. I told them, "Our moms will have dinner ready for us, so please just take us home." But they just kept driving, and we got more and more afraid the farther we got from Kitzingen.

When we arrived at the *Gasthaus*, I got an idea about how we could get away. After we were seated, I asked to be excused to go to the restroom, and I told Alice to come with me. But instead of the restroom, we went to the kitchen, and told the owners what had happened to us. I asked them if they would please hide us and tell the soldiers that we ran out the back door. Thankfully, the owners went along with my plan. After the owner told the soldiers that we had gone, they went outside and looked for us, but after a few minutes they got into their car and drove away.

We waited until we were sure they were gone, then we thanked the owners and left. We were still scared, so the last thing we wanted to do was hitchhike. But we had no choice. We were too far away from home to walk, so we had to get a ride. We stood on the side of the road for a long time, but this was a country road, and there were very few cars going toward Kitzingen. None of them stopped. It was getting dark, and we were terrified.

When a car finally stopped, we saw that not only was the driver an American soldier, but he was black. Now what? What should we do? Alice said, "No way, I am not getting into that car."

I said, "So what do you want to do? It's going to be pitch-dark soon, and there may not be another car that will stop. Also, there's only one of him and two of us. You sit in the front . . ."

"Oh No!" she said.

" . . . And I will sit in the back. I'll take my shoe off, and if he tries anything, I'll hit him over the head."

Finally, Alice agreed to get into the car. I told the man about our ordeal. I emphasized that the bad guys were two "white officers" and so we thought that we would be safe. Luckily, that man had a sense of humor, and over-looked my racist remark. He spoke good German and was amused by our story. After a while he made us feel comfortable and relaxed, and he stopped the car when we got to our exit. Before we got out of the car, he said, "I know a really nice little *Gasthaus*. Would you like to have dinner with me?"

"NO!" We both yelled, and scrambled out of the car as fast as we could. We could hear him laughing, but we didn't think he was funny, and ran for home as quickly as we could.

That was the last time I hitchhiked. I continued to ride my bicycle to visit Nadia. After a time, Nadia's cast was removed, and she joined her mother in England.

My First Full-time Job

I was helping out at home from the time I can remember with things like translating, filling out forms, letter-writing, gleaning, cooking, household chores, and any other tasks that Mama needed done. Also, I babysat evenings and during summer vacation.

My first real job was as an apprentice at Wachter's *Metzgerei* (butcher shop). I was 14 years old and had just graduated from the 8th grade with high marks.

I did not want to work at a butcher shop. I wanted to go to high school, but Papa would not allow that. I also knew that I could do office work, or any number of more interesting jobs. However, my parents insisted that I take that job; not because it paid much. I only got 10 *Deutsche Mark* a month, and I had to work 10 to 12 hours a day, six and-a-half days a week. My parents wanted me to work there because Mrs. Wachter had promised that she would send meat home (which of course was out of date meat). Also, she said that I could eat as much *Wurst* und *Brötchen* (sausage and rolls) as I wanted. The promise of getting meat was just too tempting for my parents, and so I went to work there. I had no choice.

I rode a "Butcher's Bicycle," which is a heavy bicycle with a small wheel in front so that a large basket can be attached to the handlebar. That's how I transported meat from the slaughterhouse to the shop which was about a four-mile round-trip. They usually over-filled the basket, and I had to pump hard to get the bicycle moving. It took all the strength I had to keep the bicycle upright and hold on to the handlebar.

Most times I had to ride twice a day between the store and the slaughterhouse because we ran out of something, or the out-of-date meat had to be returned to the slaughter house. (Frau Wachter kept her word, and sent some of that meat home with me.) I also rode that bicycle when delivering meat to customers all over town, and running errands for Mrs. Wachter.

After the store closed, I had to carry the carcasses of beef and pork (which hung, on hooks, on the wall during the day) into the walk-in cooler. Then all the cut-up meat and sausage in the display case, had to be wrapped and put into the cooler.

I was so hungry for meat, that sometimes I cut a piece off the carcass, and ate it raw. I was careful how much sausage I ate because Mrs. Wachter kept a close eye on that.

Next, I had to wipe out the display cases and counters, take the wooden pallets, which were behind the counter, outside and scrub them. After that I got on my knees to wash, and wax the shop floor.

The job I hated most was killing rats. There was a rat infestation in that area of town. So, I had to set-up rat traps in the storage room before I left for home. Then first thing in the morning, I had to empty those traps. Sometimes, not all of the rats were dead, so I had to kill them. I felt sick to my stomach every time I saw a rat, still alive, caught in a trap, crawling around and dragging the trap with him. I hated to kill that poor rat; he was trying so hard to stay alive. I found dead and dying rats every morning.

Next, I had to put the pallets back behind the counter, take the carcasses of meat out of the cooler, and put them back on display in the shop.

Every other Sunday morning, I worked at the Wachter's home. I helped with cooking breakfast for the family, and the slaughterhouse crew. I washed dishes, cleaned the kitchen and dining room. I also got to eat a big breakfast of sausage, bacon, eggs, and *Brötchen*.

After I had worked in the shop a few months, I asked Frau Wachter, "When am I going to start learning to be a sales clerk?"

She said, "Next year you will work at the slaughterhouse. You will learn how to butcher the animals and cut them into carcasses. Then, you will refine your carving skills. After that, you will come back to the shop and learn how to work with customers. It takes at least three years before you can call yourself a sales clerk."

This was not at all what I wanted to hear, and certainly not what I wanted to do with my life. The thought of killing animals was repulsive. I knew the Wachters were just using me as cheap labor in the guise of 'Apprentice'. Frau Wachter already had a sales clerk. She was a middle age single woman, and very fussy, especially about her long and pointy nails. I never knew her first name. Everybody, including Frau Wachter, called her Fraulein Spiegel.

About a year went by, when I noticed a lot of spider veins all over my legs.

My mother was concerned and took me to see Dr. Hubschman. He was horrified and asked me what I was doing. After I described my job, he got angry at my mother for letting me work so hard and told her that I had to quit that job right away or I would damage my legs permanently. That made my mama cry. She said, "I sorry, but Nina have to work, we need meat and money."

Dr. Hubschman told her, 'Nina can work for my daughter. She needs a nanny for her little boy. They will pay her more than twice as much as she is getting at the butcher shop, and you can buy some meat. First however, she has to stay in bed for two weeks."

He prescribed some medication, and miraculously, the spider veins disappeared. They never came back, even during my pregnancies.

I enjoyed working for Dr. Hubschman's daughter. I did light housekeeping and simple cooking. The work was easy, and the little boy was well-behaved.

I remember one incident: the daughter and her husband went to Paris for a few days. When they returned, they were going on and on about the new and wonderful things called, "potato chips" and how very thin and crisp they were. I did not know what they were talking about. But to please them, I decided to cook potatoes for them. (I thought, how hard can it be to fry very thin potatoes?) Of course, I knew nothing about deep frying. So, my thin fried potatoes were mushy, oily, and nothing like real potato chips. I did not realize just how far off my potatoes were from the real thing, Mr. and Mrs. were too nice to tell me. After I came to America and tasted a potato chip for myself, I felt very foolish, but also thankful to that young couple for not laughing at me. They just told me that my potatoes were good, but different from the potatoes they had eaten in Paris.

I had to quit the nanny job when we were notified that our immigration visa number was getting close.

Our agreement with our sponsors, Mr. and Mrs. Cohen, in Sherwood, Oregon, was as follows: I would work for them as a maid for at least one year, and my parents would take care of their farm, and animals for the same length of time.

Mama and Papa decided that I should get a housekeeping job with an American family. That way I could learn how the Americans cleaned house, and practice speaking English, which I had learned in school, but never had a chance to use.

So, I went to work as a maid for an American G.I. family, who were stationed in Kitzingen.

They didn't have many possessions, and no washer or dryer. Their apartment had wall-to-wall carpets, but they did not have a vacuum cleaner. I had no idea how to clean carpets because all we ever had were bare floors. The Mrs. told me to sweep the carpet with a broom, which of course stirred up a lot of dust, and made the dusting more difficult. I cleaned the house, made the beds, washed windows and dishes, prepared food, and so on. The hardest job was doing all of the laundry by hand. Also, everything had to be ironed, including the sheets. But I didn't mind, I was used to hard work, and I was learning a lot.

The biggest problem for me was, the man of the house had amorous intentions. Whenever we were alone in a room, he would stare at me and lick his lips, or walk by me too closely. I tried to discourage him by glaring at him, and by jerking away from him when he tried to touch me. I stayed out of his way as much as possible. I always had to be on my guard, which made me very nervous. I did not tell my parents because I had always handled things on my own, and I did not want to worry them. I didn't tell his wife for fear of making the situation worse or losing the job.

So, I just kept it to myself and hoped the man would eventually leave me alone.

One day, while his family was away, he came home early. I felt very uncomfortable, and I knew that this would not go well. Sure enough, he started getting very friendly, telling me how sexy and beautiful I looked, and how much he liked me. When I told him to leave me alone or I would tell his wife, he got angry and tried to grab me.

I stopped what I was doing, and ran out of the house.

When I got home, I told Mama what had happened, and she told me that I did the right thing by getting out of there. I never went back. Not even to collect my wages.

Oh, I almost forgot; while working for that American family, I tasted Jell-O for the first time. I spread it on my bread, and it tasted great. When the Mrs. saw me, she laughed and told me, "That is not the way to eat Jell-O. You eat it out of a bowl, like soup." I was dumbfounded. How could anybody afford to eat something that tasted so wonderful by the spoonful's?

I could hardly wait to get to America and see what other wondrous things I would find.

My Grandfather's Prison Story, 1920

In 1918–1920 Lenin seizes power in Russia, and formed the Collectives. The farmers had to turn over everything they produced to the Collective. The Communist Party was supposed to distribute the food equally to everybody. However, like everything else that is forced upon people, it is open to corruption. The warehouses were full of food, and yet people went hungry. After 1924, under Stalin's rule, the warehouses were empty and starvation was rampant. Many people starved to death. This turned neighbors against neighbors.

When I was about 14 years old, Mama told me the following story: "Your grandparents had a big farm near Sulin, Ukraine. Their main production was wheat. After the Communists took over, your grandparents, like everyone else, had to give all the wheat they harvested to the Collective.

One year, after the harvest, your grandfather did not give all their wheat to the Collective. He hid one sack in the barn. Grandfather was a very religious man. (Mama did not know which religion; she just knew that they worshiped on Saturdays) and this act weighed heavily on his conscience. But, he had a wife, four children, and other family members who depended on him, and he did not trust the Communists to feed his family.

Your grandmother was a generous woman. When she baked bread, she shared it with her family, close friends, and with hungry children who were not part of her family.

A neighbor noticed her generosity and suspected that your grandparents had extra wheat. So, she reported them to the authorities.

Two communist officials came to the house and demanded to know where the wheat was hidden. Your grandfather would not tell a lie, but he refused to tell them his hiding place, even when they beat him. The men searched the house and barn, and knocked holes in the walls. But they did not find the wheat. When they threatened to harm his family, your grandfather could no longer keep quiet. He told them that the wheat was in the barn, inside a barrel, under a block of ice.

The officials confiscated the wheat. Your grandfather was arrested and put in prison.

Your grandmother took food to the prison every day; she knew that Grandfather would not be fed otherwise. She did not know that your grandfather never got that food.

Grandfather was a man of many trades. He was a farmer, carpenter, shoemaker, and a handyman. He was also the only dentist in his small village. One day, the jail-keeper's wife had a severe toothache, and came to your grandfather for help. After he treated her, she asked what she could do for him. Grandfather, who was dying of starvation, asked only for a crust of bread. She told her husband to give Grandfather all the bread he wanted. Which he did.

Your grandfather ate too much bread. After going so long without food, he could not digest the bread. And so, he died in agony!

No one told your grandmother that her husband had died, so she kept going to the prison every day. She was never allowed to see him, but they took the food she brought. This went on for many weeks. Finally, one of the guards took pity on her, and told her, "*Babushka*, don't come here anymore. Your husband is no longer in this world."

Grandmother never got to see your grandfather's body, and she never found out where he was buried."

Here ends the story that Mama told me. I never knew my grandparents, and I wish that I had asked Mama to continue, and tell me what happened to my grandmother and the farm.

I only remember Mama telling me that my grandmother had lived a very long life, and that she was over 100 years old when she died.

My Grandmother

My 15th Year

The 15th year of my life was a very exciting one. My dream was coming true. We found out that our visa to America had been approved!

We sold and gave away our few belongings, had a going away party and said "goodbye" to all of our friends. I was sad and a little afraid of the unknown. But the excitement of finally having my dream come true outweighed the other emotions.

We took a train to München (Munich), Germany, where we were interviewed, examined and cleared to go to America.

I had my first airplane ride, and we arrived in New York two weeks before my 16th birthday.

I also had two marriage proposals, (sort of). Shortly after my 15th birthday, I got my first proposal:

A Russian man, who lived in England with his father, came to Germany looking for a wife. He was supposed to be courting another girl, but instead he spent a lot of time at our house. He brought me gifts, took me to the movies, and visited often with my parents and me.

We even went on a train trip to Frankfurt.

When the train stopped at a small village, a group of school children got on, and sat down in the seats close to us. They were all excited; laughing and talking. I was certain that they were speaking German, but I could not understand everything they were saying. I could not recognize many of their words. I was astonished. If they were speaking German, why could I not understand them? Finally, I figured out that they must be speaking *Plattdeutsch* (Low German), or some other German dialect. This was the first time I had ever heard anyone speak German with such a strong dialect.

I enjoyed being with that man and all the attention I was getting. He was a very nice and gentle man. He was in his twenties, but looked older because he was getting bald, and was overweight. He was also very shy.

One day when he came for a visit, Mama and Papa went for a walk and left me alone with him. He sat down next to me, and we talked for a while. Suddenly, he leaned over and tried to kiss me. I was shocked. I moved my head so the kiss landed on my cheek, and then I pushed him away. He looked at me with the saddest eyes, and I realized that he had been courting me all along. I told him, "I am sorry, but I don't want to marry you, or anyone. I am too young for that."

He said, "No, I am sorry." Then he got up and left.

Front, L to R: Mrs. Klimusch, Bill, Nina, Mama,
Back: Man from England, Papa, and Mr. Klimusch

I was crying when Mama walked in. She was furious with me. She said, "You knew that man was looking for a wife. You led him on, and took up all of his time. Why did you do that? Now he has to go back to England without finding a wife."

I told her, "Mama, I am sorry. I was just having fun. I wasn't thinking about marriage. I don't want to get married." She stopped yelling and walked out.

My parents and the man must have talked things over when they were outside, because when Mama came back in, she was no longer mad at me. She just told me to go outside and play.

My second marriage proposal was actually an "arrangement" which was made at our "Going to America Party." My parents and a lady friend of theirs decided that after we got to America her son Friedrich would come over as our guest. Then he and I would get married, and we would sponsor Friedrich's mother and brother. I am not sure how much of that was Vodka talking. Friedrich and I didn't really know each other. We had only met a couple of times. He was about 20 years old, dark, and very handsome. I was impressed with his good looks, and we both agreed to write.

In the beginning, we wrote to each other often; but as time went on, I wrote less and less, and finally I stopped writing to him altogether. I had too many interesting things to do in America to be thinking about a boy in Germany, whom I barely knew.

—20 years later, I saw Friedrich again when my parents and I visited friends from Germany who now live in New York. Friedrich and his mother had also managed to come to America. They owned a bar in New Jersey, and invited us to a party. Friedrich was still handsome, but also full of himself. I realized that we were two very different people.

While we were in New York, we stayed with our friends, Mr. and Mrs. Schmidt, who now lived in Queens. Their apartment was very nice, and in a good neighborhood. We also visited the younger Schmidt family, who had been our neighbors when we lived in Kitzingen. They now lived on Long Island. I liked that area, it was rural, and yet, it was close to New York City.

Among other things, I saw the Statue of Liberty and Radio City Music Hall. I also ate my first whole lobster in a lovely restaurant.

I got to see one of my best childhood friends, Alice. She used to live in *Schützenplatz*, in one of the barracks next to ours, and she now lived in Brooklyn. I was shocked at her living conditions. Her neighborhood was very run-down. There was graffiti on many of the buildings and everything looked dirty. The building she lived in was very old. We walked up several flights of stairs to get to her apartment. Alice was very pretty, but had never married. She still lived with her mother Lina, just as she had in Germany. Their apartment was small, but very clean. Even so, they had cockroaches. They said that they could not get rid of them because of their dirty neighbors. I was sad to see her living in such poor conditions, but she didn't mind. She was happy to be living in America.

All of our friends in New York were very glad and thankful to be in America. They all felt that their lives were easier and better than in Germany. Of course, we were glad that we lived in Oregon; the best place of all.

Coming to America, 1954

G oing to America was my dream, a dream to hold onto when things looked hopeless.

The dream became possible after President Truman signed the first United States Refugee Law, the "Displaced Person's Act of 1948," allowing the legal entry of people displaced by World War II into America. The Displaced Persons had to have sponsorship from people in America who could provide them with gainful employment, because government welfare was not allowed.

We were very lucky to get sponsors. Gottfried and Anna Frank, the people with whom we shared a covered wagon, had family in America who had sponsored them. After the Franks got to America, they found Mr. and Mrs. Cohen who vouched for us and guaranteed that we would not be a burden to the government for five years, and we agreed that we would work for them for at least one year.

We had no money to pay for our transportation to America. Thankfully, the Lutheran Council of Churches lent us the money.

We also had no papers, other than the identification papers we had received in Poland, and registration papers from Germany. We needed birth certificates before we could come to America. We were told to go to the pastor in our church. There we swore, with our hands on the Bible, where and when we were born and baptized. Our statement was typed up and our pastor signed it. We hoped that this would be enough to get our passports and visas. Thankfully, it worked.

After we got all of our documents approved, I was so excited! I would tell everybody I saw, even perfect strangers, that we were going to America. Some people told me, "America is wonderful and rich and the land of opportunities."

Others asked, "What do you think you will find in America? Streets paved in gold?"

I told them, "Almost anything will be better than what we have here in Germany. No matter how hard we try, you will never accept us as equals. You will always look at us and think, *Ruskies* go home."

I remembered the time we were told that a lot of food was wasted in America, and that the gleaning would be plentiful. That alone sold me.

The fact was that in Germany we had worked very hard just to survive. After more than nine years of hard work, we had only a few meager possessions.

The day finally arrived. We got our letter to report to Munich. After waiting for so long, it was hard to believe that it was really happening. Mama and Papa asked me to read the letter to them again and again, just to make sure that it was real.

We were not given much time to get ready, but we didn't need much time. We had been ready for nine years.

Papa built a crate in which we packed our few possessions and shipped it ahead to Mr. and Mrs. Frank, in America. Then the suitcase was packed and waited by the door until we departed for Munich. We sold or gave away the rest of our stuff.

Our going away party was bittersweet. We were happy to leave for America, but also sad to leave our friends behind. I knew that our friends were happy for us, but also a little envious because they too were waiting to have their visas approved. I remembered the going away party for Anna and Gottfried Frank and how I felt. I wanted so much to change places with them.

In Munich, we had to go through very thorough physical exams and interviews. We spent several days and nights in

Our going away party, Nina, top center.
Friedrich, leaning into his mother's face.

a large dormitory room and slept in small cubicles on army cots. We waited nervously until everything was approved. All the while we kept dreading that something might go wrong and we would be sent back to Kitzingen.

We were relieved when they told us that everything was in order, and we were approved to go to America.

The next morning at the airport, we lined up and waited for our final passport and visa checks. Then we waited in another line to board the airplane.

It wasn't until after we were actually on the airplane that I dared to believe our dream was really coming true. *We were really going to America!* I was happy and excited, but also a little afraid because I had never flown before.

After I relaxed a little, I became aware that all the people on the plane were refugees, and they, too, were eager to meet their dream. Everyone was in high spirits. It was a joyful party and we were all celebrating. People were milling around and visiting with each other, talking about where they were going and what they were going to do when they got there. A very handsome young man came over and talked to me. I don't remember his words, but I do remember feeling special and very grown up.

We had heard about the big statue that welcomed immigrants from all over the world and we were excited and anxious to see her.

When we flew above New York and saw the Statue of Liberty, we all cheered and hugged each other. I was staring out the window in awe, and my heart was beating fast. Some people were crying, and others were laughing, but we were all happy to see America!

Much later when I did some research, I found the Statue of Liberty Inscription.

Quote from "The New Colossus" by Emma Lazarus: (unveiled in 1903)

"Keep, ancient lands, your storied pomp!" cries she
With silent lips.

"Give me your tired, your poor,
Your huddled masses yearning to breathe free,
The wretched refuse of your teeming shore.
Send these, the homeless, tempest-tossed to me,
I lift my lamp beside the golden door!"

New York

Our plane landed in New York on January 19, 1954. We had to go through immigration control, passport check, and retrieve our luggage. But I don't remember much of that. I was impatient to get out of there as fast as possible, so I could see America.

Finally, our bus left the airport. We were on our way to the train station and I got to see what America really looked like.

The first thing I noticed were all the cars—the roads were full of them. Then I saw the tall buildings, and I understood the word "skyscrapers." How did those buildings not fall down? There were many bright lights and so many people and beautiful colors. All the cars and people seemed to be in a big hurry, and there was so much noise. Everything was overwhelming.

We knew that when we got to the train station, we had to wait several hours before we could board the train to Chicago. There, after a two-hour layover, we would be taking a train to Portland. Our final destination was Sherwood, Oregon. Mama realized that we did not have enough food for the journey. We looked around inside the train station but could not find any food for sale.

Raya Schmidt, a friend of my parents (who was also traveling from Kitzingen) and I went out of the station to search for a store. I am still amazed at how brave, or stupid, we were. I could speak only a little bit of English and Raya spoke none.

We had to walk a long way before we found what looked like a grocery store, and with help from a stranger, we were able to buy some food.

Then we got lost. The store was very large and had two exits. In all the confusion we took the wrong exit and came out on a different street without realizing it.

The farther we walked the more confused we got. Finally, we figured out that we must be going in the wrong direction and we got scared. We did not know which way to turn. Who could we ask for help? So many people, but they were all in a hurry and looked annoyed with us because we were in their way. We just stood in the middle of the sidewalk, afraid to move.

We saw a lady with a friendly face who was not in such a hurry. I approached her and said, "We need help, we are lost, we need train station. Please help."

She understood me and was very kind. She led us all the way back to the train station. She even made sure that we found the right waiting area for the train to Chicago. Who says that all the New Yorkers are cold and unfriendly? When we got back, we were glad to see our families and told them all about our first adventure in America.

Chicago

We boarded our train, and all was well until we got to Chicago. There we had another long wait for the train to Portland, Oregon. Again, we needed food, and could not find any for sale in the train station.

We saw a restaurant, and Papa decided we should go in and see how much it would cost to eat there. I still remember the looks we got when my parents, my eight-year-old brother, and I entered. We looked like four ragamuffins carrying a cardboard suitcase and some bags.

The restaurant was beautiful. All the tables were covered with white linen tablecloths, and the waiters were dressed in tuxedos. It was obvious that we did not belong there. I was so embarrassed.

But to my surprise a very friendly maître d' greeted us, and seated us at a table, and a waiter brought us water and menus. I could not recognize most of the words on the menu, but I could recognize the numbers, and I knew that we could not afford anything on that menu. I told Papa how much the food cost and he decided that we had better leave.

When we got up to go, the maître d' came over to see what the problem was. I told him, "We not have much money."

The kind man suggested we have some soup and bread. He told us the price, and Papa said we could afford that. The waiter brought us soup and lots of bread. It had been many days since we'd had anything warm to eat. We ate all of the delicious soup, and Mama saved the leftover bread for later.

Two hours later we boarded our train to Portland. Again, we had a long way to go, and after a while our bread ran out. The conductor kept coming through calling, "First call to dinner. Second call to dinner."

But we knew he was not calling us because we could not afford to eat there.

When the train stopped we saw a woman on the platform selling food. We called to her and she came to the window. We bought some bread and sausage, enough to last us until we arrived at our destination.

Portland

After we arrived in Portland, we were happy and relieved to see our friend Anna Frank. She introduced us to our sponsor, Mrs. Cohen, and we were overcome with gratitude to this wonderful lady who took a risk in sponsoring us, strangers whom she had never met. She just had Anna's word that we were trustworthy. Mama and Papa kept bowing to her and saying, "Thank you, thank you," over and over.

Mrs. Cohen drove a big station wagon with room for all of us and our few belongings. Soon we were on our way to our new home in Sherwood.

Our ride from the train station along the Willamette River and through Lake Oswego was beautiful. We enjoyed the view, but we couldn't fully appreciate it because we were tired and anxious to see our new home.

I longed for a bath and to sleep in a bed. It had been a long time since we'd had either. During our long journey, we had slept in an upright position and had taken sponge baths at the train's bathroom sink.

Ten years later, at age twenty-six, I became a citizen of the United States of America.I still remember the pledge I made:

"I pledge allegiance to the flag of the United States of America and to the Republic for which it stands, one nation under God, indivisible, with liberty and justice for all."

That was a very proud and emotional moment. The words were powerful and meant so much to me. I felt very grateful that I finally belonged to a country, and I hoped that America would be my home for the rest of my life.

Working for Our Sponsors

We finally arrived at our destination: the outskirts of Sherwood, where the Cohen's owned 30 acres along the Tualatin River.

After we turned off the main highway, a private road led us past someone's farm and through the Cohen's filbert orchard. Then we stopped on a gentle slope from where we could see a lovely valley with several buildings.

Mrs. Cohen explained that the first building on the right was a guest house, and next to it was the main residence. A little farther to the left, we saw a big barn and a smaller barn. Down the lane was the original farmhouse which was rented out. Beyond that was the caretaker's house where my parents would live. She said that my room was in the basement of the main residence where the Cohens lived.

We could see the Tualatin river curving along the perimeter of the property with gentle hills beyond. We also saw several big trees sprinkled throughout the acreage. Our new home looked like paradise to us! I could not believe that we would be living in such a beautiful place.

The house my parents lived in had four bedrooms, a large living room, a kitchen and (to their amazement)

Husky, watching over our sponsor's main house and guest house

an indoor bathroom. It was fully furnished. My parents loved their new home. This was a mansion compared to the two-room barrack and outhouse we'd had when we lived in Germany.

I loved my own private room in the daylight basement of the main house. The room had an outside window, a comfortable bed, a dresser, a desk and a chair, and it was nicely decorated. I even had my very own bathroom.

At the bottom of the stairs before entering my room was a large open storage area where "Mack," a big beautiful macaw parrot lived on a perch in the middle of the room. He and I became good friends. Every time I walked down the stairs Mack greeted me by whispering, "Hi Mack," and I whispered, "Hi Mack" back to him.

My parents' job was maintaining a barn full of laying hens, looking after some sheep, and taking care of whatever tasks were needed on the farm.

My job was cleaning the main house and guesthouse, do the washing and ironing, and some light cooking. The Cohens often went out to eat. It was not hard work, and Mrs. Cohen was very patient with all of us. Anna Frank, who worked for them before we arrived, showed my parents how to do their job, and Mrs. Cohen showed me how to do mine. She also taught me many new English words.

She had a great sense of humor. One day I came into the house shouting," Mrs. Cohen, Mrs. Cohen, the um . . . the, the man chicken is attacking the woman chicken." After she stopped laughing she assured me, "It's okay, the rooster is just doing his job."

I didn't understand her answer, but I just let it go.

Mrs. Cohen had taught me how to cook simple American meals. One day, I was going through a recipe book and a picture of a lemon meringue pie caught my eye. I had eaten lemon meringue pie one time and I loved the taste. I thought maybe I could bake that pie.

I checked and found that I had all the ingredients. I couldn't understand all of the instructions, but I thought, if I just mix all of that stuff together and bake it as directed, it should be okay. When I took the pie out of the oven it did not look at all like a lemon meringue pie. It looked like a blob and felt like rubber to the touch.

Just then, Mrs. Cohen came into the kitchen and saw me crying. I told her what I had done, and that I was sorry that I had wasted so much food. Being the goodhearted lady, she was, she tried to console me. After she took a very small bite of the rubbery mess and managed to swallow it, she said, "It tastes okay, but I don't think we should serve this to Mr. Cohen." With that, she gave me a hug and left the room. I could tell that she was having a hard time keeping a straight face. But the ultimate insult was that even Husky the dog, who ate everything, would not eat my pie.

The Cohens were wonderful people. I am guessing they were in their sixties. She was tall and handsome, and obviously once a great beauty. He was short and on the pudgy side. He was Jewish, and she was Catholic. They had no children. They were devoted to each other and I never heard them argue.

Mr. Cohen owned a furniture manufacturing business in Portland. Their main production was school furniture. Mrs. Cohen was in charge of the farm.

I enjoyed the beautiful surroundings. Our living conditions in America were so much better than they had been in Germany, and I loved all of the luxuries. I had a radio in my room which was my entertainment. I heard the same popular songs that I had listened to in Germany coming from the *Gasthaus* on the hill. It gave me a strange connection between falling asleep to the music in Kitzingen and sleeping in my very own room in America.

However, I had no contact with people close to my age, so I was lonely and missed my friends in Germany. My only American friends were Mack, the beautiful macaw parrot, and the dog. I enjoyed taking long walks along the river with Mack sitting on my shoulder, nibbling my neck and whispering, "Hi Mack" in my ear. My other friend, an Alaskan Husky dog named "Husky" followed along on our river walks.

My brother, Bill, was eight years old and too young to be my friend.

—Recently Bill told me that he had not been lonely because he had the Frank children, who were close to his age, to play with. He also enjoyed going to school, and had friends there as well.

We were very isolated because there were no towns or stores within walking distance. In order for us to become self-sufficient we had to have a car and I needed to take driving lessons.

I studied the manual and got my driver's permit. Then Mrs. Cohen hired a driving instructor who came to the house, and picked me up for my lessons. My driving test was in Oregon City on very steep roads. I failed my test the first time because the teacher had not shown me how to stop and start on a steep hill with a stick shift. Once I learned how to work the clutch, the brakes, the gas pedal, and shift gears all at the same time. I took the test again and got my driver's license.

Mama and Papa bought a black 1941 Chevy four-door sedan. I was thrilled. In my wildest dreams I never thought that I would be driving a car. I felt like a bird that was let out of the cage. I was free to go wherever I wanted. What a great feeling.

Someone told me about a German choir group in Portland, which I joined. One evening a week I drove to Portland for choir practice. We mostly sang for our own pleasure, but occasionally we performed in front of a live audience. I was the youngest of the group. I remember taking a trip to Seattle with the choir group and performing at a concert hall. We all stayed in a fancy hotel. I was very impressed, and felt very grown up. I shared a room with Herta, another Russian/German refuge. She was just a few years older than I, and we had become good friends.

I was not so lonely anymore. I really looked forward to my weekly outings. Herta, some other young people and I usually went for coffee after choir practice. It was comfortable to be with someone close to my age who spoke both English and German.

There I met Erwin, who was also a Displaced Person from Ukraine. He was about eight years older than I, and wanted to be more than friends. He even took me home to meet his mother. She was a very nice lady and welcomed me. But shortly after, he enlisted in the Army and left before our romance had a chance to blossom. I wrote to him occasionally, but after a while I got busy and stopped.

I found out that the choir group was hosting a dance and I really wanted to go. The only problem was that I didn't know how to dance. The last time I went dancing was in Germany, and I had stepped all over my partner's feet. I told Mrs. Cohan my dilemma and she suggested that I try Arthur Murray Dance Studio in Portland.

I went to the studio, and told them, "I want to learn to dance today." The instructor laughed and said, "I can't do that in one lesson, but I can try to teach you how to follow a dance partner."

He told me to relax my body completely, hold onto my partner's left hand with my right hand, place my left hand on his shoulder blade, bend my knees slightly, keep my feet out of his way, and follow his body movements. We kept practicing that until I got it right.

At the dance I did what the instructor taught me and it worked. I was able to follow everyone I danced with, and I really enjoyed myself. I continued with my dance lessons at Arthur Murray's until I learned the basic dance steps to most ballroom music.

Driving home from choir one night, it was late and I was in a hurry to get home. The speed limit through Lake Oswego was 25 miles per hour. Since there was no one on the road, I decided that there was absolutely no reason why I should drive that slow. So, I just continued to drive 35 mph. I saw a policeman parked up ahead, but I kept on driving the same speed.

When the policeman pulled me over, he asked, "Do you know what the speed limit is?"

I said, "Yes. 25 miles per hour."

"How fast were you driving?

"35 miles."

"Did you see me parked on the street?"

"Yes."

"Then why did you not slow down?"

I said, "Nobody was driving on road, no reason I drive so slow. I drive same, if you are on road, or not on road."

He just stood there and looked at me with a very puzzled expression. I don't know if he had a problem understanding my broken English, or my broken logic. Probably both.

He asked," Are your parents going to be mad at you when you get home so late?"

I said, "No, I work and live in sponsor's house. Now they are sleeping."

He stood there for another minute or so, obviously not knowing what to do with me. He scratched his head. Then, he finally just shook his head and said, "Well, at least you're honest. But you must follow the speed limit, whether you think it's logical or not. Do you understand that?"

I told him, "I understand. I am sorry. I be more careful next time."

He was a very nice man, and he let me go with just a warning.

—I didn't get a ticket until I was about 21 years old. Ironically, that ticket was for driving 35 mph in a 25-mile zone. My next ticket wasn't until I was in my fifties. Guess what? I was driving 36 mph in a 25-mile zone. Those were the only traffic tickets I ever received.

Later in life I was involved in two accidents, both caused by a deer.

The first one happened when I was driving home from Reno. It was twilight. Suddenly I saw a deer standing in the middle of my lane, headlights approaching in the left lane, and a ditch on the right side of the road. I stomped on the brakes as hard as I could, but I hit the deer and killed him. There was some damage to the front end of my car, however, my passenger and I were not hurt.

Many years later, I was driving on a curvy two-lane road through a wooded area. Suddenly, a deer jumped out of the bushes from the right-hand side of the road, and landed on top of the hood of my car. Then, the deer somersaulted, crashed through the windshield of an oncoming car, and landed in the passenger's lap. The deer died, the passenger was in shock, but none of the people were hurt. My car just had a dent on top of the hood. In both cases I was able to continue driving home, and had the car repaired the following week.

After about ten months of working for our sponsors, Mrs. Cohen and I decided that I was not cut out to be a domestic.

One day, she asked me, "How would you like to work in a hospital?"

At first, I was speechless; then I said, "Can I really do that?"

She said, "I can arrange that, but you will have to take a training class at the hospital and then pass a test. If you can pass that test, you could be working at St. Vincent's Hospital as a nurse's aide."

I hugged her and thanked her for doing that for me. Mrs. Cohen also told me that she knew some friends who lived near the hospital, and she would ask if I could live with them.

Mama and Papa, 1955 and after

Shortly before I left the Cohens, Mama found out that she was pregnant. Her doctor told her that she could not work around chickens while she was pregnant because she would be susceptible to catching a disease that was easily transmitted from chickens to pregnant women.

Mama was very upset. She was 40 years old, and felt that she was too old to have a baby. Mostly, however, she did not want to leave the Cohens and renege on our sponsorship agreement. They had been so good to us, and Mama did not want to disappoint them.

She asked me to arrange a meeting with Mrs. Cohen, which I did. Mama told me to ask her if she knew a doctor who would perform an abortion. I got upset when I heard what she was saying, and I did not want to ask that question. But she insisted, and I interpreted what Mama said. Mrs. Cohen was horrified because she was a devout Catholic.

We both insisted that Mama keep the baby. Mrs. Cohen told her not to worry. She would sell the chickens, and release my parents from their agreement.

When I interpreted what Mrs. Cohen said, Mama started sobbing, and thanked Mrs. Cohen again and again.

I can't even imagine how desperate Mama must have been to ask that question, and to have me interpret. She was a very private person, and we never talked about intimate things like that.

We never discussed the incident again. However, I do know that she was very relieved that she did not have to have the abortion. I also know how very much she loved my little sister after she was born.

Mama gave birth to a beautiful baby daughter at St. Vincent's hospital in March, 1955. I was with her during her labor. I also got to name my baby sister. I named her Lydia for her Russian heritage, and Jean, in case she wanted a name that sounded more American.

Our friend, Gottfried Frank, helped Papa get a job as a cement finisher. Papa worked there until he retired at age 65.

Another friend lent my parents some money, and they bought a little one-bedroom house on Center Street in Tigard.

Mama went back to work soon after my sister Lydia was born. She cleaned other peoples' houses, and took my sister to work with her.

Neither Mama nor Papa spoke English when we arrived, I did the translating for them. But two years later, after I married and moved out, Mama had learned enough English to get a driver's license. After a few years, both of my parents could communicate quite well in English. Mama's famous saying was: "Why you no eat?" Everyone who came to her house had to eat, hungry or not.

A few years later, Mama became an American citizen. Papa could not get a driver's license or become a citizen because he could not read and write. His parents had died when he was young. His uncle raised him, and did not allow him to go to school.

Less than fifteen years after coming to America, my parents sold their little house, and built a beautiful home with a daylight basement in Tigard Heights on one acre of land with a great view. They did most of the work themselves. When they were finished, they owned their home free and clear. They also put my sister Lydia through college.

Mama and Papa lived frugally. They believed that renting, and paying interest, was like throwing money away. Their pleasure was not in buying things or going out to eat. It was in saving money, and watching their bank account grow. They knew the power of money, and that having money was essential for having security. They never owned a credit card. Mama always said, "No borrow money, only to buy house. When you no have money for this, you no need this."

Mama was in her sixties when she had a stroke. She was paralyzed on the right side and could not speak. The following day, her speech came back. First in Russian, then in German and finally in English. She could also walk with a little assistance.

Mama was never the same after her stroke. But she managed alright, until she had another severe stroke when she was 84. Papa and my sister put her in a nursing home, and Mama hated that.

One day when I came to visit her, she was sitting in a wheelchair. When I gave her a hug, she looked at me with pleading eyes and said, "Ninotchka please, I want to die. Please Ninotchka, help me."

My heart hurt for her, and I kept hugging and stroking her, but all I could do was tell her, "Oh Mamutchka, I understand, and I wish I could help you, but I can't. Only God can do that."

Those were the last words that Mama ever spoke!

She never talked again. It was as though she had left her body. From that day on she just sat there with a vacant look in her eyes. She did not recognize any of her family again. Mama died a few months later, September 11, 1998. I got to the nursing home just in time to close my mama's eyes.

Papa was lost without her. After she died, he did not take care of himself properly. He developed pneumonia and died 14 months later, November 11, 1999.

Even now, I miss them very much.

Before Mama and Papa died, they had achieved the American Dream. They owned a lovely home, and had a substantial amount of money in the bank. They also saw their children married, seven of their grandchildren grow up, and two of their great-grandchildren born.

In spite of low wages and no insurance, they never relied on the government or anyone else for a handout. I have always been proud of my mama and papa for their courage to come to America. For working hard. And for being self sufficient

As I look back, I realize how very fortunate we were to have wonderful people like the Cohens as our sponsors. I have heard of people who were sponsored by farmers that lived in remote areas. The sponsors worked the immigrants like slaves. They kept them isolated, and the immigrants had to stay because they didn't know anybody, and had nowhere else to go.

High School in America

After my parents left our sponsors and moved into the one-bedroom house they bought, Papa added two more bedrooms and I moved in with them.

I was 16 years old, and commuted from Tigard to St. Vincent's hospital in Portland, where I worked from 3 p.m. to 11 p.m. as a nurse's aide.

In the mornings, I went to Tigard High School. The councilors determined that I had the equivalent of a high school education. However, even though I had taken English in Germany, I needed much more help, and they recommended that I take English, Journalism, and History—all English-related subjects.

I was very confused about English spelling. In Germany, if you could pronounce the word properly, you could spell it easily. You just had to remember a few spelling rules. The English language has many confusing words that sound alike, but are spelled differently; also, there are many words that sound the same but mean different things. The grammar was also very confusing to me. All I could do was listen and memorize as much as I could.

I still have a problem pronouncing some of the sounds, my *Th* comes out like *T*. In Germany the *V* sounds like *F*, and the *W* sounds like V. So, if a *W* and a *V* are in one sentence, my tongue tends to trip over itself.

My school experience in America was much different from what it had been in Germany. I enjoyed going to Tigard High School. The students were friendly and curious. They wanted to know where I had come from, and what school was like in Germany. I was not bullied, and I never noticed any discrimination, as I had in Germany. The only thing that bothered me were the frequent interruptions. I would just be getting into the subject matter when a bell rang and everyone had to assemble in the gym. There were frequent "rah-rah" sessions for sports and other things which did not interest me. I just wanted to learn English and go to work at the hospital.

I could not relate to any of the kids, even though I was their same age. They seemed so much more innocent and carefree to me. I thought that the boys were very immature, and the girls were way too emotional over things that, in my mind, were not important. I thought, "I hope I don't have any daughters. I don't understand the girls now, so how could I have patience with them as their mother?"

After that school year ended, I decided not to return to high school because I often worked a second shift from 11p.m. to 7a.m. whenever they needed someone to watch a patient overnight. I had to get some sleep before my regular shift started at 3p.m., so I didn't have time for school.

Later, on my days off, I took an English class for adults, which was a big help.

I also took a modeling course. When I enrolled, I told them that I did not want to be a model. I wanted to learn how to act like a lady. I wanted to know proper manners, how to eat, stand, sit, and how to apply makeup, etc. Just the basic things that I had never been taught; which was what they concentrated on. The modeling course helped me a lot with my self-confidence.

Working at St. Vincent's Hospital, 1954–1958

Our sponsor, Mrs. Cohen, had arranged an interview for me at St Vincent's hospital in Portland. I filled out an application and was given a manual to study. Then I was told that I had to take a two-week Nurse's Aide training course. Also, there would be an exam at the end, and if I passed the test, I would get the job.

I still could not speak English very well, and I didn't understand many of the words in the manual, so I just kept reading it again and again, until I had it memorized. I was glad that they demonstrated a lot of the things in class that we were supposed to do on the job. I paid very close attention to what I saw, and tried to apply that to the things I had memorized.

When I took the test, I passed it with a score of 97. I missed getting 100 because I didn't understand the question: "On admission, what is the first thing you do?"

The answer is: "Take the patient's temperature, pulse and respiration." (TPR). I'll never forget that.

I was hired, and moved in with Mrs. Cohen's friends, who owned a beautiful old three-story home near the hospital in Portland Heights. There was a small maid's apartment on the third floor, where I lived. In lieu of rent. I cleaned their house and did their laundry on my days off from the hospital. That arrangement worked very well until I could move in with my parents.

My first station was the Women's Surgical Ward 4 South. I had to go through the Birth Center to get to that ward. When I got off the elevator, there was a sign that read: "No one under 16 allowed in this department." I was 16 and barely legal to pass through.

Most of the surgeries on 4 South were hysterectomies. At that time, they used ether for anesthesia. The women reeked of it when they came back to the ward. The smell of ether made me sick to my stomach. So, every time one of my patients threw up, I ran for the nearest restroom and did likewise. I hoped that eventually I would get used to it, but I never did.

After a few months they transferred me to Men's Urology. Shortly after I started working there, one of the student nurses said to me, "Come along and I'll teach you how to irrigate a catheter."

I had no idea what she was talking about, but I soon found out. She flipped back the covers and there, in all their glory, were the man's privates. I was glad that the patient was unconscious and didn't see my bulging eyes. But soon I got used to doing what was needed, and saw it as just another body part.

One night as I was getting off my shift, a young man came running up to me yelling, "My wife is having a baby."

I said, "That's wonderful."

He said, "You don't understand, she's having it now!"

I still did not know what he was talking about, but there was an urgency about him, so I listened closer, and he pointed to a car. I went with him, and sure enough, his wife was definitely in labor. I ran back to the hospital to get help. By the time help came, the baby's head was protruding. They delivered the baby right there in the car, and I got to watch. I thought that was the most awesome thing I had ever seen.

My next assignment was 2 North. It was the "overflow" of the hospital. There were emergency admissions, surgeries, skin diseases, patients going through delirium tremors and dementia, patients with breathing problems. And anything else you can imagine.

Working there was never boring. We were always short of help, so I had to do many tasks that were usually done by RNs, such as setting up oxygen tents, changing dressings, cleaning out tracheotomies, doing charts, etc.

I also learned how to handle difficult patients.

For example, visiting hours were 6 to 8 p.m. During that time, the nurses took turns going down to the cafeteria. One evening as I was going on break, I noticed that there were still a lot of visitors in the hall, waiting to see the patients.

I also noticed that one of my patients had gotten out of his restraints and was walking down the hall. He was quite a sight in his short, open-in-the-back, hospital gown. I caught up with him as quickly as I could and asked, "Mr. Brown, where are you going?"

He said, "I have to catch a plane," and continued walking.

I tried to get him to go back to his room, but he wouldn't listen. He was much bigger than I, and clearly delusional, so I knew I had to play along with him to get his cooperation. I spotted a wheelchair and got an idea.

I grabbed the chair, and ran after my patient yelling, "Taxi, taxi, anybody need a taxi?" That got his attention, and he stopped. When I pulled up to him, I asked, "Where are you going sir?"

"To the airport."

"Get in, and I will take you to the airport." I breathed a sigh of relief when he got into the wheelchair.

I wheeled him next to his bed, and told him, "Please sir, get on the airplane, and I will fasten your seatbelt."

He climbed into the bed, and I quickly fastened his restraints. When I got back out in the hall, I got a round of applause from the visitors. I thanked them, but I was just glad that they didn't think that I had lost my mind.

I hurried on down to the cafeteria for my break. I was craving a cigarette, and I knew that one of the doctors or nurses would give me one. I reminded myself to buy a pack of cigarettes and quit mooching them.

I loved working on 2 North, because every day was different.

I often worked a second shift, as a private nurse, whenever they needed someone to watch a patient at night. Mama and Papa needed the money, and I got a better hourly wage than on my nurse's aid job.

There was one big room of eight men, and most of them were not really sick. They had skin lesions, and needed their dressings changed several times a day. A very nice, soft-spoken man from the Philippines was the dressing nurse. He was old enough to be my father, and he treated me like a daughter. He loved to gamble, and when he won, he would always bring me a little gift. On his days off, I was assigned to that room. I enjoyed taking care of his patients. Most of those guys were usually in a good mood and were always teasing me. They loved to see me get embarrassed and blush.

One day I greeted them with, "This is beautiful day. Let's go play hickey."

They started laughing and clapping. They just went on and on, saying how great that would be. They all wanted to be first, and yelled, "How soon can we start?"

I thought that was odd, so I went out of the room, and asked one of the nurses to tell me what I had said. When she explained the difference between "hickey" and "hooky," I was so embarrassed. Of course, I meant to say, hooky.

That was not the only time using slang got me into trouble. I was under the delusion that slang would make me sound more like an American, and I wanted so much to be a real American. Eventually, I realized that using slang just made my English worse.

Working on 2 North had its downside, like changing diapers, and handling bedpans. The worst job, however, was washing and tagging patients after they had died, and then taking them down to the morgue. After a while, I got used to that as well, and it became just another job that needed to be done.

We admitted a raging drunk man who had been stabbed in the stomach by his wife. They placed him in my care room, and put him in restraints. The man was losing fluids from both ends, and needed constant cleaning. In order to change his linens, I had to loosen his restraints. Every time I did that, I had to wrestle with him.

During one of the wrestling matches, I lost, and he fell out of bed, dragging me with him. I was pinned to the floor with the man on top. Thankfully, one of the other patients pressed his "Nurse Call Button." Within a short time, a nurse came in and helped me get my patient back to bed. The wrestling matches continued for another hour or more. But I had learned my lesson and asked for help whenever I had to clean up my patient.

That was New Year's Eve. I was glad when my shift finally ended. As soon as I got off work, I quickly changed my clothes and hurried to the hospital parking lot.

I had a date with Herta, a friend I had met at a German choir group. She and I were going to a dance hall in Portland. They had a great Band, and did not serve alcohol. Although some of the men brought in their own and sneaked it into the soft drinks. The dance hall had bodyguards, so it was a safe place for unaccompanied women. We loved to go there and dance. Herta and I never let any of the guys sit at our table. That way we could dance with different men. It was more fun than dancing with just one guy, especially if he didn't know how to dance well. That night we had a great time. We did get a little bit tipsy and got a lot of "happy new year's kisses" from the guys we danced with. But, as always, at closing time, Herta and I left the dance hall together without men.

I was introduced to Pat, another nurse's aide, by the nursing supervisor. Pat didn't have a car and needed a ride to work. Since we both lived in Tigard, with our parents, the supervisor asked if Pat could ride with me. I agreed. I was glad to have the company because it was a long commute.

Pat was about four years older than I. She had dark hair, was a little on the chubby side, with a spring in her step, and a quick laugh. We became good friends, and most of the time, she went with me wherever I went.

One beautiful Sunday, Pat wanted to go to the beach, instead of going to work, and I just couldn't resist the temptation. So, she devised a plan. We would both call in sick. Pat would pretend that she was my mother, and I would pretend that I was her mother. The stupidity of that plan was that we hadn't taken my accent into account. Of course, I did not sound like her mother, and she certainly did not sound like mine. However, we thought that our plan had worked, and we had a great day at the beach.

The next afternoon, when we arrived at work, we both had a note clipped to our timecards, telling us to see the nursing supervisor. We knew why we were in trouble, and we entered the office with our heads bowed down. We got a good tongue-lashing, and a warning that if we ever did that again, we would be fired. I was very relieved that I was not fired on the spot, and of course, I never did that again.

There wasn't really much we could do after we got off work at 11p.m. We didn't want to just go home and go to bed, we needed to unwind. Sometimes we headed to downtown Portland and dragged Broadway, which was the popular thing to do in those days. We drove around and around looking at boys and practiced our flirting skills. Once in a while, we would stop the car and talk to them, but we never picked up anyone.

Our favorite hangout became, "Peter Pan's Restaurant," on Barbour Boulevard. We got acquainted with four boys who hung out there also. They were closer to Pat's age, but to me they were just immature kids. We enjoyed talking with them. That's where I practiced my English and picked up my slang.

Our coffee klatches with the boys were harmless fun, except for the day Mama woke me up, and asked, "Nina, were you drinking last night?"

I saw that she was very upset and scared, which scared me too.

I told her, "Mama, you know I don't drink."

She said, "Go look in your car."

I went out and saw that my whole backseat was full of street signs. I was shocked and flabbergasted. How did those signs get into my car? My next worry was, "How am I going to get rid of all those signs?"

After I calmed down, I suspected that the "Peter Pan Boys" were behind this stunt. But how did they know where I lived? I realized that they must have followed me. I was very upset with them, and couldn't wait to see them, so that I could give them a piece of my angry mind. But for now, all I could do was throw a blanket over the signs, and drive to work.

I told Mama, "Don't worry, everything will be all right. I will take care of this."

That evening, I was crying and at the same time yelling at the boys in my broken English. "You do bad thing, stealing signs and put in my car. My mama afraid, and I afraid to drive with signs. We are from country where people are very afraid of *Polizei*, and stealing is very bad."

They were surprised that I was so upset, and kept apologizing. They said that they didn't mean to scare my mother and me. They just thought that it would be funny. They took the signs out of my car and promised that they would never do anything like that again. This just proved to me how immature those boys were, and I was surprised how little fear they had of the police.

Another time those boys were a big help to me.

One afternoon on the way to work, my car suddenly started running poorly. I pulled over as soon as I saw a wide spot on the side of the road. I turned off the ignition and opened the hood, but I had no idea what to do next. I gave up and tried to turn the car back on, but it wouldn't start. I was near panic. How were we going to get to work? We had no way of contacting the hospital and we didn't dare show up late for our shift, for fear of getting fired.

Pat and I decided to hitchhike to the hospital and worry about the next step later. We had no trouble getting a ride. Maybe it was because we were wearing our nurse's uniforms? The driver was a nice man and he took us right to the hospital entrance.

All afternoon I kept worrying and thinking: "How are we going to get back home, and what am I going to do with my broken-down car?" I had no answer and I had no idea what to do. Finally, I came up with a very "iffy" plan. After work, I asked a co-worker to drive us to Peter Pan's Restaurant. I was really counting on the boys being there, and that one of them would know how to fix my car. I was relieved that two of the boys were there. When I explained to them how the car sounded, one of the boys said that he knew what was wrong.

When we got to the car, he found the problem and was able to fix it. What a relief.

Afterward, we were sitting in the car, and Pat and the boys were each drinking a beer. I didn't like the taste of beer, but I had a swallow of Pat's because my mouth was dry. Just then, a police car pulled up behind us. The policeman came up to the car and asked us what we were doing there. I told him that the boys had fixed my car and that we were just talking.

He said, "I can smell alcohol. Are you drinking?"

I told him, "I only have one swallow of beer."

He asked, "How old are you?" I lied and told him I was 18. Everybody else told the policeman that they were 20. In spite of our pleadings, he gave all of us tickets for underage drinking.

The following week, we had to appear before a judge in his chambers.

I told the judge that I was actually 17. I said the reason I had lied about my age was because I did not want to involve my parents, or scare them. Besides, they could not speak English, so I had to handle things on my own. I told him that I only had one swallow of beer. I explained that in Germany I could have all the beer I wanted, but I did not like alcohol. None of the kids I hung out with in Germany drank. Maybe that was because alcohol was not a forbidden fruit.

I said, "Maybe if it be same here in America, kids also not be drinking."

The judge said, "You may be right, but in America under-age drinking is against the law and you cannot drink in public."

I promised that I would never do that again. He could see how afraid I was, so he let me go with just a warning.

I gave all the money I earned at the hospital to my parents. Then Mama would give me enough money for gas and lunch. Sometimes, she gave me some extra money and told me to go buy myself something nice to wear. I would go to Lerner's Dress Shop in Portland and look at all the beautiful things. I wanted so many of them, but I only had a little amount of money and I couldn't decide what I wanted most. I was afraid to choose the wrong thing and then regret it when I got home.

I knew how important money was. We had lived for many years without having enough money for food and other necessities. So, most of the time, I bought nothing, and gave the money back to Mama.

I didn't need a lot of clothes because most of the time I wore a nurse's uniform. When I really needed something, I would go to the Goodwill Store and buy it there.

Part II

Married Life and Family, 1955–1980

Meeting Don Carmichael, 1955

I met Don in 1955, when he was admitted to St. Vincent Hospital because of blood poisoning he got, while working on the railroad, as a cook's helper. He had accidentally stuck a fork in his leg, but instead of cleaning out the wound he put flour on it, to stop the bleeding.

Don became my patient. He was a tall good-looking man, but I wasn't sure if I liked him. He was always pressing his call button and making a nuisance of himself. I was busy with other patients and didn't have time for his games. One day he told me that he was hot, and asked me to remove his rubber draw-sheet, which went across the middle of the bed. I told him, "That is against hospital regulations, and it has to stay on." The next day he complained to one of the nuns, and she told me to remove the draw-sheet.

That did it. After that, whenever I refilled my other patients' pitchers with ice water, he got tap water. When I gave him his back rub, I dribbled cold alcohol on his back, and then ran my nails up and down his back. I also kidded with the other patients, but ignored him. I had never done anything like that to a patient before, so when he was discharged, I never expected to see him again.

However, three days later when I got off work, Don was waiting for me in the parking lot. He called to me and asked if I'd go have coffee with him. I was surprised, and all I could say was, "I don't go out with strangers."

He said, "Wait a minute, I think you know me pretty well. You must have read my chart."

He was right. I knew that he was 28 years old, that he was single, what kind of work he did, where he lived, and so on. After a little more persuasion, I agreed to go with him for coffee.

We went to a restaurant and talked. I had a good time. He said all the things a young girl would want to hear, and he had very good manners.

When he brought me back to my car, he tried to kiss me, but I turned my head and the kiss landed on my cheek. He looked at me for a moment, then asked, "Will you marry me?"

I was speechless and just stared at him. I laughed, and told him, "You are crazy. There is no way I will marry you. I haven't known you long enough. I am only 17, and too young to get married."

I walked away, and again assumed that I would never see him again. But I was wrong.

He was still working on the railroad, and whenever he was in town, he would be waiting by my car. My friend Pat was usually with me, so all three of us would go to a Café.

When he got a job as a shipping clerk in Portland, he came by the hospital more often. This caused a problem. Don did not like having Pat around, and Pat kept telling me that I should stop seeing him. She did not like Don, and thought that he was too old for me. I was torn between the two for a while.

But Don was a charmer and he kept coming back. He made me feel special. He kept telling me how much he loved me and how wonderful I was. He did not give up, even when I tried to break up with him several times. Today they might call that "stalking." But at that time, I felt flattered that someone cared that much about me.

After a while Pat gave up trying to convince me that Don was not right for me, and made arrangements to ride with someone else. Sadly, that broke up our friendship, and I seldom saw her again.

Don and I saw each other almost every day. He followed me home after I got off work, to make sure that I got home safely. He kept asking me to marry him again and again. After a few months, I finally gave in and said, "Yes." I think the main reason I agreed to marry him was because no one had ever made me feel so wanted and special.

We set the wedding date for June 1, 1956.

We never talked about money, or things that couples should talk about before they marry. My thinking was, "He is much older than I, so he must be smarter. He also obviously loves me a lot, so things will be all right."

It's hard to believe how naive I was. I should have listened to Pat, and recognized that he was not good husband material. He was 28 years old, worked at a minimum wage job, and lived with his parents.

However, I must have had an inkling that I might be making a mistake, because the closer the wedding date came, the more apprehensive I became. I kept asking myself, "What am I doing? Do I really want to marry this man? Where will we live?"

By the middle of April, I had done nothing to get ready for the wedding. No invitations had been sent out, no place was selected for the wedding, and I hadn't even thought about a dress. Most importantly, I had no money, because I gave all the money I earned to my parents. I suspected that Don did not have much money either, so how could we have a wedding?

I had made up my mind to either postpone the wedding, or cancel it, but I just didn't know how to break the news to Don. I thought, "If I wait long enough, the decision will be clear. Since nothing was arranged for the wedding, we'd have no choice but to postpone it."

Then, a complication arose.

My parents kept telling me that they did not like Don. They wanted me to keep writing to Friedrich, the boy I had met in Germany, or wait for that nice German boy, Erwin Zander, until he came back from overseas. There was also Hans, the son of my parents' friends, whom I had met a couple of times. He seemed interested in me, but I wasn't interested in him. So, I ignored my parents.

One evening when I got home from work, my parents were waiting for me, and I could tell that they were angry. They started right off by telling me, "We forbid you to marry Don. A friend of ours told us that Don has been married before, and has three children."

I said, "No. I don't believe that."

Instead of talking to me, and telling me who had told them that story, and then letting me confront Don, Mama and Papa decided to beat me into submission. Mama slapped me twice, then Papa started hitting me with a leather belt across my back. Between each stroke, they asked, "Will you stop seeing Don?"

I just got more stubborn, and kept telling them, "NO!"

After several agonizing minutes, that felt like hours, Mama told Papa to stop hitting me. Then they told me that I had to quit my job at the hospital and get a day job closer to home. They also took away my car keys, and told me to go to bed. I could not sleep because my back hurt, and I was upset and angry at my parents.

I don't know what they were thinking. I was 18 years old, I had worked for the past four years, and had lived on my own for some of that time. What made them think that beating me was the way to get me to obey them.

—Looking back, I know that they were just trying to protect me, and that was the only way they knew how. I just wish that they had talked to me reasonably. The outcome might have been much different.

The next morning when I got up, I was still wearing my nurse's uniform. Mama told me to call the hospital and tell them that I quit my job. We didn't have a telephone at home, so I had to walk up to the highway and use a payphone. I told my supervisor that there was an emergency at home, and I could not come in to work.

After that, I stood there, not knowing what to do. I just could not go back home. All I had on was my nurse's uniform, white stockings, white walking shoes, and a jacket. I had also taken my purse along.

I decided to call Don. His father answered the phone and said that Don was at work. I told him what had happened to me the night before, and that I did not want to go back home. But I had nowhere else to go. He told me to take a bus to Portland, and wait in the park by the bronze statue, where he would pick me up

He drove me to their house. After Don got home, I showed them the welts on my back. They were horrified. I asked, "Can I stay with you until I have enough money for an apartment?"

They insisted that Don and I should get married. Don's mom said, "You planned on getting married anyway, why not do it now? The timing is perfect."

Don's brother Walt, and his wife Joanne happened to be visiting from California. They suggested we drive to Stevenson, Washington, where there was no blood-test required, and they would be our witnesses.

I was certainly not in any mood to get married, but I felt trapped. What could I do? I couldn't go home, and I had nowhere else to go. Also, there was no room for me in Don's parents' house as a single woman. So, reluctantly I agreed.

I borrowed some clothes from Joanne. The four of us drove to Stevenson, and Don and I got married. It was April 21, 1956. Don was 29 years old, and I was 18. The ceremony was performed by a judge. It was quick and simple.

Afterwards I couldn't believe that I was really married. I can't remember whether the four of us went out to dinner, or if we went back to Don's parents' house, and Don's mother made dinner for us.

We had no money, so there was no honeymoon. Our honeymoon night was spent in Don's very small bedroom, at his parents' house.

The next morning, I was too embarrassed, so I stayed in bed as long as I could. When I finally had to get up, and opened the door, I saw Don's whole family, his parents, his brother and wife, and Don's younger brother Sandy, lined up at our bedroom door. They were all laughing and teasing me. Walt leered at me and asked, "How was your wedding night? Did you have a good time? Did you have fun? Are you feeling like a married woman now?"

I wanted to sink through the floor and disappear. I was so mad at Don because through all of that teasing, he stayed in bed, under the covers, and pretended that he was sleeping.

Later that day, I called the hospital, explained my situation to my supervisor, and asked for a few days off. Don's brother gave us some money as a wedding present. Joanne gave me some of her clothes and a few necessities, so I could get by for a few days. Don's parents gave us enough money to rent an apartment, and most of the items we needed.

We found an apartment on Glisan Street, in Northwest Portland. It was on the second floor, in an old three-story building. It was shabby and small, but it was furnished and cheap, and I scrubbed it from top to bottom. Most importantly, since I did not have a car, it was within walking distance of the hospital where I worked. It was also close to Don's work. He was still working as a shipping clerk in Northwest Portland.

Two weeks later I tried to pick up my clothes and car from my parents, but they were still mad at me and refused to let me have them. We had to hire an attorney, who wrote a letter demanding that they release my property. When we went to pick up my things, they barely spoke to me. They gave me my clothes, but not the car.

I was not happy, being estranged from my family. A few months later I invited my parents to dinner. They were very nice. Papa even complimented me, and told me that my dinner was the best meal he'd ever had. I still remember what I served that night: I had heated up two large cans of

"Dinty Moore Beef Stew." Of course, I made sure that they did not see the cans.

I was glad when Papa told me that I could have my car back, but the most important thing to me was that the family was on speaking terms again.

Married Life and Surprises

I soon found out that my husband had a lot of debt, which was something unheard of in my family. I had a hard time coming to terms with that, and I was disappointed with him.

My parents never bought anything on credit, except their first house. To them paying rent or interest was the same as throwing money away. Mama taught me, "If you no have money for this, you no need this."

Don and I lived paycheck to paycheck. So, imagine my surprise on Christmas day, when I saw a room full of gifts. "Where did all of this come from?" I asked.

Don stood there beaming. "I just love you so much, I want to give you the world."

Besides clothing and other personal stuff, there was a whole set of camping gear, tent and all.

"Where did you get the money for all of this?"

"I charged it at Meier and Franks."

I stood there, not believing what I'd heard. "This is not a gift. Not if we have to pay for it most of the year."

I insisted that he return most of the stuff.

Afterwards, I felt guilty. How could I tell my husband how to handle our finances? After all, the man is the head of the family. (This was drilled into me as a child).

But I couldn't live with creditors hounding us, so eventually I had to take over managing the money. Every extra cent went toward paying off Don's debts, even if we had nothing but beans to eat at the end of the month.

We were both driving old junky cars, and when one of the cars broke down, it was not worth fixing. We would then buy another old car which would also break down, and so it went.

—Jumping ahead to 1960: When the car I was driving had a major problem, we decided that we needed to buy a more reliable car. But Don's credit was bad, and I had no credit. The only way we could buy a newer car was with a co-signer. We asked Papa and were surprised when he agreed to sign.

We bought a used, 1958 Chevrolet station wagon. It took us two years to pay it off. We were relieved when there were no more car payments.

But, one month after the car was paid off it broke down and needed a new motor. The estimate was $300, which we didn't have. I hated to go into debt again but we had no choice. I got a loan from Moore Business Forms, where I worked at that time, and had a new motor installed.

After I paid off the loan, I opened a savings account. I continued to make "pretend car payments" and put that same amount of money in the bank. That's how we paid cash for all the rest of the cars we ever bought.

Two or three years later, we discovered that the floor in the back of the wagon was rusted-out. We were shocked. Wondering how long it had been like that while we were driving around with our boys in the back. We traded the car in for $300, paid the rest in cash, and bought a new Buick station-wagon.

Don and I lived in our apartment for about six months. One day, a policeman came to our door. He told us that the woman in the apartment above ours had been raped the night before, and asked if we had heard anything. We told them that we hadn't, and he went away. After that, I didn't feel safe living there.

I hated to pay rent. My parents had taught me that paying rent was like throwing money away. We started looking for a house to buy, even though we had no money for a down payment. We found a house for rent, with an option to buy, on Center Street in Northeast Portland. It was an older ranch style house, with two bedrooms, a large kitchen and living room. Newly painted inside and out, and located in a good neighborhood.

The house was farther away from where we both worked, but it was close to Don's parents, which was handy because we spent a lot of time at their house. We bought some inexpensive second-hand furniture, just enough to get by. I used an old wringer washer at my in-laws, and line-dried our clothes at home. (We didn't have a washing machine until after I had my second baby).

I really liked Don's parents, Bea and Walter. They insisted that I call them Mom and Dad, which I did. Bea was more of a girlfriend to me than a mom. I loved being with her. She stayed up and watched scary movies with me, even though she didn't like them. She was game for anything. She listened to me when I was mad at Don. Then, she would tell me all the bad things he used to do. She also told me that Don had been married before and had a son.

When I confronted him, Don admitted that he had been married. But he said that the baby was not his. I told his mother what Don had said, and she assured me, with tears in her eyes, that it was his son. I didn't know whom to believe, so I just let it go.

On Don's birthday, I decided to give him a surprise party. It was my day off, but Don had to work. I told him to come to his parents' house after he got off work for dinner. I invited my parents and some friends. Bea and I made a big dinner, and I baked a birthday cake from scratch. All the guests came and we waited for some time, but no Don. We finally ate, and the guests went home.

Don showed up at his parent's house after 9 o'clock. It was obvious that he had been drinking. His parents and I were furious and questioned him, but he never told us where he had been.

By now I was convinced that I had made a mistake marrying Don. It was clear that we were not right for each other. But I was too stubborn to go back to my parents, and admit that they were right. So, I stayed and told myself that I had married this man for better or worse and had no choice but to stay with him.

Don was a charmer; he really had the "gift of gab." He knew just what to say to make me feel special, telling me how pretty I was and how much he loved me. He would tell me how sorry he was after he did something wrong, and that it would never happen again. And somehow, I believed him every time.

Fifteen months after our marriage, I found out that I was pregnant. So, now I knew that I had to stay and make the best of my situation.

Working at the hospital while I was pregnant was very hard on my legs and back. The problem was, I had poor circulation in my legs. By the time I got off work I was in a lot of pain. Don massaged my legs every night, which gave me some relief. I continued to work until my legs and back hurt so much that I couldn't take care of my patients anymore and had to quit.

I got a job at a dry-cleaning shop, but that was too hard on me also, because I had to stand on my feet all day.

After that, I sold Sarah Coventry jewelry in the evenings and weekends, and helped my mama with her house-cleaning job two days a week. I worked with Mama until my belly got too big. But continued to sell jewelry up to the weekend before our son was born.

My labor pains started in the middle of the night. I was afraid, but told myself, "Millions of women have had babies. If they could do it, I can do it."

Don's mom wanted to come with us, so we stopped on the way to the hospital and picked her up. I was in labor for over eight hours, and was not given any medication for pain. I was glad that Bea was with me. She helped me through my most painful contractions, by encouraging me to breathe deep and relax.

Barry John was born in Portland at Providence Hospital April 23, 1958. He was a beautiful, strong and healthy baby.

After I was released from the hospital, Bea insisted that we come stay with them for a few days. I was very thankful, because I had no idea how to care for a baby.

Bea and her friend, Vera, had given me a baby shower the month before. They had presented me with a beautiful bassinet, which they had decorated with ribbons and lace. (I used that bassinet for all of my babies). Other friends had given me enough baby things so I was all set.

Bea was a wonderful grandma. She absolutely adored Barry, and took care of him when I went back to work.

I found a job selling Avon products door to door. My district was in a poor part of town. The women didn't have much and they wanted everything. They ordered a lot of products, but when I went back to deliver and collect, they didn't have the money to pay me. I had to ship back a lot of the merchandise. But I made enough money to subsidize Don's meager wages and somehow, we got by.

Bea's Death

Don's mom had severe diabetes. She was on insulin, had to be careful with her diet, and had frequent infections in her feet. When Barry was about nine months old, Bea caught a cold, and it kept getting worse. We called the doctor on a Friday afternoon, he said, "Just keep her hydrated, use steam to ease her congestion, and bring her into my office on Monday morning."

Early Monday morning, Don's dad called us. He sounded very upset. He said, "Mom is much worse and I don't know what to do." We told him that we would be right over. When we got there, we saw that Bea was really struggling to breathe. We called the doctor and he came to the house right away. As soon as he got there, he called an ambulance, but by the time the ambulance arrived, Bea had died!

We were all in shock; including the doctor. How could she be dead from a cold? Later, the doctor told us that she had died of pneumonia.

I would not let the ambulance drivers take Bea's body. I kept clinging to her, and hugging her. I whispered over and over." Wake up. Please wake up." I told her that I needed her, she was my only friend and the dearest person in my life, and that I didn't know how I could live without her. Don had to tear me away from Bea, so that the ambulance could take her.

I missed Bea so very much. She was my best friend, my teacher, my confidant, my support. A wonderful mother-in-law, and the best grandmother in the world. Even as I am writing this, the page looks blurry through my tears.

Walter was devastated. He had relied on Bea for so much. We helped him make the funeral arrangements, and with Don's brothers' help, took care of the funeral costs.

Don's dad had worked as a mechanic for a car company for over 30 years. He had never made much money, but he was afraid to change jobs. When he retired, they gave him a pocket watch, instead of a pension. Bea and Walter lived off of his Social Security money.

Don's parents had been renting the house they lived in for many years. After Bea died, the house was too big for Walter. The family bought a small mobile home for him, and parked it on a cousin's property.

Walter lived for several years after Bea's death, but he was very unhappy without her. He was always concerned about Sandy, his youngest son, who was a grown man, but still depended on his father's help. When Walter died, we made sure that Sandy got what few possessions he owned.

Moving from Town to Town

During the years 1958 to 1962 I gave birth to four children, Don worked at six different jobs, and we moved seven times.

About two months after Don's mother died, Don lost his shipping clerk job in Portland. A short time later, he got a job as manager of a small variety store in Keizer, and we had to move. We gave the Center Street house back to the sellers. Then we rented a drafty old house in Salem, near

Portland Road, for about three months, until we found a better house on Menlo Drive in Keizer.

We liked living in Keizer. Don joined the Lions Club, and we met some nice people, including Ken and Jeanette Harvey. (Jeanette and I have remained friends to this day).

We also met Tom and Ila and enjoyed their friendship. I liked Ila right from the start. She was a very happy, easy going person, and fun to be with. She made me realize that there was more to life than work and responsibilities. We enjoyed their fun parties and going boating with them.

Our second son, Brian, was born on a Sunday afternoon, July 12, 1959, at Salem Hospital. Barry, who was 15 months old, loved his little baby brother.

Later that year, Don was transferred to manage a store in Albany. I hated to move away from our friends, but felt that I had no choice. I did not like Albany. I felt isolated. I did not know where to get a job or find a babysitter. Don worked long hours, while I kept busy taking care of Barry and Brian, the house, the yard, and mowing the large lawn with a push mower. We lived there for a couple of months, and then Don got a job as a manager of an "88 Cents Store" in Portland.

We moved into a two-bedroom duplex in Northeast Portland. It was an old building, but nice and clean, and in a good neighborhood.

I got a job as a secretary at a sewing machine store. I did their bookkeeping, and made appointments for the sales-people, who demonstrated sewing machines in people's homes. I liked my job, but I didn't like leaving Barry and Brian with a babysitter that I did not know. I had no choice because Don didn't make enough money to support us. All of Don's 'manager' jobs paid little more than minimum wage, so I had to work.

Again, we were throwing our money away by paying rent. So, we bought an old house with nothing down on a Land Sales Contract. Our monthly payments were less than the rent we were paying for the duplex. The house was located in Portland, near the Burlington Fred Meyer store. It was very old, so old in fact, that it had been built with square nails which we discovered when we tore down a wall. It needed a lot of work, but I didn't mind hard work. We spent every evening working at that house, removing a wall, patching holes, painting, and cleaning. Even though I was pregnant again, I worked hard, and enjoyed it, because this was our house, and I hoped that we were building for our future.

Our third son, Donald Jr., was born September 29, 1960, at Providence Hospital in Portland. The night before we had been at the Burlington house painting. When we got home, I was so tired, I went to bed without bathing.

The next morning, I woke up with labor pains. I couldn't go to the hospital dirty. So, I took a shower, washed my hair, and then got Don out of bed. He said, "I have to make some phone calls before we can leave."

He was on the phone for a long time, while I was moaning with pain. When we finally got to the hospital, they took me directly to the Labor Room, and Donny was born 20 minutes later!

While I was in the hospital, Don moved our possessions from the duplex to the Burlington house. We had given our notice and had to vacate the duplex before the first of the month. When I got home, there were boxes everywhere. Most of them were still unpacked, but at least the bed was made, and I was thankful for that.

I was surprised when Mama brought Barry and Brian back the following morning. She helped me unpack some of the essential kitchen supplies and then left. There I was, with a brand-new baby, two toddlers, and a lot of unpacked boxes. Somehow, I managed to take care of them all.

When Donny was about two months old, I went back to work at the sewing machine store.

Sometime in 1961, Don was transferred to the '88 Cents Store' in Salem. We sold the Burlington house for about the same price we had paid, and moved back to Keizer. Don had rented a house for us on Arnold Street, which was in a very poor area of town. It was a small, two-bedroom, with a big backyard. Even though I didn't like the neighborhood, I was glad to be back in Keizer.

There was a dark maroon, solid colored, wall to wall carpet in the living room. It showed every spot, and I had to vacuum it every day. I learned the hard way that I didn't dare sleep in, the boys would get rambunctious and have pillow fights, break things, or get into things they shouldn't.

One morning when I got up, I couldn't believe my eyes. There was cottage cheese all over the furniture and the maroon rug. The boys had had a cottage cheese fight.

Another morning, the boys woke me, yelling, "Look mommy, kitty. Look mommy, kitty." When I opened my eyes, there was a dead mouse dangling just above my face. I had set a mouse trap the day before, and the boys found the trap and the dead mouse.

On a beautiful sunny day, Barry, Brian, and I, were playing ball in the backyard, while Donny was lying on his tummy on a blanket. I ran into the house to answer the phone, and was gone for just a few minutes. When I got back, I saw that Donny had crawled to the edge of the blanket, and was eating potato bugs. I did not know how many he had eaten, so I got concerned and called the doctor. He told me, "Don't worry. Potato bugs won't hurt him. They are high in protein." This was not the first, or last, of such calls I made to the doctor. It seemed like the boys put everything they touched into their mouths.

I was getting unemployment, and hoped that I would continue getting it for a little while longer, so I could stay home with my babies. However, about two months later, the employment office sent me to Moore Business Forms for a job interview. I didn't really think that I would get that job. I was twenty-three years old, had three little children, and a spotty work history. But the test they gave me, showed that I had a high aptitude for proofreading. Really? A Russian-German woman with a heavy accent, working as an English proofreader? I thought, "They will never hire me." When they interviewed me, I foolishly told them, "I am a good work-horse." So, I got the job.

I found out that proofreading meant more than just checking for spelling errors. We checked size and style of type, margins, spacing, number of copies, and so on. We were evaluated for accuracy, and we had to meet a standard on how many jobs we read. It was intense, but I liked that job and I was good at it. I was grateful that it was not physically strenuous work, and that I didn't have to stand on my feet all day. Also, the hours were good. I worked from 8 to 5, with Saturdays and Sundays off. The pay was good and they provided health insurance. The only downside was that, once again, I had to leave my children with an unknown babysitter.

Our next-door neighbors appeared to be very poor. They had several little children who were frequently at our house.

I felt sorry for them, because they were always hungry and dirty, and their clothes looked like rags. I decided to go through all of my children's clothes, and give any extra clothing we had to the neighbors. My reasoning was, I had a washer and dryer, and I would just wash my boy's clothes more often.

Those children did wear the clothes I gave them, but they were never washed. They just kept wearing them, until they too looked like rags. I got angry with myself. I thought, "How could I have been so stupid, giving my children's clothes away?"

I was upset at the children's mother, and I wondered why she didn't take better care of her children, but I didn't really want to know. I was overwhelmed with my own responsibilities, and I did not want to take on anyone else's problems. I did learn a lesson however. I realized that some people will always be poor, and just giving them things is not always the answer.

After a few months, Don lost the '88 Cents Store' job. I don't remember the reason he got fired. I just know that every time he lost a job, I lost a little bit more respect and confidence in him.

Next, Don got a job selling something to small businesses. He was part of a team of men who worked out of town during the week, and came home on weekends. He liked that job. He and his buddies could do as they pleased after work. I, on the other hand, learned how hard life could be for a working, single mother, with three small children, and no family living nearby.

One night, I saw a 'Peeping Tom' looking in my window. I got scared and called my friend, Ila. She sent over her teenage son, who looked like a mature man, and he spent the next two nights at our house.

The following weekend when Don got home, I told him, "I no longer feel safe in this neighborhood. We have to move. You also have to find a better paying job in town."

The job he had now, was barely paying his expenses. The men worked on commission. By the time he paid for gas, motel, food, and entertainment, there was very little money left over to bring home.

I was really mad at him, and said, "How can you leave us alone all week long? I work full-time, we have three little children, and I am pregnant again. I need help and there is nobody close enough to help me. How can you not see that? You are supposed to be the head of the family. You need to put your family's safety first. Why do I have to tell you this? How can you leave me with all the responsibilities?"

Don told me that he was sorry and promised to do better. He also agreed to look for a job in town.

Thankfully, within a short time, Don found a job as manager of a variety store in Keizer.

Will Avenue House, 1962 to 1969

Don had been in the Navy before I knew him, and was eligible for a VA loan. Our credit was good now, so we started looking for a house to buy. Soon we found a very nice ranch-style home for sale on Will Ave. (now 7th. Ave.) in Keizer. We paid $500 down, which my parents had lent us, and got a VA loan. We moved into the house on New Year's Eve, 1962. I remember that date because our friends were at the Lions Club celebrating while we were moving.

I loved that house. There was a big fenced backyard with a large play area plus a vacant lot next door. Big walnut trees grew along the back fence. The house had an attached drive-through garage and a storage shed. It was nicely land-scaped and had awnings on all of the windows. There were three bedrooms, a living room with a fireplace, and a dining room plus a kitchen with a nook. All the rooms were pan-eled in pine. There were also two add-ons: a TV room, and a playroom which was great for our three little boys.

I barely had time to unpack and settle in before our fourth son, David Scott, was born January 15, 1962 at Salem Hospital. During the delivery, my blood pressure was erratic. Later, the doctor told us that I should not have any more children, at least for a while. Don decided to have a vasectomy, and that solved that problem.

I was on a two-month unpaid maternity leave from Moore Business Forms and I had saved up just enough to get us by for the two months. Don was still working as a manager at the variety store in Keizer, so all was well and going according to plan.

But four weeks after David was born, Don came home and told me that he'd lost his job. I was devastated. But all I remember saying was, "Oh no. Not again!"

I felt panicked. We had bills to pay, four children to feed, and no money coming in. I had to do something quick. I called Bob, my boss at Moore Business Forms, and begged him to let me come back to work. He said that he could not put me back in proofreading for another four weeks, but he would try to find something else for me. About an hour later Bob called back and offered me a job in the file room. I accepted it gratefully.

I called the employment office for a babysitter and they sent Martha Hutchens the next day. I liked her immedi-ately. She was 17 years older than me and had a warm and cheerful personality. I hired her on the spot. She was the best babysitter I'd ever had. We remained close friends until she died many years later.

I did not know how strenuous that filing job would be, especially for someone who had given birth recently. The files were floor to ceiling and wall to wall around the entire room. I had to climb up and down a ladder with an arm load of folders, push the existing files apart, and squeeze in the new folders. My arm and leg muscles burned and my stomach felt like it was being torn apart.

I was glad that I had Martha. She came to our house to care for the children, and she kept the house clean. During the week, I just had to shop for groceries on my way home, cook dinner, and clean up. I did whatever else needed to be done on weekends.

Don got a job selling sewing machines which paid a small salary plus commission—not a good job for a "non-starter." Martha told me that on many days Don would go back to bed after I had left for work and sleep until noon. One day two men from the sewing machine company came to our house while Don was still in bed. They fired him on the spot and took back their van.

When I got home and found out that he was fired—again. I was furious. I asked, "How can you be so lazy? You know how hard I am working and how much my body is hurting."

He just stood there with his head down and had no answer. He looked so pathetic. I actually felt sorry for him, and just walked away.

Don applied for a sales job with Seitz Hardware Store in Salem. I was surprised when Mrs. Seitz called me at work. She told me that she wanted to come to my home and interview me, that day, right after I got off work. I agreed, and called Martha. I asked her to have the house and children especially neat that day.

Mrs. Seitz was very surprised at how clean and organized my home was, and how well-behaved the children were, and so, Don got the job. To this day, I don't know why it was necessary for her to inspect our home before she hired my husband.

Don worked at Seitz Hardware for a few months, but he was not happy there. He said that he felt like he was being watched all the time. Sure enough, a short time later, he lost that job. He told me, "They accused me of stealing bolts and screws."

That didn't make any sense to me, and I didn't care about the reason. All I could think about was, "Oh my God, he is out of a job, again."

Early on in our relationship Don had told me that he hated to see a woman cry. He said that his mother cried a lot just to get her way, and he couldn't stand it when she did that. So, I made sure that I did not cry. I just toughened up whenever there was a problem. When I worried about things and couldn't sleep at night, I would get up and scrub kitchen cupboards or floors. That didn't solve the problem, but it helped to calm me. However, keeping my emotions in check finally caught up with me.

I started having heart palpitations. When they became severe enough, I went to the doctor. He examined me, but couldn't find anything wrong other than an irregular pulse. He asked, "Do you have a lot of stress?"

I told him," Yes, but not any more than usual."

He was concerned about the irregular pulse, and sent some heart medication home with me, just in case I needed it.

The following day after dinner, I don't remember what set it off but, I got very nervous and started pacing the floor. I felt like I was going to lose my mind, and that I was walking a tight-rope. On the left side I saw a very deep dark hole, but the right side was light and bright. I felt that any moment I could fall to either side. Suddenly, tears were flooding my eyes and running down my face. My children were frightened because they had never seen me cry, and they couldn't understand what was happening. Don got concerned also, but he didn't know what to do.

I told him, "Take care of the children. I'm going into the bedroom."

I closed the door and threw myself on the bed. My body started shaking uncontrollably. I was moaning, deep sobs were coming out of me, and my body was convulsing. This went on for quite awhile. All the pent-up emotions and all the crying that I had suppressed for so many years, were pouring out of me. When my sobs finally subsided, I felt like a very heavy load had been lifted from me, and I dozed off for a while. When I came out of the bedroom, I assured my frightened children that Mama was okay and everything was all right.

I told Don, "From now on, if I really feel like crying, I will do it. So, don't tell me again that you can't stand to see a woman cry." He just stood there and had nothing to say.

After that incident, I never had heart palpitations again. I did allow myself to cry when I needed to, but most of the time I cried in private.

A month went by and Don could not find a job close to home. I could pay the mortgage, utility bills and babysitter, but after that there was very little money left for food. My wages were not enough to take care of everything. So, when Don told me that he could get a job that required traveling during the week, and being home only on weekends again, I agreed to listen.

He told me that he would be selling insurance policies to small businesses. He said that this was a great opportunity and that he would be making a lot of money. I was not happy about him being gone again, but we really needed the money and I felt that I had no choice but to agree.

Before he could take that job, we had to buy new tires for his car. The old ones were almost bald and wouldn't last long. Our friends, Ken and Jeanette, loaned us $150, and Don took the job. (I made sure that we paid off that loan as quickly as we could).

The promise of making a lot of money never materialized. Again, by the time he paid for gas, food, lodging and whatever else, there was little money left. This was just like the other out of town job. But Don was always sure that next week would be better. I really wanted to believe him, so I went along with his promises.

This went on for more than three months. With Martha's help, I got along pretty well, but we barely had enough money for the necessities.

Then came . . . The Big, Infamous Storm, October 12th, 1962.

It happened on a Friday, shortly after I got home from work. Don was out of town and I was alone with our four little boys. I had no way of getting in touch with Don. There were no cell phones then and I didn't know the name of the town where he was working that day. At first, I was not too worried because it was just a big wind. Then some roofing shingles crashed through our kitchen window, and there was broken glass all over the kitchen counter and floor. Now I knew that this was getting serious!

I told the boys to go into the playroom, the most protected room in the house. There were no windows, but there was a door to the outside. Then the power and telephone went out. I gathered up bedding, food, water, baby supplies, and whatever candles and flashlights I could find and made us a cozy area in the playroom. The boys were four, three, two, and nine months old, and they did not understand what was happening. They understood camping, so I told them that we were "pretend-camping." That worked only for a little while. Then they started getting scared because they could hear the wind howling, and they could feel that I was worried. The baby started crying and the boys became unruly. I was beside myself.

Suddenly there was a knock on the door. I was afraid to open it, but then I heard Ken's voice. Ken knew that Don was out of town and he'd gotten worried when he couldn't reach us by phone. He drove through the storm to see if we were okay. He said that they had not lost power at their place and it was nice and warm. He insisted that we go with him. That was a wild ride. The wind was blowing hard, and stuff was flying at us from all directions. Ken and Jeanette's house was close by, and luckily, we arrived there without a scratch. We spent the night at their house, feeling safe and comfortable. I will never forget their kindness.

We woke up to a beautiful sunny day, but what a mess there was everywhere. Many people had lost their roofs, and some lost their homes. When we got back to our house, I was relieved that our damages were minimal. We had a broken kitchen window, our fence was down, and all of our awnings were torn to shreds. There was a lot of debris all over our roof and yard, but everything else was fine.

Our insurance company sent us a generous check. We fixed everything ourselves, and put most of the insurance money in the bank. That was our first real savings account.

Don came home two days after the storm. He knew that I would be mad, so before I could say anything, he started talking right away. He said, "I could not get home any sooner because the roads were closed. And I couldn't call you because the telephone lines were down. I was worried sick about all of you, and I never want to be away from you again."

The next day he quit that job.

Martha got a job as a janitor in a high school. I hated to lose her, but I understood why she took that job. Her husband had developed a heart condition and was on disability. The janitor job paid more and came with health insurance benefits.

I don't remember what Don was doing. I'm assuming that he was looking for a job because I had to find another babysitter.

A friend's daughter babysat for a while, but she was too young to handle four little boys. Martha told me that she had stopped by our house one day to see how the babysitter was doing. She found out that the girl had been changing David's diaper on the kitchen counter and that he had fallen on the floor and hit his head. By the time I got home, David was okay, but I let the babysitter go.

Don hired the next babysitter. He took the boys to her house and picked them up. At the end of the month the sitter called and told me that she was blind, that the boys were too active, and that she could not care for them any longer.

I was horrified. How could we have let a blind woman babysit our four little boys? When I confronted Don, he shrugged his shoulders and had nothing to say.

Don finally got a good job. He started working for a bread company, delivering bread to stores. That was the best paying job he ever had. The only drawback was he had

Wednesdays and Sundays off. The rest of the days he had to be on the job by 5 o'clock in the morning.

I had to get up every morning at 3:30 AM, make his breakfast, pack his lunch, and try to get him out of bed, which was not easy. It took three tries before he finally got up. But I didn't mind doing that. I was glad he was finally making enough money to support us.

This also meant I could quit my proofreading job and stay at home with my children. It was clear that I needed to be home because my children were showing signs of stress. Barry started to stutter and was constantly blinking his eyes; Brian would sit on the couch and bang his head against the back cushions; Donny and David cried a lot.

I asked Barry what was going on, and he told me that the babysitter was hitting them. When I pointed out that I also spanked them sometimes, he said, "But that's different Mom. You love us."

His words took my breath away. The next day I gave my notice at work. Shortly after I started staying home with my boys, all of their symptoms disappeared.

Don often stayed away from home. He was either fishing, hunting, or coming home late from work. A few times I was told that Don had been seen with other women but, when I confronted him, he denied everything. Sometimes when he couldn't convince me of his innocence, he would be remorseful, and swear that he would change. Other times he would threaten to kill himself, if I didn't forgive him. I always forgave him. I felt that I had no choice. We had four little boys who needed their father.

Also, now that he was supporting us, and I could stay home with our children, it was easier to live in denial and pretend that all was well. Don was very good at convincing me that I was the only woman he loved.

We did have good times. We learned square dancing and ballroom dancing. We played cards with friends and went to the Lion's club for dances and special occasions. Once in a while we all went fishing, even though our two youngest babies were still wearing diapers.

On one of our fishing trips, Barry and Brian didn't want to stay in camp with me. They wanted to follow Don when he went upriver to fish. Don agreed to let them come. But he did not watch them, and Brian fell into a deep pool of water. He couldn't swim and nearly drowned. Thankfully, a teenage girl came along and pulled Brian out. After that, the kids and I stopped going fishing, until the boys learned how to swim

I joined the YWCA and took the boys with me. Tuesdays were 'Mom's Day Out." There were games for the kids while moms enjoyed activities such as playing volleyball. They also had a swimming pool, and that's where the boys took swimming lessons.

Barry started school when he was six, followed by Brian, then Donny. Keizer school was only about two blocks from our house. At that time, all of the children who lived within a mile walked to school.

All of our boys loved grade school and I loved the time I had with them at home. I grew a garden and canned vegetables. I hung our clothes out to dry to save electricity. I also planned our menus according to the sales at the grocery store and cooked everything from scratch. Every day was cleaning day. There were also specific tasks: Monday was wash day. Tuesday was ironing day because Don wore starched, white cotton shirts to work. Wednesday was grocery shopping day. I even had time to do some arts and crafts.

One day, I realized that I was not a citizen of the country I called my home. I had been so busy earning a living and taking care of everything, I didn't even think about the fact that I was not an American citizen. I applied for citizenship, studied a manual about the laws and branches of government in America, and then passed the test.

In a ceremony at the courthouse, with several other immigrants, I remember crying as I pledged allegiance to the flag of America, and received my Naturalization Certificate.

On the 21st day of December 1964, I became a citizen of the United States of America.

I felt that now I really belonged here, and that America was truly my home.

I must have been very excited that day because when I got back to my car, I discovered that I had locked myself out. I had never done that before, or after, in my life. I called our friend Ken and he came to my rescue with a coat hanger. I don't remember where Don was on that day.

I enjoyed staying home with my sons, but I knew that once our youngest son David started school, I needed to go back to work. We were living very frugally and we could certainly use more money. Don came up with the idea that I should get a license to sell real estate. I told him that I didn't think that I could do that, but he insisted that I could. Finally, I said that I would think about it.

In the meanwhile, the Salem Health Department needed a Russian translator. Someone recommended me, and they asked me if I would volunteer to translate once or twice a week for a home call nurse. She made house calls on the

'Old Believers', a Russian community in Gervais and Woodburn. I was glad to help, as long as it was during the time my older boys were in school and I could take David with me.

The nurse and the Russian people were grateful for my help because they could not understand the previous interpreter. He was a college student who was learning the Russian language, but he could not pronounce the words properly. I spoke Russian in their dialect, and even though I did not know the exact medical words, I could explain things to the women by using simple words until they understood.

They trusted me with intimate subjects like birth control. Their church and their husbands forbade them to use birth control of any kind, but some of the women knew that they could not take care of, or afford, any more children. They were desperate to know how to prevent any more pregnancies. The nurse told them what to do, and assured them that their husbands, and their pastor, would not be told.

The community also had a big problem with intestinal worms. The women trusted me to interpret this to the nurse, who, until that moment, was not aware of that problem. I was glad that I could be helpful with some of their medical issues.

But soon, the Russian people started calling me at home at all hours and asking me for help. There were many times I couldn't go and help them. I felt bad, but I could not leave my children alone, and I could not afford a babysitter.

The nurse asked the Health Department to put me on the payroll. They suggested that I put in an application, which I did. But, the 'Powers that be' said that I was not qualified because I did not have a college degree. The nurse and I felt that this was totally illogical and unfair. She told them that, but they said they had to follow the rules.

How ironic. I was more than qualified as long as they did not have to pay me! Their decision made me feel worthless. Two weeks later, I quit volunteering. School was out for the summer and I needed to be home with my boys.

Don kept nagging me to get a real estate license. He told me, "I have seen how selling comes very naturally to you, and you might just as well sell something that brings bigger commissions." I still didn't have confidence in myself and felt that my English was not good enough, but he kept assuring me that I could do it. I finally agreed after Don promised that he would take care of the boys while I studied. The following week I enrolled in the Norm Webb Real Estate School.

Our first lesson was Real Estate Law, which was way over my head. I kept thinking, "What am I doing here? I don't belong in this class." During the break a woman came up to me and asked me if I understood what Norm Webb was saying. She said, "I am a teacher, and I am confused. I don't understand many of the legal words, and the difference between a trust deed, a mortgage, and a land sales contract."

I told her, "I am familiar with a land sales contract because we have purchased two houses that way, but I do not understand the rest of it."

It was encouraging to hear that a teacher also felt confused. I thought, "Maybe by studying hard I can learn this stuff after all."

The only time I could study was in the evenings after I locked myself in the bedroom. The first lesson was the hardest. When I opened the manual, all I could see were many pages filled with words that I did not know. I was overwhelmed and asked myself, "How am I going to learn this when I don't even understand what I am reading?" Then

I remembered the manual I had memorized before getting the nurses aid job at St. Vincent Hospital. That was 14 years ago, when I could barely speak English. I decided, "If I could do it then, I can do it now."

I kept reading the lessons over and over until I finally became familiar with the legal terminology. Then I memorized most of the material.

Norm Webb was an excellent teacher. I passed the real estate exam and got my license in 1968.

I loved selling real estate, and surprisingly made money right from the start.

My Four Sons, Early Years

Sadly, when I look back at my four sons' childhood and youth, I only remember bits and pieces. My heart hurts as I look at their pictures.

When I became a mother, I was too young and inexperienced. Having to work full time and taking care of most

Barry, Brian, Donny, David

everything else, I did not have much time to hold and nurture my boys. I missed so much during those years. My biggest regret is, leaving my children with strangers while I had to work.

My first son: Barry John, was born 1958 in Portland, two years and two days after his father and I were married. However, Barry told our friends and perfect strangers, "I was born two days after my Mommy and Daddy got married." In those days, that was very embarrassing.

Barry walked and talked before he was nine months old. He had a lot of privileges as the number one son, but he also had a lot of responsibilities. We put him be in charge of his brothers, even though he was not much older than they. Of course, his brothers did not want him to be their boss. When I look back, I realize just how unfair it was for all of them. Later in life he turned out to be the most responsible of my sons.

Second son: Brian Donald, was born 1959 in Salem hospital. My labor pains started Sunday morning, but this time I knew that it would take a while, so Don and I had breakfast and read the paper before going to the hospital. Brian was born about two hours later without incident. He had red hair, and green eyes. When the nurses found out that his father was part Scotch, they dressed him in a Scottish Kilt. He looked so cute when they brought him to me.

Barry and Brian were both happy babies, but they were typical boys and got into everything. One day I found Barry kneeling on top of the bathroom sink, in front of the medicine cabinet, and Brian standing on the toilet lid with white drool running down his chin. Barry told me he thought that the aspirin was candy, and he gave some to Brian to try it. Not knowing how many pills Brian had swallowed, I took him to the hospital to have his stomach pumped. That was the first of many such incidents.

Brian was a very curious boy, he had to examine everything he saw. He too started walking and talking early. One of his first words was "kinky." So, my nickname for him was Kinky. He became attached to his baby blanket and took it with him wherever he went. He was between four and five years old, when he accidentally left his blanket at Grandma's house. My parents lived fifty miles away, so we grownups decided that this would be a good time to break Brian's dependency. That was a mistake because without his blanket, when Brian got upset, he would sit on the couch and bang his head against the back cushion. Sadly, I was not smart enough to realize that he had anxiety issues. The blanket had been a comfort to him, and we should not have taken it from him. But that is what we did in those days; break "bad habits" as soon as possible.

Third son: Donald Murdick Jr., was born 1960 in Providence Hospital in Portland, 20 minutes after we arrived. We almost didn't get to the hospital on time. He was a beautiful chubby baby, with blonde hair and blue eyes. He slept through most nights, right from the start. He was a happy child. Even when he was crying, all I had to do was hug, or tickle him, and he would give me a great big smile.

We named him Junior because we had not picked out a boy's name. I was sure that the baby would be a girl, so we chose a girls' name (Julie). After Donny was born, we had to make a quick decision, and Don liked the idea of naming the baby after him.

Donny never met a stranger. He craved attention, and loved telling stories. He would talk to anybody that stopped to listen. When he was about five years old, he went around the neighborhood, introduced himself, and told the neighbors, "We four boys are all brothers, we have different colored hair, but we have the same mother and father."

The neighbors told me this, and other stories, when I went around the neighborhood collecting for "The March of Dimes."

Fourth son: David Scott, was born 1962 in Salem hospital. I had problems before and during delivery. My blood pressure went above 200 several times. The doctor was concerned, and told us that we should not have any more babies for a while.

David was gorgeous. He had black hair and dark eyes. He too was a happy and healthy baby. He was about three years old when one of the boys made him drink furnace oil. That time, the doctor told me not to induce vomiting, because the vomiting could damage his brain. He said to give him an anti-vomiting medication. But by the time I could give him that medicine, it was too late, and he did throw up! He was delirious all night, while I put cold compresses on his head, and prayed. In the morning, the fever broke, and he slept peacefully most of the day. The next day there seemed to be no after-effects.

David was about six years old, the boys were playing "Cowboys and Indians," and David was shot in his right eye with an arrow. When I saw David holding his hand over his eye and blood pouring out between his fingers, I almost passed out! I was afraid that if David moved his hand, his eye would fall out. I forced myself, with all the strength I had, to stay calm. I grabbed a towel and pressed it on top of David's hand, then I told him to remove his hand. I took a deep breath and slowly lifted a corner of the towel inch by inch. I started breathing normally when I saw that his eye was still attached. The arrow was blunt, so David did not lose his eye. But it was bruised. He had to stay in bed, with both eyes bandaged, for two weeks, which was a big ordeal for an active six-year-old. But he was good, and the eye healed well. Thankfully his eyesight was not affected.

When the boys were toddlers, I would take them on nature walks. We would examine pretty rocks, flowers, and especially bugs of all kinds. The goal was to make the boys unafraid of crawly things. I did not want them to grow up as "sissies."

So, it should not have been a surprise to me to find crawly things in the house.

Sometimes, when I picked up the boys' dirty clothes, a mouse or a snake would crawl out, which always startled me and made me jump. That was bad enough, but the day I opened the refrigerator and saw a mouse running around inside, was over the top. I yelled and slammed the door shut. The boys came running, and asked what was wrong. When I told them that there was a mouse in the refrigerator, they just looked at me and said, "So why are you yelling?" That's what I get for having four sons that are not sissies.

—40 years later; I found a roasted mouse in the bottom of our toaster. The sickening part was that we had eaten the mouse-toast twice, before I found the dead mouse. This time I could not blame it on my sons. This time it was one of our cats, who brought the mouse into the house.

I seldom went shopping with my little boys because it was too much of a challenge. For example:

I was shopping at Meier and Frank, holding the two younger boys' hands, while the two older boys were supposed to be following me. We were walking away from the escalator, which the boys had really enjoyed riding. When I heard a commotion behind me, I turned around but couldn't see Barry and Brian. I looked farther back, and saw them standing by the escalator. I also noticed that people were walking down the escalator steps. When I got closer, I realized that my two boys had stopped the escalator. I thought, "they are only five and six years old, how could they stop an escalator?" I certainly had no idea how to do it.

I yelled at them, "Don't you ever do that again." Barry said, "But Mom, we just wanted to see how those stairs moved."

Another incident happened when we were in a plumbing store. This time my two youngest sons, Donny 3, and David 2, were with me. I took my eyes off the boys for just a moment while I was talking to a salesman. Suddenly I heard someone shout, "Ma'am, Ma'am."

I turned, and saw one of my sons standing by a toilet, which was on display, and pulling down his pants. I ran over to him as fast as I could, and pulled up his pants before any damage was done. To be fair, my son told me that he had to go potty, but I told him, "Hold on, I'll take you to the potty in just a minute." Then I got distracted.

Shopping for the boys was also a challenge. When they were younger, I bought them new school clothes every year, and they were satisfied. As they got older, they wanted brand name clothes, which we could not afford. When they were old enough to pick strawberries and beans, I told them that whatever money they earned, they could spend on clothes, or on whatever else they wanted. Working in the fields was good for them. It was hard work, but they also had fun being with their friends. They could see what their money would buy, and were proud of themselves that they had earned it.

We never had a problem with the boys being picky eaters, nor did I ever have to force them to eat. They ate whatever food I put on the table. They also knew that there was no point in whining. We seldom had junk food in the house, but there was always plenty of wholesome food available; soup, milk and sandwich stuff, as well as fruit. Nobody ever had to go hungry.

I usually bought food that was on sale, and made my menus accordingly. I always cooked homemade meals, and when I had the time, I baked. We very seldom, if ever, ate in restaurants. Hamburger was cheap, so we ate a lot of that. The boys' favorite dish was, what I call "slumgullion," a thick hamburger stew, consisting of whatever food there was on hand. I browned onions and hamburger, and added canned tomatoes and vegetables, and served that, with bread and butter or potatoes. The boys loved it, and I felt good about feeding them a healthy meal. We never had leftovers.

I make slumgullion to this day. Only now, I stir-fry chicken wild mushrooms and vegetables, and serve it with brown rice or quinoa.

The boys loved "Popeye The Sailor Man" cartoons, and how Popeye was so strong, because he ate spinach. So, they decided that they loved spinach too. Later, at school lunches, they ate their spinach and everyone else's. The only thing they did not like was squash. I don't know where they got the idea that squash tasted bad. Later, when they tried squash and liked it, they asked me, "Why didn't we like squash when we were children?"

I told them, "You had to have something you didn't like. That way, you could be like all the other kids, and go on and on about how you hated a certain food."

People have asked why I didn't teach my sons to speak Russian or German. There were a couple of reasons. First of all, their father spoke only English. Also, it was important to me that the boys learned to speak English well, and without an accent.

I wanted them to sound like Americans. That is something I never achieved. No matter how hard I tried, I have never lost my accent.

Fir Cone House, 1969–1980

We had outgrown our Will Street house. The rooms were small, and there was only one bathroom, which was not enough for six people. (Listen to me, being picky. The one who grew up using an outhouse in Germany).

Being a real estate agent had its perks. I found a house that had been repossessed by the bank. The selling price was $18,500 for the house and two adjoining lots. Even in those days, that was a great price.

We sold the Will street house to one of the men in my office, and bought the house on Fir Cone Drive in Keizer. It needed a lot of work, but the structure was sound and the work was mostly cosmetic.

It was a 3,000 square foot, daylight basement house, with five bedrooms and three bathrooms. The property was on a hill and had a great view. We could see as far as the gold statue on top of the State Capital in Salem. There was only one house nearby, which was across the street. Mr. and Mrs. Friesen, an older, childless couple lived there. Otherwise, we were surrounded by land.

We scrubbed the house from top to bottom, removed black motorcycle oil in one of the bedrooms, and scraped off used gum, which was stuck on most of the hardwood floors and kitchen cabinets. We hired painters to paint the whole interior, before we moved in.

We had to buy the house on a land sales contract because the bank could not clear the title. One year later, after the title cleared, we got a VA loan. We put in a new kitchen, updated the bathrooms, put in carpets and new window coverings. Then we landscaped the yard.

It took a while for the boys to get used to the new house. They kept going back to the Will Street house, which was more than a mile away, and peeking in the windows; until I found out and put a stop to it.

The boys had to switch grade schools and they did not like that. But the move worked out well for Barry, our oldest son. When he got into middle school, the following year, he knew the kids from both grade schools. He won easily when he ran for school president. He even got to see San Francisco, where he attended a school president's conference.

When our friend Martha's husband died, she sold us their pickup and camper. Don was still working for the bread company, and had Sundays and Wednesdays off. If we wanted to go camping, we had to leave as soon as he came home from work.

We would camp overnight, and come back the next evening. I had to do all of the packing, and unpacking. It was also up to me to do all of the cooking and cleanup while we were camping. For me this was not fun, but I loved the outdoors, and felt that it was important to expose the boys to nature. We went camping as often as my real estate business allowed.

My restful vacation was one week a year, when Mama and Papa kept the boys so that Don and I could go off by ourselves. I know it was hard for them to watch four boys for that long. But that's the only time Mama and Papa ever watched them; other than when I was in hospital having my babies. They lived in Tigard, which was over fifty miles away, so regular babysitting was not an option. I appreciated their help during that week very much.

Early one summer, Don sprained his ankle and couldn't work. He had to take his vacation because he had used up all of his sick leave. The boys were about 11, 10, 9, and 8, and had just started their summer vacation. We decided we might just as well go camping for a week. Don couldn't drive because the truck had a clutch. I had never driven that pickup, and it had been a long time since I had driven a car with a stick shift. But I decided to give it a try. It was much harder than I thought. As we drove east on Highway 22, a strong wind came up, which made the camper rock from side to side. I had a hard time keeping the pickup on the road.

We had planned to go to a campground that we knew, just outside Sisters, but it was closed because there was still too much snow on the ground. So, we decided to drive to Ka-ne-ta Hot Springs Resort, which was much farther. When we stopped for gas, I asked if there was a shortcut to the campground.

The man said, "Yes there is. Go up the road, turn left at the top of the hill, and you'll cut off quite a few miles."

He did not tell us, however, that as soon as we turned left, the road dropped straight down. It was very steep and narrow, barely two lanes wide, with a drop-off into a ravine on one side, and a cliff that went straight up on the other side. The road was also very curvy. I didn't want to use the brakes too much, so I tried to shift down. But every time I stepped on the clutch, we picked up too much speed before I could shift into a lower gear. I had to leave the truck in high gear, and keep using the brakes.

Another problem was that the boys were up in the camper and jumping around, this made the camper rock back-and-forth, which of course made it harder for me to steer. It was a very wild ride. Thankfully, the brakes did not give out, and we got to the bottom of that long hill in one piece. I think I aged five years during that ride.

The boys had a great time at the Hot Springs. They had never experienced a hot water lake before, and they just loved it. Even on the overcast days, they wanted to go swimming. We all enjoyed that camping trip.

On the way back home, we went by way of Mt. Hood, which was a shorter route, but there was also a chance that there would be snow on the road. Thankfully, the roads were clear, and by the time we got past Mt. Hood, I was an expert at using the clutch and stick shift.

All four of the boys were handsome and popular. After they became teenagers, girls were constantly calling the house and being a nuisance.

This is just one example: One day I thought I heard a girl's voice, so I knocked on the boys' bedroom door. David opened it just a crack and made it obvious that he did not want me to enter. When I pushed the door open, I didn't see a girl, but I noticed a purse on the desk. I opened the closet door and, sure enough, there was a girl.

It was not clear whether the girl was there for David or Donny; they shared the bedroom and were both in the room. I told the girl to leave. Then I questioned the boys. They said that they didn't know that the girl was in the closet. Really? Who would believe that story?

I told them, "From now on if you invite a girl to the house make sure you stay in the family living areas, not behind closed doors." But they insisted that the girl came over uninvited, and they didn't know what to do with her.

One by one, the boys got their Driver's License. When Mama and Papa bought a new car, they gave us their old car for the boys to share. A few months later the boys got into an accident and totaled the car. I can't remember who was at fault, but I do remember that they healed well and had no lasting injuries.

Aunt Froysa's Visit from Russia, 1978

My mama's sister Froysa came to America for a visit in 1978. I will never forget the joyful reunion between Mama and her sister.

From 1977 to 1982, Leonid Brezhnev, was Russia's Head of State, and Communist Party leader. Jimmy Carter was the U.S. President. During that time, the relationship between Russia and the United States was less strained, and why my Aunt was allowed to visit. Before then, it was rare for Russians to travel to America.

Mama had been writing to Froysa for many years, and kept inviting her to come for a visit. It took several years and a lot of paperwork between the U.S.A and U.S.S.R authorities before Froysa was finally permitted to travel.

Aunt Froysa must have left for America the moment she got permission. She did not even wait until Mama and Papa were notified. None of us knew that she was coming until she landed in New York. Then the immigration office tried to call my parents, but could not reach them because they were visiting friends in California. (It was Mama and Papa's first, out of state, vacation).

The only other contact number Aunt Froysa had was Mama's best friend, Anna Frank, who lived near my parents. Luckily, Anna was home. She assured the immigration officer that Froysa would be picked up at the Portland Airport.

When Anna called me, she was so excited. She yelled, "Nina, your Aunt Froysa is coming this afternoon!"

I was confused-- how can this be? It took a while for my brain to process this information. I kept asking, "Today? Really? Are you sure?"

Anna kept saying, "Yes. Yes. Yes. I have already called your parents. Your mama is overjoyed, and they will be home as soon as they can."

My next concern was, would I recognize Aunt Froysa? Would we be able to understand each other? I spoke Russian with Mama and Papa, but I knew it was a mixture of Russian and Ukraine. Would my aunt speak the same dialect?

I did not need to worry. The woman coming off the plane was the stereotype of a Russian woman. She was on the stout side, had a round face, and wore a "*babushka*" on her head. She marched with her shoulders back, and her head held high. She did not seem to be afraid, or intimidated, in any way. I was amazed at her courage. She was about sixty years old, had traveled all the way from Russia by herself, and she did not speak one word of English. When we met, I was relieved that she and I could communicate very well.

First, I had to assure her that our car and home did not have any listening devices. Only then did she speak freely about the conditions in Russia. She told me that they had to be very careful about what they said, because there was always someone listening; many people were sent to Siberia for speaking out against the government.

She said that she lived in a small house in a little village near Millerovo, Ukraine. Her house had only one light bulb, and no plumbing. There was only one well that supplied water for the entire village. There were no stores in her village. They grew their own vegetables, and had some chickens. She and her husband worked on a Collective farm. They had enough food to eat, but not much of anything else. They had to do what the Communist Party told them, and not question their authority.

But people rebelled against the cruel communist leaders in any way they could. They resented that the party leaders had special privileges and were more prosperous. The majority of the people had no incentives for working hard, that's why they worked as little as possible.

The cost of their electricity was very high. Their electric meter was read only about every six months. So, Aunt Froysa, and others, rebelled by disconnecting the meter for several months in between the readings.

Before she left for America, a communist official came to her home, and talked to her privately. He ordered her to keep her eyes and ears open, while she was in America, and to report anything "of interest" to him, when she returned to Russia.

Her assigned destination point was my parents' house in Tigard. She had to get permission from the U.S. government, if she wanted to travel outside a twenty-five-mile radius. I lived in Keizer, which was about 50 miles away. I told her that I would stay with her at Mama and Papa's house, until they got back from vacation. But she would not hear of it. She insisted that she would go home with me, and I could not talk her out of it.

I knew that one of my mother's concerns was the bathroom situation. Mama said that Froysa had only used an outhouse all her life. Mama was worried that Froysa would be uncomfortable using the bathroom inside the house.

But, after I showed Aunt Froysa how to flush the toilet, she had no problem.

She was puzzled about some things. She asked, "Why you cover floors with rug, do you have holes under there?" I assured her that we did not have holes. We had hardwood floors, but like most people at that time, we covered them with carpets.

We had a large maple tree in our backyard. She wanted to know, "What grows on that tree?"

"Just leaves."

"Why?"

"For shade."

She just shook her head and said, "That is a waste. You get shade from fruit trees, and then you also have fruit to eat."

I told her, "You are right, but we do have fruit trees on the other side of the house."

She was amazed at the size of our house. She asked," Why only one family live in so big house?" I did not know how to answer that.

Mama arrived the following day. I can still see the two of them in my kitchen, crying tears of joy while embracing each other; two sisters who had not seen one another for over thirty years. I will never forget my mother's radiant face.

Mama took Froysa to see the Pacific Ocean and Mt. Hood, but Froysa did not want to see the sights. She was only interested in seeing the stores. During the two weeks Froysa stayed in America, Mama took her shopping every day. She was fascinated with all the stores.

The first time she saw a supermarket, she stood in awe, it was as though she were standing in a grand cathedral; she stared at all that food, and all those choices. She had never seen so much food in her life. She was also amazed that everything was out in the open, and that she could touch everything. The first two days she just kept walking around and around the store not believing what she was seeing. She asked, "Are they not afraid that people will steal this food?"

Mama told her that there were security cameras, and that most people had enough money, so they did not need to steal.

In the following days, every time Mama took her to the store, Froysa would pick up an item and examine it, then she carefully put it back. She would then walk another step or two, pick up another item, ask what it was, and Mama would explain. She marveled that so much of the food was already cooked. Every day, she would find new items to examine, while Mama would stand by patiently, and answer her questions.

Froysa's regret was that she could not tell anyone in Russia about the wonders that she had seen in America. She was afraid of the Communists. She had heard of people who bragged about America. They were taken away, and never returned. She did not want to be one of them, so she had to look for negative things to report about America.

Two of those included: America does not have free health care, and people have to pay for higher education.

Aunt Froysa's husband was a heavy drinker—like so many other men who felt powerless under communist rule. He kept calling and telling her to come home. He told her that he was sick and needed her. She did not want to leave, but she knew that the Communists were pressuring him, so she had to obey. She left America one week before her originally scheduled departure of three weeks.

Froysa told us, "I know that the Communist officials are forcing my husband to make those phone calls. They want me to come home sooner than expected, so that I can tell everybody that things in America are very bad, and I could not stay there any longer. And that I am very glad to be back home in Mother Russia."

Mama tried to send only items that were on the "allowed list" home with Froysa. They spent long hours in the fabric store buying patterns, and many yards of all kinds of fabric. Things not allowed included: expensive and finely finished clothing, electronics, jewelry, and anything that would show off America's quality merchandise, and superior workmanship.

But my brave and stubborn aunt picked out items she wanted, and were not on the allowed list. She asked that those boxes be sent through the American checkpoint. She was confident that the packages would arrive safely that way, and not get stolen as they would be at the Russian checkpoint.

Later she wrote that her plan had worked, and she received all of the items.

At the airport, it broke my heart to see Mama and Froysa crying, and clinging to each other. They did not want to let go. They knew that this would probably be the last time they would see each other.

They were right. Mama never saw any of her Ukrainian family again.

Mama's sisters.
L to R: Shura, Valentina (Mama)
Front: Froysa

Don had worked for the bread company for about four years, the longest time he had ever held a job. But just as I was beginning to feel secure, he came home and told me that he had lost his job. He said, "A female sales clerk at the Fred Meyer store complained that I had flirted with her, and said some things she didn't like. The Fred Meyer manager insisted that the company fire me, or he would cancel bread delivery to the store. So, the company had no choice but to let me go."

I was beyond mad, I was furious. How could he be so stupid? I asked, "How could you jeopardize that good-paying job?"

He just hung his head, and told me that he was sorry. I didn't ask, nor did I want to know, what he had said to the sales clerk that got him fired.

After about two months, Don managed to get another job; this time with a non-union bread company. He got less money, but it was still better than any of his previous jobs.

A little while later, I got a telephone call from a Teamsters Union representative. He said, "Tell your husband that if he keeps that non-union job, he will never work in a union shop again."

I couldn't believe that he was actually threatening us. I got angry and told him, "We have four sons to feed, and right now, that "non-union company" is paying for our food. So, unless you want to take over feeding my children, don't call or threaten me again."

I was surprised at myself. Where did I get the nerve to talk back to that union man? However, I was glad that I did. We never heard from that man again.

A couple of years went by, we were financially stable, which was a great relief to me. Even though there were signs that

Don was unfaithful, I tried to ignore them, and continued to live in denial.

Sadly, Don lost that bread delivery job as well. He would not tell me why he was fired. But by now I was so used to him losing jobs, that it didn't shock me anymore. I was glad that my real estate business was doing well, and that we didn't have to worry about paying our bills while Don looked for work.

It took a while, but Don got another delivery job. This time with Reeser's Fine Food in Tualatin. It was about a 30-minute commute from our house, but it was mostly free-way driving.

Reeser's was a good company to work for. We went to one of their parties and I got to meet many of the employees. Everybody loved the owner and told me that they enjoyed working there. I really hoped that this would turn into a permanent job for Don.

I guess there must have been too many temptations at work, because Don came home later and later every week. I would feed the boys and wait to have dinner with Don. It got to be seven, then eight, or later. At first, I questioned him but he always had a reason for being late. Finally, I just accepted it. I ate with the boys and put Don's dinner in the refrigerator until he got home.

One night he called me after 11 o'clock and sounded very drunk. He said that he was sorry to be so late, but he would be leaving for home shortly. I did not want him to drive home drunk, so I told him to stay there, and get a room.

I called my friend Martha and told her that I had to take a change of clothes up to Don, and asked her to come with me. Very early the next morning, we drove to Reeser's. We sat in the parking lot and waited.

A few minutes later, Don drove in and get out of his truck. I saw him laughing and high-fiving with one of the guys, and I could hear bits of their conversation. They were talking about the great time they had the night before. Finally, I honked my horn. The minute Don saw me he totally changed. He went into his "Oh, I've been a bad boy" act, and slowly came to the car with his head hung down to his chest.

All of a sudden, I saw clearly what Don really was. I knew that he had been putting on an act for the past twenty-four years. I knew he was a charmer with lots of sweet talk, but a man with no real substance. Now I realized that he would never change, unless I did something drastic. When he came to the car window, I just handed him his clothes and drove away.

That night when he came home, I told him in no uncertain terms, "I will not be your mama anymore. You are the man of the house and I expect you to act like it. I will no longer keep trying to wake you in the mornings. That is not my job. You will get up when the alarm goes off. It is up to you to get yourself to work. I expect you to come home at a decent hour and be a father to our sons. They are teen-agers and need their father."

I hoped that this time he knew that I meant every word, and I think he did.

He did hear the alarm in the mornings, and he was able to get up on his own. I was surprised because his mother had told me, after we were married, that Don would never hear the alarm.

For twenty-four years I woke him every morning. Even when I was in hospital, after given birth to my babies (those days we had to stay in hospital for three or more days). I would set my alarm clock. Get out of bed. Use the telephone in the hallway. Let the phone ring until Don answered.

Then keep him on the phone until I was sure that he was awake and out of bed, before I went back to bed.

All those years, I had felt that it was my duty as his wife to make sure that Don got to work on time. Even when Mama and Papa went to Germany for a visit, I couldn't go because I had to stay home and make sure that Don got up. Our oldest son Barry went with them instead.

Getting home in time for dinner lasted only a little while. Then the excuses started again, and he was coming home late again.

Several months later, Don lost the Reeser's job. Of course, I asked him why he was fired. But he would not tell me. I suspected it had something to do with him coming home late. But I wasn't sure, so finally I just had to let it go.

My smoking habit, which had started while I worked at St. Vincent's hospital, was now an addiction. The more stressed I was, the more cigarettes I smoked. Somehow, I convinced myself that they were helping me overcome my stress. I had to have the cigarettes with me at all times. I was definitely a chain smoker.

Next, Don got a job as a clerk at the Oregon State Employment Office. I was glad, because this meant that he would be working in town, with regular hours, and he would be home at night. Several months went by. He said that he liked the job, and all seemed to be going well.

Then, someone told me that many times Don did not get back to work until well past his lunch hour. When I questioned him, he said that he was tired, and sometimes fell asleep in the car after he ate his lunch. I just knew by the way he acted that there was more to that story. I was pretty sure that he was having another affair. All of the memories of his infidelities came back.

I finally had enough. The boys were almost grown, and I was making enough money selling real estate to support the family. I decided that I no longer had to put up with Don's laziness, his womanizing, and his lies. So, I asked Don to leave.

I told him, "I want you to move out. I don't want a divorce, but I no longer trust you, believe you, or respect you. Without those three things, I cannot love you. I really hope that you can change, and if you do, you can come back, and we can start all over again."

He started making his usual promises, but he could tell that they were falling on deaf ears this time. He checked into a motel nearby. But two days later he came home, begging me to forgive him. He volunteered to see a psychiatrist, if I would just give him another chance.

This was something new. Don actually admitting that he had problems, and that he could not change his behavior on his own. That gave me hope. Maybe this would work.

Don started seeing a well-known psychiatrist, that my friend Inge had recommended. He also went to group meetings, which the psychiatrist had prescribed. I asked several times if I could go too, but he did not want me to come with him, and he would never tell me what was discussed in those meetings.

About three months went by, but nothing was changing. I still felt hurt and alienated from Don. Finally, I insisted that I go with him to see the psychiatrist. I told him that I only wanted five or ten minutes of the man's time. Don reluctantly agreed.

I went in alone. The psychiatrist was polite, and said that he was glad to see me. I told him why I was there, and how I felt. He listened patiently and nodded. But he didn't say anything. After a while I said, "I just have one question, can my marriage be saved?"

He said, "No."

His answer shocked me! I could not believe what I heard. I asked, "Why not?"

"I cannot tell you. Don is my patient and anything that we discuss is confidential."

I was speechless, I always thought that psychiatrists did not give such definite answers. I expected him to ask, "And what do you think will save your marriage?" But he didn't, and he had nothing more to say to me. He did not even suggest that Don and I go to marriage counseling.

I got up on shaky legs and walked out of his office. I felt like my world had collapsed. I was in shock, thinking, "What do I do now?"

In the car I asked Don, "What did you tell the psychiatrist?"

Silence. Don would not tell me. I asked again, and again, but there was only silence.

After we got home, I told him, "If you can't talk to me, and tell me what is going on, then there is no hope for our marriage, and you have to move out."

Don just looked at me and shrugged his shoulders.

I felt like something had died inside of me. I was numb. There was no anger, no hate, and no love. I knew that I had to be strong and let him go. I had no choice in the matter. I could no longer live in denial and pretend nothing had happened. I knew I could not be intimate with Don. It was as though all of my feelings for him had drained from me. I saw no point in arguing and, it seemed like neither did he.

Many years later, I read somewhere, "The opposite of Love is not Hate. The opposite of Love is Indifference."

We had just bought a nice rental house in Keizer. It had three bedrooms, two baths, living room, family room, a double garage, and was in a good neighborhood, not far from Fir Cone house, and it was vacant.

I told Don, "You can move into the house we just bought." Don just said, "Okay."

I surprised myself by telling Don, "Take Brian, Donnie and David with you. They are too big for me to handle on my own, and need their father. You need to be a real father to them and take care of them."

The words just came out of my mouth. I had never even thought about letting my sons go. But deep down I must have known that I was in no condition to take care of my big boys.

—In retrospect, all I can say is that I must have been at my wit's end and at a breaking point, and my self-preservation instinct took over. I had been responsible for people ever since I could read and write, and I just could not carry the burden anymore.

The boys were 18, 19, 20 and 21 years old. Barry was already married and living in Salem. They had made it clear that they did not need their mama anymore. They did not listen to me, and I did not know how to guide them. The boys were troubled teenagers. We had tried counseling with them, but that did not do much good. I did not know what else to do. I had lectured, pleaded and yelled at them, but nothing I said or did seemed to make any difference.

I remember shaking Brian one time, and yelling at him, "Don't you know how much I love you? I see you putting yourself in danger, and I feel like I am losing my mind."

Brian just looked at me and said, "Then, just don't love me so much."

When the boys got home, I told them, "Your Dad and I are separating for a while, I want you to go and live with your father, but anytime you are ready to obey my rules, you can come back and live with me. I love you very much, but I just can't handle things the way they are."

Don and I never had any big arguments in front of the boys; we always made sure that they were either asleep or away from the house when we had our "discussions." Even now, there was no mention of a divorce. The boys did not seem to be traumatized, or concerned, and agreed to go with their father.

Divorce, 1980

After Don and the boys moved out, Fir Cone house became too big and empty. I had never lived alone, and I was very uncomfortable being alone; especially at night. I couldn't sleep and I worried over every creak and groan in that house. They all sounded like footsteps to me.

I was also feeling guilty. "Did I do the right thing, asking Don to move out and to take the boys with him? How could I do such a thing?"

I was disappointed that none of the boys came back home. Much later I found out why. While they lived with their father, they had very little supervision. They did not have to follow rules and could do whatever they wanted. So, of course, they did not want to move back in with me, I had rules, but I did not think that I was overly strict. I just wanted them to do what was best for them and their future.

After a few weeks, I couldn't stand living alone anymore and asked my friend Martha, if she wanted to move into my daylight basement. She agreed, but she told me that it would be two weeks before she could move in.

In the meanwhile, Nila Palmer, my secretary at Red Carpet Realty, was flying to Rancho Mirage to house-sit for a friend and asked me to come with her. I gladly agreed to go for one week.

Nila and I had a great time. The house was beautiful and had a big, totally private, swimming pool. The weather was perfect, and we went skinny dipping every night. Nila was 15 years older than me. She had led an interesting life and I loved hearing her stories. During the day we talked, went sight-seeing and shopping. In the evenings, we played cards, or went to the Eagles, a club we both belonged to. The time just flew by.

When I got back to Portland, I was surprised to see Don waiting at the airport. A friend of mine was supposed to pick me up, but Don told her that he would do it. As always, he was a smooth talker, but it had no effect on me this time. I did not hear any change in him. I wanted him to tell me that he was working hard and taking care of the boys, and that he would be more of a help-mate to me if we got back together again. But he just said the same things he had said many times before. Also, Don still would not tell me why the psychiatrist said that our marriage could not be saved. So, when we got to the house, I thanked him, and just walked away.

I was glad when Martha moved in. I could sleep much better, knowing that someone else was in the house. When I got home from work, I would talk to Martha for hours. She used to babysit for me, so she knew Don very well. She knew all of his faults and she was glad that I had finally left him. She kept encouraging me to stay strong and not change my mind. She reminded me of the time when I had asked Don to move out, after I found out that he had been cheating. But after two days I gave in to his pleadings and promises that he would always be faithful, and let him come back home.

I knew that Martha was right. This time I needed to be sure that Don had changed, before we got back together again. I don't know if I would have stayed strong without Martha's help.

A couple of months went by and I found out that Don had a lady friend, which did not surprise me. I was not jealous, but my hope for a reconciliation was dwindling fast. What was I thinking? Why did I think that Don would change?

I knew that I had to stay busy in order to keep my resolve strong. During the day I didn't have a problem. I was managing Red Carpet Realty and that kept me busy all day. However, in the evenings and on weekends, when I was not showing properties to potential buyers, I felt lonely and I missed my family, even with Martha in the house.

I had several close female friends who were great listeners and ego boosters. Jeanette Harvey, my longtime friend, came into my office one day and surprised me by telling me that she and Ken were getting a divorce. My friend, Mable, was separated from her husband as well. There was also Mickey, a widow, who was a friend of Martha's, and a lot of fun to be with. At that time, all of my friends were older than me, because I felt that I had more things in common with older women.

Sundays were the loneliest for me. I found out that the Eagles club had a Sunday afternoon bowling league. I loved bowling, so I signed up as a substitute. That way I could bowl when they needed me, and when I was available. After that my Sundays were not so lonely anymore.

One Sunday, there was no bowling. I was restless, and had nothing to do. I called Ron Treece, who was divorced, and a part time salesman at my office. I asked if he'd go to the coast with me for the afternoon. When he agreed, I drove to his house in West Salem, and then he drove his car to Lincoln City. It was a beautiful, calm sunny day just right for beach walking. Ron took me to a place where he and his family used to stay and walk the beach. We parked in the motel parking lot and went for a walk.

As we were walking along the ocean, I couldn't believe my eyes. I saw my son, Donny, with a girl. I was very surprised, and we walked over to them. After we made the introductions, I told my son that Ron was just a friend, and that we were here for the day. We stood and talked for a while. Then we all walked back to the motel where Ron and I had parked. I didn't think about how it would look to my son when he saw that we were parked in a motel parking lot. I knew that Don was dating a woman, so I didn't think that I needed to convince Donny that Ron and I were not sleeping together. As a matter of fact, at that time, sex was the farthest thing from my mind. But of course, Donny didn't know that. I suspect that my son must have reported the incident to Don (I never found out for sure). Looking back, I wonder if this was meant to be. What are the chances of my running into my son, on that particular and somewhat isolated beach?

About two or three weeks later, Martha came upstairs and woke me up. She was very excited and said, "Nina, did you know that your divorce announcement is in the newspaper?" (They did that in those days).

I was stunned! I said, "My what?"

She handed me the paper, and sure enough, there was Don's and my name in the "filing for divorce" column. I couldn't believe my eyes. We had never talked about getting a divorce, and I had not been served with divorce papers. I thought, "How could he do this?"

I felt betrayed. I also realized that I was still hoping that Don would change, and we could be a family again. This was so final. That is not how it was supposed to be. I wanted a change, not a divorce. I realize how naive I was. Don had not changed in all the years we were married, so why would he do it now? I suppose that I had been waiting for a miracle.

I called Don and asked, "Why did you do this?"

He replied, "My lawyer suggested that I file first."

"Your lawyer told you to do this? And you listened to the lawyer without first talking to me? We have been married over 24 years. I gave you four sons, and this is how you treat me? You trust a lawyer instead of me? How could you do such a shameful thing. Why did you not talk to me first?"

Don had nothing to say. After a long silence, I just hung up the phone. I sat there feeling that my world had collapsed. My marriage was really over. What do I do now?

That happened on a Sunday morning. I cried and talked to Martha all morning long, and she kept assuring me that I was better off. But, the severity of the betrayal would not go away. I went bowling that afternoon, hoping it would distract me, but it just kept festering. I kept asking myself, "How could he do this? He knows that stabbing me in the back is one of the worst things that could happen to me. How could I have been married to a man like that for such a long time?" This just kept going over and over in my mind.

That Sunday afternoon, Ron Treece was my bowling partner. There was a bar in the bowling alley. After bowling Ron offered to buy me a drink. Hoping that a drink would calm me down, I accepted. But my mental state was very fragile and alcohol made it worse. I took two swallows and the alcohol went right to my head. I got very dizzy and sick to my stomach. I went into the bathroom and tried to throw up, but I couldn't. I just sat there hugging the toilet, too dizzy to get up. Finally, Ron sent a woman in to see what had happened to me. She found me and helped me out of the bathroom.

I left my car in the parking lot and Ron drove me home. I was still dizzy and nauseated and I had dry heaves all the way home. Ron went downstairs, told Martha what had happened, and then he left. She came upstairs, helped me undress, and stayed with me while I kept crying and asking over and over, "How could Don do this?" until I finally fell asleep. The next morning, I felt better. I had gotten the venom out of me and I knew that I had done the right thing when I had asked Don to leave. His betrayal was proof of that.

The following week someone gave me the name of a good divorce attorney. I made an appointment for a consultation which cost me $60. After I explained my situation to the attorney. He said, "I can't believe that I am talking to a woman. Your story sounds just like the stories of my male clients. I am certain that I can get you a 70/30 asset split."

I told him that I did not want to go through a nasty divorce, and that I wanted to make this as easy as I could on my sons. He said, "I understand, but you should get at least a 60% split. If you can do that, then you don't need me. And since there are no minor children involved, all you and your husband have to do is agree on the property settlement. Then your husband's attorney can finalize the divorce."

I thanked him for his advice and told him that I would see what I could do.

I had already given Don the pickup and camper, the extra furniture and kitchen items when he moved out. Now we divided the money in the bank, and the four rental properties. I let him keep the house he lived in, and I kept the Fir Cone house. It was important to me to have a home where my children, and their children, could come. I felt that my roots in America were in that house.

After we agreed on the property settlement, we paid his lawyer, and the divorce was finalized July 17, 1980.

Four months later, Don married his lady friend. Shortly after, they moved to a town in Washington, where Don finally got his wish and bought his own business. I was told that it had something to do with cement.

He had wanted to buy his own business for years, but I did not want to risk the money. I knew that in order to be successful in business, you had to be a hard worker and a self-starter, and Don was neither. Sure enough, he was out of business in about two years.

My Sons, Later Years

At the time of our divorce, Barry, my oldest son, was already married to Glenda, who was his high school sweetheart. Glenda was perfect for him. She was kind and nurturing, and a good homemaker.

When Barry was about seventeen years old, he got a wart on the inside of his knee. When it got really big and started bothering him, he showed it to me.

I remembered the witch in Germany who got rid of my warts, and decided I would try her tricks. Barry was surprised when I told him that I could get rid of that wart.

I told him to sit down at the table. I lit some candles, cut off a piece of bacon, and started rubbing it on his wart. He thought that I had lost my mind, but I told him to trust me. Since I didn't know the words the witch had used, I just made up some words. I said, "You are a nice little wart, but I don't want you anymore, I want you to go away."

I told Barry to repeat those words, while I continued to rub the wart with the piece of bacon. Again, Barry looked at me like I was crazy, but I told him, "If you want to get rid of that wart, do what I say."

After a while, I told him to take the bacon down by the creek, at the end of our road, and bury it. I assured him that the wart would be gone when the bacon had rotted. Two weeks later that big wart was gone!

Barry's girlfriend, Glenda, was with him when I performed my "witchcraft." She was impressed after she saw that the wart was gone and told my son, "Wow, your Mom must really be a witch."

Barry, holding son, Matt; Brian, Donny, and David

Glenda married my son. Later, when she was pregnant, I predicted the date the baby was going to be born. When the prediction came true, she was convinced that I indeed was a witch. I let her think that, but actually, I am pretty sure that I just got lucky when I predicted that date. Or was I? We will never know, because after that, I stopped pretending that I was a witch. I thought I'd better quit while I was ahead.

I never had to worry about my oldest son. I have always been proud of him. Even though my other sons tell me, "Barry broke all the rules just like we did, but he was never caught."

Barry enjoyed school. He was a good student, and was elected school president in middle school. He liked all sports, but he was outstanding in football. In his senior year, he and his team went to state finals, and came close to winning the title.

Barry got a two-year college football scholarship. After graduating, he got a job as a guard at the state prison. He had always wanted to be a policeman, and thought that the guard job would prepare him for that. But he soon discovered that he did not like working with criminals.

He went to work for a steel company in Salem, and was promoted quickly. He then became a company representative for a large steel company, covering Washington Idaho and Oregon. He was a good provider, and Glenda was able to stay home with their two sons, Matthew and Nathan. She too contributed financially, by babysitting at home. She loves children and became a second mother to the children she cared for

Grandson, Matthew, went through college, earned a Bachelors' degree, two Masters', and is now working on a Doctorate. He married, Anna, who is an Episcopalian priest. She was transferred to Fresno, California, and Matt is working there as a librarian. He does not like living in Fresno, he misses his family, and is hoping that they can return to Oregon soon.

Grandson, Nathan, who looks very much like his uncle David, was married for a short time. He has two sons: Aiden and Kyler. They are identical twins; both are smart and handsome boys. He shares custody with his ex-wife, Alicia, and is an excellent father.

Update: after many years of being single, Nathan became engaged to a lovely Ukrainian girl, Alla. I was very happy when they married in June of 2017, and had a son, Maksim, in March of 2019.

My second son, Brian, has a loving heart and is a loyal person. He loved two women in his life, but sadly he never married. I always felt that he would have made a wonderful father. I base that on my observations of how protective he was of his little brother, David, and how much he cares for his niece and nephews.

Brian was teased in school about his red hair and he has never gotten over that. I wish I would have done more than just tell him that his hair is beautiful. We should have told him that his hair is special, and is proof that he's a descendent of Vikings, who were very brave and fierce warriors. Maybe that would have helped him with his self-esteem.

Brian has always been a reliable worker. He had several jobs, one of those was as a carpenter, and for many years he was a truck driver.

Update: Brian hurt his back and is on disability. Thankfully he is able to care for himself. I bought three rental houses several years ago, Brian now lives in one of the houses, and pays us whatever rent he can afford. Knowing that he is safe and has a home, takes a lot of worry off of me.

My third son, Donald, had many friends at school, and he loved acting. A few years after graduating from high school, he married, Karen, a woman with three children. The marriage ended in divorce a few years later. But the blessing from that marriage is my beautiful granddaughter, Brianna, who gave birth to a son, Clayton.

"Clay-Clay" is a very loving child. I love the way he hollers, "Gram-Gram," and runs into my arms every time I see him.

Donny is now married to Sondra, a very good and hardworking woman, who is an excellent partner for him, and a good grandmother for Clayton.

Donny was a good salesman, which did not surprise me because he was born with the "gift of gab." From the time he could talk, I thought that someday he would have a career as a salesman, a politician, or a preacher.

He has had several jobs throughout his life, but he thrived as a salesman and branch manager for "Garten Services," who employ mentally challenged people. He loved his job, and loved the people at Garten; they were all his buddies. It was a rewarding career and he felt that he was making a difference in their lives.

In the last few years, my Donny has been having major health issues. He has Diabetes, and Hepatitis C-3. He has gone through two years of very intense chemo. treatments, and is now going through the third and final treatment. His liver is badly damaged, and he has lost all of his teeth. We are hoping and praying that this clinical trial treatment will work. He is very brave, and always in positive spirits when we talk; which is a comfort to me. However, I know that his nausea is severe, and the treatments are poisoning his body, I can't help being worried about him. I tell myself, "Where there's Life, there's Hope." But I pray, "Please Dear God, don't take another one of my sons from me!"

Two years later: amazingly Donny's Hepatitis is in remission, and we hope that his liver will recover. He is grateful to be working again. He is now manager for a large storage rental company, and likes his job. I am glad that I could help Donny and Sondra during this terrible time. They are living in one of my rental houses, and paying whatever rent they can.

All of my handsome sons, not only had different colored hair, they also had very different personalities. Barry is strong, reliable and a good provider. Brian is sensitive, and tender hearted. Donny is everybody's friend, and has the gift of gab. David wanted to please everybody, and he loved dogs (Snoopy was his favorite).

—Personal note to my children: When the time comes to settle our estate, please do not argue over money, or any of our belongings. Be generous with each other. We have made out a Trust, and tried to be fair in how we want our estate to be distributed. I hope that you will accept our decisions. I love all of my children equally, and unconditionally. I know that Ron feels the same about his children. I see no reason why we would ever disinherit any of our children, unless we had dementia. In which case, we would want you to take that into consideration, and be fair with each other.

My Brother and Sister

Bill Streich is seven years younger than I, and was born in Germany. He married when he was twenty-one years old. He and his wife divorced when Bill was in his forties, and he has never re-married. He is a good man. He was the owner of a roofing company, and has always been a good family provider. He has two beautiful daughters, Angela and Courtnay; both are smart business women and are married to two great guys. His son, Jared, recently received his doctoral degree in botany. Bill is very proud of his children, and rightfully so.

In 2015, Bill became a proud grandfather to Angela's daughter, Esme, and three years later, to Angela's son, Spencer.

Lydia Jean is 17 years younger than I, and was born in America. She grew up to be a beautiful woman. She finished college and married David, a boy she met at college. She worked for Multnomah County as a Food Inspector for many years. I was told that later she became a teacher and worked with special-needs children. She and David never had children of their own.

Sadly, because of an inheritance dispute my brother and I, and our families, have not spoken to Lydia since after Papa's funeral. I wish her well, and I hope that she is happy.

L to R: Nina, Bill, Lydia, Papa and Mama, at Lydia's wedding

Losing David

My youngest son David, my tall dark and heartbreakingly handsome boy was very popular in school, especially with the girls. He begged for a drum set, and we bought him one. He took lessons and became a really good drummer. When he was about 17 years old, he started going steady with Tammy, a beautiful blond girl who was also warm and kind. They made a lovely couple.

After high school, David joined the Marines and graduated from boot camp. He was very proud of that accomplishment. One day, David and I were having an argument over something trivial. He turned to me and said, "You can't tell me what to do, I am a man now."

I replied, "You may be a man to everyone else, but to me you are, and will always be, my baby. Even when you are a hundred years old."

David glared at me and slammed out of the house. Half an hour later he came back with tears in his eyes and said, "I am sorry. I love you Mom."

We hugged, and I was glad my baby boy was still inside that very strong and beautiful young man. After David

David, on the drums

came home from Boot Camp, he seemed changed. I don't know whether the Marines "made a man out of him" or if they broke his spirit. He was much more serious and he was also drinking too much.

In March of 1982, David went to Washington to visit his father. Two weeks later, he called to wish me Happy Easter. He said, "Mom, I love you very much and I will be home in a day or two."

I told him, "I love you too and I want you to be safe. Please don't hitchhike. Get the money for bus fare from your dad, and tell him that I'll pay him back."

That was the last conversation I had with my son.

In April of 1982, there was a knock on my door. I opened the door, and saw a policeman standing on my porch.

He asks, "Can I talk to Don Carmichael?"

"Which Don Carmichael, Senior or Junior?"

"Probably Senior."

"Don Senior is my ex-husband and he does not live here anymore."

"Are you alone?"

I tell him, "Yes."

I got extremely nervous. There was a big lump in my chest. I did not want to hear what the policeman had to say, but I invited him in.

I don't remember exactly what happened after that. I know that when I was told that my son David was killed, I started moaning and kept on moaning, until I could not catch my breath. I felt like my heart had stopped beating, and my head would explode. I also felt like I was losing my mind.

I remember taking a deep breath and saying, "No. No. This can't be true." Another deep breath, "He is not dead.

You have the wrong person." Another very deep breath, "My son is alive. He can't be dead."

Every time I thought of the words, "David is dead," I felt that I would go mad. I had to let my mind go into denial in order to stay sane. When the pain would get unbearable, I told myself, "No, David is not dead. He is only 20 years old; this is a horrible mistake."

I don't know why David decided to hitchhike. Don told me later that he had given him bus money.

David got as far as the Tigard exit, off I-5. Then, while trying to get another ride, he got too close to a car. He was hit. And run over by a second car!

His body was too badly mangled. The family was not allowed to see him. A close friend of the family identified his body.

My biggest regret is, I did not get to hold my son, and say goodbye. When I think about it however, I wonder if I really want to carry the picture of my son's broken body in my mind the rest of my life. I don't know, I think not, but without seeing him, it took years for my mind to accept that David was really dead. So, there is no good choice here.

We had a military funeral for David. I was honored when they handed me the American flag, and very proud of my son—even as my heart was breaking. To this day I cry every time I hear a bugler play Taps.

I couldn't believe that we were really burying my David. I wanted so much to open the casket and see my son's body, but I couldn't. The pain was so overwhelming, I had to push it away and tell myself that all of this was not real—my son is not dead.

After the funeral, I invited family and friends to come to my home. I pretended that this was just a party, and I had to play the role of a good hostess. I could not let anyone see me grieve.

I know that living in denial was keeping me sane. I continued to see David everywhere I went. I was disappointed every time when they turned and the face was not David's.

Day after day, I kept agonizing about returning to David's grave. I felt that I should go, but I was afraid. A few weeks later, I got up the courage. When I saw David's, name engraved on the tombstone, it finally sank in, "My baby is really dead, and buried in that ground."

The pain hit so hard, it felt like a physical blow, I fell on my knees, sobbing. The desire to claw the ground was overwhelming, I just have to see my David. Thankfully, I came to my senses and forced myself to walk away.

I have never gone back to see my son's grave since that day. I don't want to feel that excruciating pain again. Sometimes that grave calls to me, but I tell myself that David is not there. He lives in my heart and in my memory, and his spirit surrounds me always.

Losing a child is the very worst thing that can happen. It is not natural. I am supposed to die before my child. His death will haunt me for the rest of my life. Could I have done something to prevent his death? Why did this happen? There are no answers; there is only pain.

I read somewhere that, "Guilt is the most painful companion of death." I agree with that.

Ode to my Son David:

They tell me that you are dead—This cannot be true.
They say a car ran over you—I hear their words,
but this cannot be.

My son is dead, why not me?

David, a Christmas Miracle

I am decorating the house for Christmas with a heavy heart. I keep thinking, David won't be here. This will be the first Christmas without him. I start whimpering, then stop myself. No, he is not dead! But he won't be here for Christmas, so he must be dead. Oh, how I miss him … No. Stop. Don't do this.

Somehow, the Christmas tree got decorated. Next, I have to decorate the mantle, and put out the centerpieces. All of those decorations are in the trunk behind the loveseat. When I lift the trunk lid, the first thing I see is a beautiful shiny Christmas card lying right on top. Puzzled, I reach for it, "Why is this here? Christmas cards don't belong here. They are never in the trunk. They are always kept in the bottom desk drawer."

I open the card. When I see the signature, I stop breathing. My heart skips a beat, and my knees buckle. I sit down on the floor. I am stunned, the Christmas card is from David! "How can this be?"

The printed words are: Merry Christmas and Happy New Year.

The written words are: "Dear Mom, I love you very much. Love, Dave."

Oh, my dear God. My tears flow freely for a very long time. When they stop, I feel drained. I place the card on the mantle. Now I know that David will be home for Christmas—even if I cannot see him.

To this day, I cannot explain how that card came to be in the trunk, a place where I would be sure to find it, just at a time when I needed it most.

My beautiful baby-boy,
trying to look like a fierce Marine

A Mother's Lament

He was so small, so sweet was he,
The most beautiful baby boy you'll ever see.

Then, he was grown.

So strong, so sure, so brave, so full of life and love, was he.

Why did I not know he would be gone so soon?

How could I not see, not feel, not hear, not know?

Am I to blame? Have I done wrong?

How could he die, and I survive?

How will I live, how will I thrive?

My son is gone!

And I can't sleep, and I will mourn,
and I will weep, for-ever-more.

Family Pictures

Barry and Glenda

David

Brian

Donny and Sondra

Don and Nina, 1971   *Mathew and Nathan*

Brianna

Clayton

Aiden and Kyler

Clayton, 10 years old

Maksim, (great grandson)

Aiden and Kyler
Ready for Ninth Grade

Nathan and Alla's Wedding

Matt, working at Mt Angel Library

Donny and Brianna

*Beatrice and Walter
Carmichael (Don's parents)*

Mama and Papa

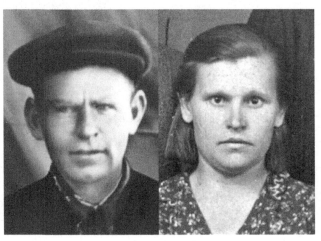

Mama and 1st Papa

Brother Bill and Nina

Ron and Nina; our first cruise

Bill's children: Jared, Angela, and Courtnay

L to R: Donny, Barry, Brian; David in front

Beatrice and Walter with Don

Barry's family, L to R: Matt, Glenda, Nathan, and Barry

PART III
Life Stories and Adventures

Selling Real Estate, 1968–2010

I was 30 years old when I got my real estate license. I kept that license for over 40 years. I enjoyed selling real estate, and was always amazed that I was getting paid for something I loved to do.

I hung my license with Joe Mooney Real Estate. I knew Joe from square dancing, and I liked him and his wife Evelyn. He had a small office in downtown Salem, next to the Army Recruiting Office. There was another older real estate agent working in his office. They were both retired from previous jobs and liked sitting around telling tales.

I told Joe that I wanted to work part-time for the first month until David started school and he agreed. But he kept me busy right from the start. He didn't like showing properties, so when someone called and wanted to see a house, he called me. I had to hurry, yank curlers out of my hair, get dressed, and take my son David to a nearby babysitter.

My first sale was an old four-plex in North-East Salem. That was the biggest commission check I had ever received. To celebrate, we spent part of the money on a color television set, which made everybody in the family happy.

I had so much fun looking at houses, sometimes I forgot I was the Realtor. It felt more like my clients and I were friends, looking at pretty houses. I never pressured my clients to buy. We would just look until they found the house they liked and could afford. Then we went back to the office. Joe answered all their questions, and wrote up the earnest money agreement.

He also took care of anything else that was necessary to close the sale, leaving me free to go out and sell more "pretty houses." At that time, there was a popular television show starring Lucille Ball. Lucy's last name was Carmichael, and her boss was named Mooney. Since my name was Carmichael and Joe's was Mooney, we had a great icebreaker. We played our parts, and our clients loved the fun atmosphere. This partnership worked great for many months.

A Realtor's merchandise is his listing. Without it, there is nothing to advertise and attract buyers. I needed a listing, and came up with an idea: I spoke Russian, so I could be a big help to the "Old Believers," living in the Woodburn Russian community. They had escaped Russia because of their religious beliefs, and many of them could not speak or read English.

That afternoon I drove out to Woodburn and knocked on doors. Within a short time, I got a lead. A woman told me that the people across the street wanted to sell their house. When I knocked on their door, the man of the house answered. I smiled and said, "*Zdrastvuiete* (hello), are you interested in selling your house?" He was surprised and pleased that I spoke Russian, and invited me in.

I met his wife, and after we talked for a while, he insisted that I join him and drink a glass of *"Kvass"*—a fermented homemade brew, that the Old Believers make in a Crockpot. I told him that I could not drink while on business. But he said, *"Kvass* is a healthy juice drink, and it is impolite of you to refuse a drink." So, I gave in.

Then he told his wife, "Go fry fish."

Again, I tried to tell him that this was not necessary. It was clear that the wife did not want to "go fry fish." But the man insisted.

While the wife was cooking fish, I got a closer look at the house. It was in bad need of repair, and I wasn't sure if it was saleable in its present condition. At that point, I should have just left. But oh no, I kept sipping the *Kvass*, and the man kept refilling my glass.

After the fish was fried, the wife called us to the table. In the middle of the table I saw a platter of fried trout. We sat down and the man said, *"Kuschai"* (eat). I looked for a plate, or a napkin, or a fork, but there was only the platter of fish on a dirty tablecloth with flies buzzing all around.

I had no idea how I was supposed to eat that fish. I convinced the guy that, since he was the man, he should start first. I watched him pick up a trout and put it in front of him on top of the dirty tablecloth. He pulled the fish apart, shooed the flies away, and started eating. So, I followed his lead and did likewise. By then I'd had enough *Kvass* so the flies and the dirty tablecloth didn't bother me too much.

I don't remember how I extracted myself from that house. I think I told them that I had to bring my broker, Joe Mooney, back with me to write up the listing.

When I got back to the office, I was in a jovial mood. Joe took one look at me and asked, "Nina, have you been drinking?"

I told him, "Well, yes and no. I was in Woodburn, trying to get a listing, and a chauvinist Russian guy made me drink *Kvass*. He told me that it was a healthy juice drink, and I had to be polite and do what he said."

Joe just stood there, shaking his head and laughing. I didn't think it was funny because my stomach was starting to reject that "healthy juice drink," and I headed for the bathroom.

I never went back for that listing. From then on, I stayed away from the Russians and their *Kvass*.

A few months after I started selling real estate, Joe moved the office to Keizer. More salespeople joined our office and he got busier. I had to do my own advertising and paperwork. However, by then I had enough experience and I didn't really mind.

Two years after I got my real estate license, I was eligible for a broker's license. This time I didn't go to school. I just studied a Norm Webb manual, took my broker's test, and passed. As I was driving to my office, I felt proud and confident, and I wanted to celebrate.

When I got to the office, there was an envelope on my desk. I was told that the letter had been left by a young woman. When I opened the envelope, a picture of a small baby, with a lot of dark hair, fell out. I unfolded a torn-out sheet of notebook paper, and these were the exact words I read, "*Nina—I'm inform you that that I had a boy, I thought you'd Like to know I had a boy. So I'm sending you a piture to show you what Our son Looks Like. So I named him after his father. I hope you didn't mind. With All my Love, Rose Anna.*"

The note was poorly written in pencil. It was clear that it was meant to hurt me. Which it did. I felt like she had punched me in the stomach. Seeing Don's infidelity revealed in writing, instead of just hearing about it, made it seem much more real.

So, the celebrating I had wanted did not happen. Instead I had to go home and confront my husband about this woman. On the way home I wondered, "How much longer can I put up with Don's womanizing."

When I showed the letter and picture to Don, I could see the fear in his face. But he recovered very quickly and denied knowing the woman. When I asked how she knew my name and where I worked, he hung his head and had no answer. It was obvious that he did know the woman. But I knew that she had lied about the baby being my husband's because Don had had a vasectomy a few years before. Since she had lied about that, she had lost her credibility. Also, I had no proof that Don was involved with her. I didn't even know where I could contact her.

I was so relieved that Don could not be the father of that baby, his infidelity became less important. Actually, I didn't really want to believe what I was seeing; it just hurt too much. So, I let it go. After all, I had four sons under the age of twelve. What else could I do? I saved the letter and the baby picture, and I've kept them to this day. The reason I kept them was because, even though the note was not entirely true, to me, it was proof that Don did have an affair and that I was not just making things up.

I stayed with Joe Mooney Real Estate for over ten years, until Joe died.

After that, I went to work at Cascade West Realty where I got a much better commission split. There were four of us in that office. We were all experienced brokers. Don Rollins, the owner and Designated Broker, let us run our own business. My hours were flexible, but I made myself available whenever my clients needed me.

Real estate was good to me. I never made a big amount of money because I could not work that many hours. I tried to be at home with my boys as much as I could. Even so, I had a good steady income. I made more money than I had ever made working for wages, and I invested some of that money wisely.

I worked at Cascade West for several years, until Don Rollins died of lung cancer, and his wife closed the office.

Then I went to work for Red Carpet Realty in Keizer. Elmer Valkenaar owned that office.

When Elmer purchased another Red-Carpet Real Estate office, on Market Street in Salem, I became the Designated Broker and manager for that office. I was told that the sales people were not getting along well, so I was a little nervous about taking on that position.

There was a secretary who took care of the paperwork named Nila Palmer and eight salespeople: four women, two retired older men, one a former Navy officer, and the other a former Oregon Parks Manager, plus Ralph, an old Realtor, and a part time National Guard guy Ron Treece, who only came into the office on weekends. When I first met Ron, I didn't like him. He seemed kind of stiff and arrogant. However, I grew to respect and admire him.

I was younger than all of the people in that office, and aware that they were all independent contractors. I was not their boss. My job was to supervise their real estate transactions, and to encourage them to be successful. I did ask them to stop gossiping, and backbiting. Whenever I heard of an argument, I would ask both people to come into my office, one at a time. I would listen to their side of the story, and then ask them to consider the other person's side for just a few moments. Most of the time that defused their anger, and peace was restored.

Many years after the first encounter with the Russian "Old Believers" (named so because of their religious beliefs) I had another encounter.

Elmer Valkenaar wrote up a sale on a small acreage to the Woodburn Old Believers. They had told him that they needed a place to bury their dead, and because of their beliefs, an American cemetery was not right for them. The acreage was zoned EFU (Exclusive Farm Use) and it needed a zone designation for a cemetery before the sale could be finalized.

Elmer asked me to go with him to the hearing, and help him persuade the Planning Commission to grant this zone designation. At first, I said, "No way, I do not want to become involved with the Old Believers again."

He kept on talking, and reminded me that I was born in Ukraine, and that these were "my people" and that they had been looking for a cemetery a long time... Finally, he wore me down and I went with him to Silverton where the hearing was held.

I had worked hard on my presentation. I pointed out that the acreage in question was not good farmland, and that it was far enough from any homes. Therefore, a cemetery would not interfere with anything. I even brought up the fact that the Old Believers came to America because of religious freedom, and how badly they needed a cemetery. I used facts and logic, as well as emotion, in my presentation.

There were too many objections from the people of Silverton, and we lost. The zone designation was denied. On the way home, I was furious. "How could they not grant the zone change? What harm could there possibly be in granting it? This was so unfair. Why were there so many objections from the neighbors?" On and on I raged.

In the end, the sale fell through, and the Old Believers did not get their cemetery.

A few months later, I noticed an article in the paper. It said that the Old Believers could not find land for a cemetery, and because they did not believe in embalming their dead, they could not bury them in a regular cemetery. So, they had to bury them in their backyards. This was discovered when a dog dug up a grave and dragged the corpse through town!

I was horrified. What a terrible thing to have happen. I could hardly wait to get to the office and show the article to Elmer. He was also upset and we wondered, "Had the planning commission granted a zone change when we asked for it, maybe the dog incident would never have happened." We really hoped that the Old Believers would now get their cemetery after all. But I never found out if they did.

I owned two houses on Mission Street. One of the renters, a tall handsome black man, came into my office every month to pay the rent. Usually he was cheerful, but this time he stormed into my private office, and before I could close the door, yelled, "Tell your husband to stop coming into my house and bothering my wife. Just because he is the landlord, he thinks that he can come into the house anytime he wants. Well he can't, and he better stop it, or else."

I saw that the salespeople had heard everything and looked alarmed. I waved them off, and quickly closed the door. I told the man that I was sorry, and didn't know that Don was bothering his wife. He saw how upset I was and calmed down. Then he apologized for yelling at me. I told him, "It's okay, I understand your anger. I am angry too." I assured him that Don would never bother his wife again, and the man left.

By this time my marriage was in serious trouble. I knew that Don was a womanizer. This incident was just a small nail in the coffin. But I was very embarrassed and had felt humiliated in front of my sales people; that really hurt.

When I got home and confronted Don, he denied doing anything wrong. Of course, I didn't believe him and told him, "What you are doing is really low and disgusting. Stay away from the renters!"

Whatever he said after that fell on deaf ears. I had heard it all before, and was sick of it.

While I managed the Red-Carpet office, we all got along pretty well and the office made good money—until the real estate crash (around 1980). Interest rates kept going up and got so high that people could not afford to buy houses. And then, when real estate values plummeted, people were afraid to buy homes. Many real estate offices had to sell or just go out of business.

Elmer had overextended himself and had to sell some of his real estate offices, including Market Street. The salespeople wanted me to buy the office, but the timing was not right for me. No one else wanted to buy it either, so we had to close our doors.

I transferred my license to Realty House, on State Street. They had a good reputation, and they offered me a fair commission split. Interestingly, Doris Seitz, (the lady who had inspected my home many years ago before hiring my husband) was one of the owners of that real estate firm. She did not remember me. Which was just as well because I did not want to remember that time in my life.

Jury Duty

A year or two after I had switched offices, I was summoned for jury duty. In those days jury duty lasted for a whole month. But on my last day I was picked again as a juror, so I served for almost five weeks.

We had to go into the courthouse and check in every morning. We then waited to see if they needed us for that day; if not, we were dismissed. I was excited about jury duty. I wanted to learn how the judicial system worked, but I was apprehensive because I knew that this would not be good for my real estate business. However, I felt that I had to do this. It was my duty to serve this wonderful country that had welcomed me.

During the five weeks, I was picked several times to be a juror. Most of the cases were just minor disputes and easily settled. However, I remember three of the cases that lasted for several days.

One that bothered me the most was a child molestation case. The boy was less than five years old, and he testified that his father had molested him. It was graphic testimony and made me feel uncomfortable. The father's testimony was that he had never molested his child, and he accused his ex-wife of coaching and bribing his son to give false testimony. As jurors we had a very difficult time deciding who to believe. After several hours of deliberation, we decided to take the child's word and found the father guilty. That night I had a hard time sleeping, worrying about whether we made the right decision. What if the father was innocent? What a terrible injustice that would be.

The next morning, I was still upset and groggy from lack of sleep. Then I read in the newspaper that the father of the child had been accused, or found guilty, twice before of child molestation. I was very relieved to see that we probably had made the right decision.

I was angry that we had not been told about the previous molestations. I know they say that it would prejudice the jurors. However, how can anyone make the right decision when they don't have all of the facts? I think that the previous accusations should have been revealed, and the man given a chance to explain. I believe that the jury should be given all of the facts. That is the only way they can make a fully informed decision.

The second case was about a real estate investment. The lawyers knew that I was a Realtor, so I was surprised when I was chosen to be a juror.

A man had sold his business and was suing his accountants because they had advised him to invest some of that money in real estate. Shortly after that, the real estate prices dropped. The man felt that he had lost a lot of money and blamed the accountants.

Of course, I sided with the accountants. I told the other jurors that not even the Realtors knew that the market was going to drop that drastically. I also told them that if the man held onto the properties, there was a good chance that the real estate market would rebound, and his investment values would go back up again, which they did about two years later. The jurors believed me, and we voted in favor of the accountants.

I liked the way the accountants had conducted themselves in court, and hired them to take care of my personal taxes for many years, until one of the partners died and the other partner sold the business.

Third case: A prisoner was appealing his sentence, and acted as his own attorney. Apparently, he had never heard the saying, "Anyone acting as his own attorney has a fool for a client."

It was obvious that he was there mainly to entertain himself. He took a long time questioning the jury. He also asked some very inappropriate questions.

When it was my turn, he asked, "Are you married?"

I said," No."

"Are you divorced?"

"Yes."

"Why are you divorced?"

I glared at the prisoner, then glanced at the judge who looked half asleep.

I surprised myself by yelling at the prisoner, "That is none of your business and I'm not going to answer that question."

That got the judge's attention, and he reprimanded the prisoner. I had hoped that the prisoner would dismiss me as a juror, I had already served my four weeks, but he didn't.

As the trial went on, it became clear that the prisoner did not have a case, and we denied his appeal. He shrugged his shoulders and smiled. He knew right from the beginning that he was not going to win. This was just something to do to alleviate his boredom. The whole thing was a waste of the court's time and mine. I was appalled that the prisoner got away with that charade.

That trial lasted several days beyond the thirty days I had been called to serve, and I was anxious to get back to my real estate business.

As it turned out, I was right to be concerned. My business definitely suffered because I did not advertise or take proper care of my clients for five weeks. However, I do not regret jury duty, in spite of the loss of money. I am proud that I did it. It was a very interesting experience, one that I will never forget. Eventually I got back on track, and my business went on as usual.

I had enjoyed working with the people at Realty House, but after my jury duty ended, I realized that I didn't really need that office. I had my own client list and worked mainly from referrals. So, I created an office in my home, and got a Designated Brokers License as "Nina Carmichael Realty".

I gave up my license when the real estate business stopped being fun. It became more like "dog eat dog." The Realtors became more aggressive. The rules changed. The buyers and sellers had to have their own attorneys to protect their interest. Before that, most Realtors tried hard to cooperate with each other and make sure that "The Sale" was fair to both buyers and sellers, and the attorneys and escrow companies took care of the legal matters. I was in my seventies, and did not want the stress of fighting with the other Realtors and attorneys.

I have one more real estate related story to tell. The following encounter occurred after I had been a Realtor for over 15 years:

I had a savings account and was always on the lookout for better interest rates. One day I saw an ad in the paper offering," Great interest rates on annuities." I went into that bank and told the teller why I was there. She introduced me to a very prissy little man with a thin mustache and, obviously dyed, jet-black hair. His name was Percy.

After Percy led me to his desk, I asked him, "What is an annuity, how does it work, and how much interest does it pay?"

Without listening closely to what I had said, or finding out who I was, Percy proceeded to explain interest to me.

He said, "The best way you can learn how interest works is to compare it to baking bread. You know, when you add yeast, the dough gets bigger. That's the same way interest works. Interest makes your money grow."

I sat there with my mouth open, not believing what I was hearing.

He then asked, "Did you understand that, little lady?"

That did it!

I closed my mouth, cleared my throat, and said, "I do not bake bread, and I don't need someone telling me how interest works. I have been a Realtor for many years, and I know what interest is."

I got up, glared at Percy, and walked out. I resisted the urge to turn around and call him a Chauvinist Pig. I could not believe that a man in the banking business could be that stupid, and I certainly was not going to trust my money with him.

Dave DeLapp, a long time Realtor, and I worked on some real-estate transactions together. I also called him whenever I needed advice on real-estate-trades. Later we were in the same writing class. He published his book "Chips" before I finished my memoir. For my 80th birthday, he and my fellow writers surprised me with a birthday party, and Dave wrote the following poem:

Ode to Nina

A wonderful woman from birth to eight oh
from four kids to career it was never "go slow"
being a beautiful woman, she produced a plenty
if she hadn't of stopped, she would have had twenty
we all sit in wonder on hearing her story
the perfect example of having guts and some glory?

Her life has been full and there's still more to come
so, in writing her story she'll always be welcome.
To honor your birthday, we all just feel fine and
all agree Nina, you don't look a day over seventy-nine.

So, when you arrive at a hundred and five
all any-one will say is, "She is still alive?"

Dave DeLapp

After Divorce

After the divorce I was so glad that I had my women friends. I don't know what I would have done without them. They kept me from being lonely and depressed. We got together often and sometimes, we went to the movies and dancing. We made sure that we always stayed together as a group and watched out for each other.

I remember one night when Martha, Jeanette, Mable and I went to a night club. I danced with a guy that made me feel uncomfortable. He kept trying to hold me too tight and putting his hand where it didn't belong. When he came back and asked me to dance, he wouldn't take "No" for an answer. When he grabbed my arm, Martha got up and yelled, "You take your hands off my woman!"

That got his attention. He stopped, looked at Martha, then at me, and again at Martha. He was absolutely stunned. He dropped my arm like a hot potato, walked away, and left me alone. Martha had sounded so convincing that even the three of us almost believed what she had said. We laughed about that many times and for a long time I was teased about being, "Martha's woman."

Another time we gave Mickey a bachelorette party. There were six of us women and no one was coming over to ask Mickey to dance. I felt bad, so I went over to the bar where a bunch of guys were sitting. I stepped between two of them and said, "We are having a bachelorette party and we want the bride to have a good time, would you guys please go dance with Mickey?"

The guys were glad to oblige and danced with her. I told the other ladies, "Okay, now it's your turn. You have to either ask Mickey to dance, or go find a guy."

Two of the ladies danced with Mickey. When it was Martha's turn, she went up to the bar, but instead of just telling the guy what she wanted, she asked, "Are you alone? Would you do me a favor . . . ? "

Before she could finish, the guy got up and walked out. She came back to the table, with her head hung low. When she told us what she had said to the man, we all started laughing. The guy must have thought that she was propositioning him, got embarrassed and ran away. As the evening went on we all had a great time, especially Mickey. The bachelorette party was a great success.

Once or twice-a-month Martha, Jeanette, and I would go to the beach and spend a night in Lincoln City or Newport. We would go to the Eagles or the Elks club and have a good time. Sometimes we went to a bar called "Winos, Dingbats and Riffraff." We would act goofy, have fun with the drunks, and laugh a lot. I was about 41, Jeanette was 49, and Martha was 58, but we acted like we were teenagers.

Later, when Martha was in a nursing home, and Jeanette and I would go to visit her, she told us that whenever she felt lonely or sad, she would read her diary, and re-live the great times we had. She reminded us of the things we had done; like the time we went with a man that we had met at the "Winos" bar to a bonfire beach party. We decided that Jeanette should sit up front with him, and if he "tried" anything, Martha and I would either look the other way, or hit him over the head—her choice. We didn't need to worry; the man was a perfect gentleman. There were a lot of people at the party. The music was great and we had a good time dancing on the beach around the huge bonfire.

Another diary entry recalled the time Martha, Jeanette, Mable and I went dancing. I danced with a guy who told me that he lived in Lincoln City, and was in Salem on business.

He said, "I rented a nice motel, but there is a snake in my room and it's bothering me. Would you come with me and help me kill that snake?"

I said, "Really? I never heard of any snakes in motels around here. I'm sorry, but I don't go to motel rooms with men."

He didn't say anything more. He just looked at me and shook his head. After he dropped me off at our table, I tried to tell the girls what the man had said to me. Before I could finish talking, Martha started laughing. Then Mable and Jeanette laughed, while I sat there staring at them. Finally, Martha said, "Don't you know what kind of snake the guy is talking about?" It finally dawned on me what the guy had asked me to do, and I felt like a fool for being so naive.

I was glad that Martha had kept a diary, it was fun remembering those times with her and laughing. Martha and I remained close friends until the day she died. Jeanette and I are best friend to this day.

One weekend I went rafting on the Deschutes River with some of my real estate friends. We had a river guide, but he was not doing a good job. The guide told us that we didn't have to wear our life vests until we got close to a big rapid.

There were two eight-man rafts, and one four-man raft. My friend Elmer, his son Louis and I were in the small four-man raft at the end of the line. Up ahead we noticed that the people in the other rafts were putting on their life vests, and we knew that we had to do the same. It was a cold day, and I was wearing two jackets. Before putting on my vest, I needed to remove one of my jackets.

But the river was too swift, and before I could remove my jacket, we were on top of "Box Car," a three-star rapid. Our raft went over the edge sideways, and all three of us fell out.

In the last moment, I pushed away from the raft because I did not want to be caught under it. That put me into a vortex.

The river held me down under water and I could not get out. I worked my arms and legs as hard as I could, but no matter how hard I tried, I could not get to the top. My strength was gone and I was almost out of air. I was afraid, and started praying, "Dear God, I have worked hard all my life and have been taking care of my family since I was a child. I am finally free and can live my own life. Please God, don't let me die now, please let me enjoy myself for a little while."

Suddenly, I realized that I was still wearing my two jackets, and that they were pulling me down. I stopped struggling, and unzipped the top jacket. That made me buoyant and, miraculously I floated to the top.

In the meantime, Elmer and Louis were back inside the raft, and looking for me. They were frantic because I had stayed underwater too long. When I finally popped out of the water, they were relieved to see me and pulled me out.

I was very cold, and couldn't stop shivering. They quickly got me to shore, where the other rafts were waiting. Somebody wrapped me in a blanket, and our guide built a fire to help me get warm. The guide felt terrible, and apologized for not reminding us to wear our life-vests. I told him, "Don't worry, I am just so glad to be alive."

After we got back home, Elmer had a t-shirt made for me which read, 'Thank you River God for spitting me back out.' I put it with another one of my favorite t-shirts, with the logo: "When God made man, She was only kidding."

My, 'When God made man, She was only kidding" T-shirt

Another adventure I remember was the time I tried marijuana:

In those days' marijuana was illegal. And I had forbidden my sons to smoke it. However, I had also heard that marijuana was not harmful at all, so I was not sure what to believe.

One of the women in my office was getting a divorce. She had been smoking pot on a regular basis and asked me if I wanted to try it. I said, "No way." But after she assured me that she knew what she was doing and that she would make sure that I was safe, I agreed. She asked me to come to her house for dinner the next day, and spend the night. When I got to her house, she had everything staged. The table was set, the stereo was on, and the candles were lit.

She lit a joint and passed it to me. Even though I was a smoker I had a hard time holding the smoke in my lungs but I soon learned. The first thing I noticed was that the flickering candles were keeping the beat to the music on the stereo. Then I felt my whole body go light. It was a nice, relaxed feeling. I talked and laughed a lot. But suddenly I could not complete my sentences. I forgot what I was saying. This was very frightening to me. I felt stupid, and I hated that feeling.

When I drank alcohol, I was always careful, and limited how much I drank. I wanted to be in control and be aware of what I was doing at all times. I felt that I could not control marijuana in the same way and I was afraid. It was good that I was spending the night at the woman's house because there was no way I could have driven home in my condition.

I was glad I had tried marijuana. After that, I could say for sure that pot was not for me. I valued my brain and I did not want to do something that would jeopardize it.

Before my divorce I asked Ron, who had gone through a divorce a few months before, "What will happen to me after the divorce?"

He said, "Everyone is different, but don't be surprised if you act as you did before you were married."

I told him, "That's ridiculous. I got married when I was 18 years old. Now I am over 40 and certainly more mature."

He was right. I did do some silly things for a little while after my divorce. However, I don't regret anything that I did during that time. I had fun and did not hurt anyone. I got married when I was too young, and it felt good to be carefree and single again.

But after a while I got the "running-around" out of my system. I was ready for something more meaningful in my life. That's when I found a beautiful river-front property, and my life changed.

But that story comes later.

Managing my own Rentals

At my parent's urging, I bought several rental properties, while I was in real-estate.

When Don and I divorced, he got the house he lived in,
and a triplex in Salem. I kept the family home, one rental
house in Keizer, and two rental houses on the corner of
13th and Mission in Salem.

The two small houses in Salem were a real nuisance to
manage. I bought them because it was known that the
city of Salem had a plan to widen Mission street, and they
would need those two houses. I had hoped that when that
time came, the City would pay me a generous amount for
my houses. But that did not happen. I had to fight with the
city, just to get a fair price.

In the meanwhile, I couldn't be too choosey about my
renters, because Mission and 13th were very busy streets.
Also, the houses were not far from the State Prison, and
most of the renters were families of the prisoners incarcer-
ated there. Many of them stayed for only a couple of months,
and when they moved out, they left a big mess.

Over a period of two years, I had to exterminate cockroaches in both houses. Remove half of a bathtub full of
dirty diapers, a bag of rotting potatoes left under the sink,
and rotting meat left on the kitchen counter. There was
motor oil on the living room hardwood floors, and twice
I had to clean up human and animal excrement in both
houses. Plus, there was always other garbage left behind
when the tenants moved.

Several times after a tenant moved, I had to patch holes
in walls and doors, and repaint most of the rooms. One of
the houses had a fire in a bedroom, which was caused by
a portable heater. The insurance company gave me barely
enough money for cleanup, and a few gallons of paint.

I couldn't afford to hire people, so in the beginning I did most of the work myself. Later when Ron and I became friends, I found that he was a good handy man and could do almost everything, including electrical and plumbing work. He helped me clean and repair the rentals several times.

When the rent on the second house was past due again, and I went to collect, again, the property looked abandoned. So, I let myself in. It looked like the renters had moved out and left everything behind. The electricity and the water had been shut off for some time, and the house had a horrible smell. The meat in the refrigerator was covered with maggots. The renters had used a bucket for a toilet, and were very sloppy with it. There was also dirt and junk scattered everywhere. The whole house looked like a garbage dump.

I had to ask Ron and my sons for help because I could not move all of that stuff by myself. Ron and the boys were gagging the whole time they were in the house, and my sons swore that they would never own rentals. As we kept hauling the stuff outside, I got more and more furious. This was the biggest mess that I had ever seen, and I kept saying," If I ever see this renter, I'll tear her apart."

I had worked myself up into a frenzy when, you guessed it, the renter showed up. She started screaming at us for stealing her stuff, and told us to get off her property. I couldn't believe she had the nerve to show her face, let alone, yell at us.

I yelled back," How dare you call this your property. This is my house, you did not pay the rent, so you are a trespasser. You left the house full of garbage and we are hauling it away."

She swore and called me a nasty name, and I just lost it. I practically jumped on her, and started hitting. I was so angry. Luckily Ron and my kids pulled me off before I could really hurt her.

—Later my sons told me they could not believe their eyes. They had never seen me like that, and they didn't think that I had it in me. But I knew that I did. I told them about the bully in the German school yard, whom I had attacked because he was hitting a small refugee boy.

The woman screamed, "I'm going to call the police."

I stared at her and said, "Don't you dare. I'll call them myself."

I went across the street to the service station and used their phone. The police must have been close by because they got to the house just as I got back. The policeman looked at the renter, and she hung her head. He said," We know each other very well, don't we?"

He asked me," What do you want me to do with her?"

I said, "Just tell her to get her stuff out of the house by tomorrow, and clean up the place, and I won't press any charges." And that's exactly what the policeman told her.

Two days later when we checked, all of her stuff was gone. We still had to haul away the garbage and clean the house, but I was glad that the ordeal was over, and that the renter was gone.

After the house was clean, I put a 'For Rent' ad in the paper. I received a call from a man who said that he wanted to rent the house. I asked, "You mean you want to see the house?"

He said, "No I want to rent it. I am a truck driver and I'm calling you between deliveries. I don't have time to see the house."

I asked, "What about your wife, doesn't she need to see the house?"

"No, we need a house, and she will take whatever we can get."

"I have to talk to your wife before I rent it to you."

"Okay, I'll arrange that and we'll call you right back."

A little while later he called me back on a three-way conference call. I described the house, and I told her that it was located on a very busy street. The wife said that everything sounded just fine, and they would take the house as is. I was not comfortable renting the house to them. This had never happened to me before, and I had to think about what to do.

After a minute, I told them, "The only way I will rent the house to you, is if you pay two months' rent, plus a large cleaning and security deposit in cash before you move into the house." I felt that this way I had nothing to lose.

They agreed to my terms, and I met the wife and her sister at the rental house the following day. She was waiting for me with a packed U-Haul truck. The wife paid me the money in cash, and we signed the rental agreement. That's when she told me that her husband was not a truck driver, he was in prison and that's why they needed a house so desperately.

She said, "My husband is innocent. Don't worry, I promise to take good care of the house, and pay the rent every month."

I was flabbergasted, not only because they had lied to me, but that the prisoner was allowed to make a conference call without me knowing that the call came from a prison. As it turned out they became good tenants. They always paid their rent on time and stayed until the city bought the houses.

Another day I went to the corner house to collect the rent. When the tenant came to the door, she could barely speak because her jaw was wired shut. Apparently, her boyfriend had hit her and broken her jaw. This was not the first time she had been beaten up by her boyfriend. I had seen her twice before with black eyes. But this time, watching the woman struggling to talk, with tears streaming down her face, made me dizzy and sick to my stomach. I had to get out of there immediately. As I was backing up, I told her, "It's okay, it's okay, just send the money when you can." And I quickly left.

I called Ron when I got home, and asked him if he would go and see the poor woman. He had met her when she moved in, so he felt comfortable going to the house. The woman let Ron call her father in California. When the father heard what had happened, he came up and moved his daughter back home.

Looking back, I think my reaction at seeing the hurt woman was brought on by memories from my childhood. I had seen Papa hitting my mama, and I felt scared and powerless then. That feeling returned when I saw that pitiful woman.

Another renter, another story: The first week of December, I went to one of the houses to collect the rent. The woman gave me the rent check. Then with tears in her eyes, she told me that she had nothing to give to her children for Christmas. All the way home I kept thinking about that woman, and feeling sorry for her. I also felt guilty about taking the rent check, even though I knew that this was business, and I should not be feeling guilty.

When I got home, I called Ron and told him what the woman had said. I asked him if he could talk to his National

Guard buddies and see if they had any extra toys their children did not want. Ron said he would do that, and the guys were happy to donate. He delivered a big box full of toys to the woman, and she was very grateful.

That same woman moved out the next month without notice. Almost all of the toys that Ron had collected from his buddies were in a big garbage pile. Ron was angry, "I begged my men for toys for this woman, and now, seeing them in the garbage, I feel like I was slapped in the face."

The woman had been in a shelter for battered women. The shelter had moved her to my house, and were paying her rent and utilities until she could get a job. After living in my house for three months, I was told that she had returned to her abuser,

One of my renters called shortly before Christmas. She said, "I don't have enough money to pay the rent and buy presents for my kids. Can I just pay half the rent this month?"

I said, "Well, you can call my bank and ask them if they will let me pay half of my mortgage payment this month."

She got the hint, and got some money from her Church to pay the rent. I was not being heartless. I just wanted to teach the renter responsibility. My mama taught me that food and a roof over our heads come first. That is what I taught my sons, and I felt she should teach that to her children as well. Two months later she moved out. But before she left, she flooded the bathroom floor. We had to replace the floor and the sub-floor. My attempt at teaching her responsibility failed miserably.

Owning those two houses taught me a good lesson. Cheap houses or apartments in bad neighborhoods are a lot of work. There is always a big turnover because of the quality of the renters.

After I sold the Mission street houses to the city of Salem, I bought a newer, ranch style, three-bedroom house with a double garage in Keizer. Later I bought two more nice houses in a good neighborhood of Keizer. I always made sure that the houses were spotless before I put them up for rent. With the better houses, came a better quality of renters. Even now, I keep the rents below market rate, and the same renters have stayed for seven, ten or more years, which has saved me money in the long run.

I learned that a landlord reference is very important. Equally important is a job reference and how much income they earn. I didn't care what color or gender they were, but I limited the number of people living in my rentals. By keeping the rent low, I got many applications and I could pick and choose to whom I rented the house.

I keep the relationship professional. I am friendly with the renters, but they are not my buddies. I am firm, but fair. I make it very clear that the rent must be paid on time. I ask that they tell me when repairs are needed, and I make sure that the repairs are done as quickly as possible. I also make sure that the security and cleaning deposit is large enough to take care of most of the damage the renters might cause. I am always happy to return the deposit when the property is left undamaged, and reasonably clean.

Owning rental property is not for everybody. It takes patience and strength to put up with dead-beat tenants. You need available cash to make repairs when needed. Don't rent out a property that you are attached to emotionally, unless you are positive that the renter will take very good care of the property.

Instead of buying more properties, I paid off the mortgage on the three rental houses, and my home, before I retired. This gave me a good supplement to my social security income, and made me feel secure.

Another reason I kept three rental houses was for security for my sons. I was making sure that my sons would never be homeless, like I was as a child.

I still own the three houses. One of them has been rented to the same couple for the past thirteen years. They recently painted the house inside and out, put in vinyl floors and upgraded the kitchen and bath. We paid for the materials and they did the work.

The other two houses are occupied by two of my sons. They are paying whatever rent they can afford. Eventually the houses will belong to them.

The River Lot and Cabin

In 1981, one of the Realtors in my office told me about a lot on the Santiam River which was for sale. He had written up a trade agreement between the owner of that lot, and an acreage that was owned by a corporation. The people who owned the lot did not want to deal with a corporation, so the Realtor needed a "take-out buyer." He asked me to take a look at the lot and see if I would be interested in buying it. I had never wanted a second home or recreational property, but this lot was only 27 miles east of Salem, so it was close enough to take a look. I fell in love with the property the minute I saw it.

The next day, I asked Ron Treece, to go with me and look at the lot. I knew he was interested in owning property on the water and I wanted his opinion.

The property was located off Highway 22 on a dead-end street. There were eight lots on the street, all were along the river. Two of the lots already had nice homes. On the other side of the road was a vacant field. The land across the river is an island, owned by the Bureau of Land Management, and overgrown by brush and mature trees. No houses can be built there.

The river lot was covered with big trees, ferns and all kinds of bushes. We followed a path down a gentle slope. Long before we got to the river, we heard the sound of whitewater, a loud roar and murmur at the same time. When we got to the river, we found a lovely sandy beach, and big rocks just right to sit on. Much of the river was whitewater, but there was also a large fishing and swimming hole right in front. The river curved around the property, and there was a beautiful view up and down river for about a mile. As I was standing on the sandy beach listening to the whitewater, the sound varied. It was a liquid sound, a solid booming noise, a whisper and an echoing, all at the same time. It seemed like there were voices murmuring to me, and taking all of my cares away. After a few minutes, I did not want to leave. I really wanted that property.

On an impulse, I turned to Ron and said, "I will buy this lot if you will be my partner and help me develop it."

He looked at me as if to say; "Lady, I don't know you that well," but after a pause, he said, "Okay."

In retrospect, Ron was right, we did not know each other well enough for a long-term commitment of this kind. However, I was not thinking about a commitment, or the future. I just knew that I wanted and needed something meaningful in my life and that this river lot was the answer. I felt like this decision was being made for me, and I had no control over it. I was certain that I was making the right decision in buying the property. But I also knew that I couldn't develop it on my own.

I had known Ron long enough to know that he was a good man. I had met his parents, and knew he came from a good family. I also knew that his ex-wife and children lived in California. He had been with the National Guard for over 20 years. I met some of his co-workers, and was told that he was respected at work.

On the way back to the office, I could tell that Ron was also getting excited about developing the property. It was all we talked about. He had gone through a divorce a few months before I had, and he too needed something positive in his life. We were anxious to start clearing the lot, so we could see what it really looked like.

The next day, I made an offer of $16,500, on a land sales contract, with $2,000 down and the rest on payments, amortized over five years. The sale was contingent on obtaining a building permit. The lot was two-thirds of an acre, and the new regulations required a full acre for an on-site well and septic tank. The property already had a septic permit, but I was concerned about finding water. I asked for an easement on the property across the road, which was owned by the original developer, just in case we did not find water on our lot. The easement was granted and the offer was accepted. I was proud of myself, but also a little apprehensive. This was the first time that I had ever bought property in my own name.

Once the sale was closed, Ron and I went to work. We selected a building spot about 50 feet up a gentle slope from the river's edge. There was a lot of brush that needed to be cleared, and several trees had to be removed from the building site. Ron and our friend, Richard, felled the trees. It was exciting to watch. The trees did not always fall exactly in the intended direction, and Richard's wife and I had to get out of the way in a hurry. We were lucky that no one got hurt.

After the trees were down, we were thrilled to see what a fantastic view we had up and down the river from our building site. We removed the limbs, saved the bigger limbs for firewood, and burned the rest of the brush. A nearby mill cut our trees into lumber, which we used when we built our cabin.

We hired someone to do the excavating, and to install the septic system. We also had the framing done, and my brother, Bill, put on the roof. After that, Ron and I put up the siding, and Ron installed all the electrical and plumbing. Then we put in the insulation.

At first, we used the river for our water supply, and brought drinking water from home. Later, we got the well drilled, which produced enough water for house use, and we used river water for irrigation.

One day, I was showing a property in Dallas when just by chance I spotted two big stacks of inexpensive cedar boards at a lumber store. We wanted our cabin to look rustic, so the cedar was perfect, and we bought all they had. Ron set-up his saw in the living room, and cut cedar to his heart's content. We did all the ceilings, walls, closets, and trim in cedar. When we drew up our building plans, we added many windows, and made sure that every room in the house had a view of the river. On the main floor was a large open area consisting of a kitchen, dining, and living room. An open archway led into a bedroom/ office area. The utility area and bathroom were off the entry.

Later, we installed a spiral staircase leading down to the basement, and into a large all-purpose room, with big windows and a sliding door to the outside. We also added a master bedroom and half-bath on the main floor.

It took us two years to complete the cabin, because we could only work on weekends and some evenings.

Ron and I had a few arguments during that time. I still remember our biggest argument. He wanted to put all the cedar boards horizontally, and I wanted them to be vertical. We argued about it all the way home. Suddenly, he started yelling at me. I couldn't believe the words that were coming out of his mouth. I yelled, "Stop."

When he did, I asked him," Who are you yelling at?" I knew that I had not said anything that should have brought about that kind of response.

He didn't explain, but he immediately apologized, and we settled the argument by compromising. We put some of the boards horizontally, most vertically, and some in a herringbone pattern. We also agreed that, if there was a good reason for doing something a certain way, I would give in. However, if I really wanted something done, and there was no logical reason not to do it, we would do it my way.

Actually, we got along very well. Building a house can be very stressful. It is definitely a good way to test a relationship, and see whether it's real, and can survive the stresses of life. I was surprised how much Ron knew about building. He had never built a house before, but he had remodeled several houses and he was not afraid to learn.

We did not take out a mortgage. We paid cash for everything as the building project went along. We welcomed any castoffs people gave us, such as old carpeting from my brother's office, a kitchen range from a friend, a wood stove, an old bathroom cabinet, a kitchen cabinet, and so on. Later, we replaced them with new items, as we saved up enough to pay cash.

When the cabin was finished, we were proud of what we had achieved. We knew we had created something permanent that would probably outlive us both.

Spending so much time together I got to know Ron better, and I could see myself spending the rest of my life with him. He was the opposite of my ex-husband in every way.

Looking back, I am amazed how trusting Ron was. He put money and a lot of work into the building project, even though the property was in my name. However, he knew my story and how hard it was for me to trust and respect another man. I am glad that he trusted me, and of course I did not betray his trust. I added his name to the title after the cabin was completed.

River view from Cabin

Ron Treece, 1981

Imet Ron when I started managing Red Carpet Realty. He was a part-time Realtor in that office. He was First Sergeant in the National Guard, a Civil Service technician, and later supervisor. Divorced, and all of his family were living in California. When I first met him; he seemed conceited and arrogant. Later, I realized that he was just shy, and covered it up with bravado. The more we talked, the more relaxed he got. But our first, so called, date almost didn't happen.

One afternoon we happened to be in the office at the same time. He told me that his birthday was coming up the following Friday. I asked what he was doing that day, and he said, "I am not doing anything."

I said, "You can't be alone on your birthday. Why don't we go and do something?" He agreed, and I told him that I would call him on Friday.

Well, that Friday evening I went to Happy Hour and dinner, with some of my real estate friends. When I got home, it was almost 10 o'clock. My friend Martha came upstairs and said, "Some guy named Ron called awhile ago, and asked for you."

I felt terrible! How could I forget to call him? I called him immediately, and apologized profusely. He told me that it was all right, and not to worry about it. However, I insisted that there was still enough time to celebrate his birthday.

I said, "It's not 12 o'clock yet. We can still go out and dance a few times." Reluctantly he agreed.

We met at "The Ranch," a fun night club I had gone to with my girl friends. They had great music, and we had a good time. We danced until they closed. Ron told me I was such a good follower, that he might ask me to go out dancing again. I was glad that I had taken Arthur Murray dance lessons, so that I could follow almost anyone on the dance floor. But I did not tell him that.

Shortly after that night, Ron told me that his parents were coming from California for a visit, and he wanted me to meet them. We set the day and time they would be at my house, but they arrived way too early. I was on top of my house clearing moss off the roof. I climbed down and apologized, but his mother assured me that it was okay. They knew that they were early. Thank goodness I had everything pretty much ready for the dinner I had planned. All I had to do was wash up, and change my clothes. The evening went well, and I really liked his parents. They were nice, down to earth, hard working, and smart people.

Later, Ron told me that on their way home, his father said to him, "You should marry that woman!"

I just laughed and told him, "Your father is a wise man."

As time went by, I discovered that we agreed about the important things in life. We have the same values, work ethic, and respect for money. But, do we love each other? I know that when I met him, it was not 'love at first sight'. I think that love grew with time, and building our cabin on the river gave us that time to get to know each other better. I learned to respect and trust him. Ron is two years younger than I, and the opposite of my ex-husband.

A few months later, when Ron asked me to marry him, I said, "Yes."

My parents hosted our engagement party. Ron's kids, Michael, Bryan and Tiffany, as well as my four sons, celebrated with us. After that, Ron moved in with me. In those days, living together without being married was immoral, and people called it "shacking up." However, I felt that living together was the most logical thing to do. There were not just the two of us, we both had families, and I needed to see how we would all get along. The only way to do that, was for Ron and me to live together.

Eventually, we agreed on a wedding date. But as that day got closer, I lost my nerve. I was afraid, and felt like I was walking into a trap. My last marriage had lasted for almost 25 years. I had felt trapped for most of those years, but I had stayed in the marriage for the sake of my children. I did not want to marry the wrong man again. I changed my mind and decided to wait and be sure that Ron was the right man for me. We canceled our wedding plans, but we did go on our Hawaiian honeymoon.

Ron and I continued to live together and I got to know his family better. His sister, Carole, and her husband, George, his brother, Ken, and wife, Carrol, are lovely people. I could see myself being friends with them, even without Ron.

We never had a problem with Ron's ex-wife. She was always pleasant to me, and even thanked me for being nice to her children. Ron's two sons, Michael, age 14, and Bryan,

L to R: Ron's sister Carole, Brother Ken, Parents, and Ron

L to R, Back: George, Ken, Michael, and Bryan
Middle: Jim, Nina, Carole, Carrol, Tiffany, and Ron
Front: Carole's daughters, Kristan and Kim

age 12 accepted me. Ron's daughter, Tiffany, age 10, did not like me. But that was understandable. She and her father were very close and I had disrupted that relationship. It was mostly my fault. I tried too hard to be a "good stepmother." I should have known that the kids did not want a stepmother. They wanted their parents back together. In retrospect, I should have just made myself as unobtrusive as possible until they had a chance to get used to me.

My sons who were practically grown men, accepted Ron right from the start. He told them, "I am not your father. You already have a father, but I want to be your friend, and if you ever need anything I will do all I can to help you."

Ron has kept that promise to my sons throughout all these years.

My parents liked and respected Ron and he felt the same about them.

I liked Ron's mother Alice. We understood each other because we both had a tough life when we were young. She lost her mother at an early age, and she too, had gone through hungry times. She understood my reluctance to throw good food away, and she agreed that being frugal was a good thing. I admired her; she was smart and tough, but also a loving mother. Pappy, Ron's father, was a gentle soul. He accepted life as it was. Even when it was his time to die, he accepted death readily. Alice continued on without him and built a life for herself. She stayed active and independent until two weeks before she died, at age 92.

Ron and I had been living together for about two years when our neighbor, Elena Friesen, talked to me and pointed out that if Ron or I got sick and had to go to the hospital, we would not have any say in one another's care. She really liked Ron. She thought that he was a good man and that he would make a good husband. She was very convincing.

I loved Ron, and knew that I was better off with him than without him. For the first time in my life I felt secure, which was very important to me. I knew he would be a good life-partner for me. He was honest, trustworthy and dependable. He came from a very good family and I liked them all.

We had talked about our children, and how we would handle our blended family. We decided that we would put each other first. Then together, we would put our children and parents first. There would be no seconds. All of us would be first. This has worked very well for us throughout our marriage.

Before I could lose my nerve, I told Ron that I wanted to get married in Reno. I was still not sure if I would be brave enough, but the following week we drove to Reno. We had not told anyone of our intention. That way, if I changed my mind at the last minute, there was no harm done. I bought a red wedding dress, which I could wear for any dress-up occasion. If the wedding didn't happen, we would just enjoy Reno and have a good time.

The next day I was certain that I wanted to marry Ron. And so, in November,1984, we were married by the Deputy Commissioner of Civil Marriages.

As part of the wedding ceremony she chose the following poem:

Indian Wedding Blessing

Now you will feel no rain
for each of you will be sheltered to the other.

Now you will feel no cold,
for each of you will be warmth to the other.

Now you will feel no loneliness,
for each of you will be companion to the other.

Now you are two persons, but there are three lives before you;
his life, her life, and your life together.

Go now to your dwelling place
and may your days be good and long upon the earth.

I love that poem. We framed it, and hung it on the wall in our cabin.

After the wedding we called our families and told them the news. Not everyone was happy. I think it was mostly because we surprised them and they felt left out. I was sorry that they were disappointed, but I knew that I had to do it this way. I was afraid that if we had set another wedding date, I would have lost my nerve again. Even as we were driving to Reno, I was not sure if I would go through with the wedding.

From Reno we drove to California and had a party with all of Ron's family at his parents' home. Then, when we got back to Oregon we celebrated with my family and friends.

We continued to update and remodel our cabin. It gave us a sense of accomplishment. We also loved traveling all over the world, until my health deteriorated.

Ron and I were in our 50's when we learned how to ski. It was a very cold and windy day and my gloves were too thin. Ron, the good man that he is, insisted that we exchange gloves. The saying, "No good deed goes unpunished" was true this time. He wound up with frost-bitten fingers. To this day his hands are pale and always cold. I tell this story just to show what a good man he is.

We have been married for over 34 years. During those years, especially the first twenty, we had our ups and downs. Ron had anger issues which I overlooked in the beginning. But as time went on, he got more impatient and angrier, and I didn't stand up for myself. I did not know how to cope with verbal abuse. Ron was aware that I was unhappy, and volunteered to go to an anger management class, but it didn't really help.

The thought of another marriage failing was unbearable. I insisted that we go to a marriage councilor. I told Ron that I needed the counseling, but I wanted him to come with me. Ron went along and listened while I told the counselor about my past and how that was affecting me now. My eye-opener was when the counselor told me, "You know, if you were a stronger woman, Ron wouldn't get away with being abusive."

I couldn't believe what I was hearing. Did I really get so weak that I allowed a man to yell at me?

But then I thought, "I know that Ron loves me and doesn't want to yell at me. There must be something that's making him do that."

We talked to our doctor and at her suggestion, Ron agreed to take Paxil, which calmed him down considerably. About that time, we found out that Ron's anger problem was genetic. It took time, patience and consideration from both of us. Our marriage grew stronger and I started feeling better about myself. Now, we speak our mind when there is an issue, resolve it, and then forget about it within a short time.

Our marriage has survived because at the core Ron and I are alike. We agree about all of the important things. We only argue about stupid stuff. He is too impatient and I talk too much. But we love, trust, respect, and rely on each other. I admire Ron in many ways and I tell him so all the time.

Ron has health issues, but he never complains, even when he is in pain. He is a good role model for me. Seeing him strong and not complaining helped me when I was diagnosed with breast cancer. He stayed by me through my surgeries and treatments and helped me to stay strong. I don't know what I would do without his help, Ron has been my rock.

Smoking Addiction

I started smoking when I was 15 years old and living in Germany. Somebody gave me a drag off of their cigarette and I was immediately drawn to it. Even though it made me nauseated, I continued puffing on a cigarette every once in a while, and I got over the nausea. I did not smoke on a regular basis until after we came to America and I started working at St. Vincent's hospital. It seemed like all the doctors and nurses smoked when I went down to the cafeteria, and they were very willing to share their cigarettes with me. Soon after, I bought my own cigarettes and I was hooked.

My addiction grew throughout the years. Cigarettes became my best friend whenever a problem came up. They were with me when I wanted to celebrate, and they helped to calm me when I was stressed. I didn't see it as a problem. Almost everybody I associated with smoked, and no one thought anything of it. Our house, cars, and clothes reeked of smoke. But that was normal for those times. We were told that smoking was healthy and sexy.

My smoking went from one pack a day to two packs, and by the time I got divorced, I was a chain smoker. When I developed a cough, I realized that I needed to cut back on the cigarettes, but I ignored the warning. By then I was smoking as many as three packs a day. I kept on smoking, even when I had a cold or the flu. Soon I started getting bronchitis on a regular basis and I knew I was in trouble. My breathing was more labored and my coughing was getting worse. I promised myself that I would quit when I turned fifty.

However, when that time came, I couldn't quit. I slowed down, and Ron and I stopped smoking in the house and in our cars. Once in a while, when I tried really hard, I could go for a day, smoking only a few cigarettes. But the next day I went back to chain smoking. For the rest of the year, I kept fighting the addiction. I tried nicotine gum, but that didn't work. I chewed the gum and smoked at the same time. Nothing I tried worked. The next time I had bronchitis, I noticed that I was spitting up blood, so I knew I had no choice. I absolutely had to stop smoking!

My friend Joe was suffering from emphysema, and continued smoking. When I listened to him struggle for every breath, I asked myself, "Do I want to suffer like that for the rest of my life?" The thought was unbearable.

I had heard of a hypnotist that specialized in smoking addiction and I thought maybe he could help me. I planned on making an appointment with him the following week, but when I found out how much he charged, I did not want to pay that price.

The more I thought about it, the madder I got. I berated myself," How could you be so weak? You are stronger than that. You have lived through so many things, and you are going to let cigarettes win? I can't believe this. You just have to make up your mind to be strong and stop smoking. It's just 'mind over matter'. You can do it."

The next morning, I was determined that I would win. I put the cigarettes out in the shed, and told myself that I was done. I started a journal. I walked the floor. I wrung my hands, I pounded my legs and told myself, "I can do it, I can do it" over and over. But I was in agony and my whole body trembled. I kept track in my journal how much time had passed since my last puff on a cigarette, and of my emotional state.

The first day was Hell. My need for a cigarette was very strong, and my head was pounding. I was sick to my stomach and my nerves felt like they were on fire. The next day, my nerves were still raw, and I still kept pacing the floor.

This went on for several days. I was constantly tempted to go out to the shed and get just one cigarette. When I resisted, I praised myself.

However, when my desire for a cigarette was unbearable, I did have an occasional puff off of Ron's cigarette, and I chewed Nicorette Gum, which helped with the jitters. By the second week, I felt that maybe the worst was over. I knew I absolutely had to stop smoking this time, and I vowed to never have another cigarette again. I was certain that I had no choice. I had to quit. I told myself over and over that my life depended on it.

My desire for cigarettes continued for many months, especially during the times when I had a cup of coffee, or a glass of wine. Whenever I finished a major task I longed for a cigarette as my reward. I resisted because I knew if I had even one cigarette, all of my hard work would be wasted, and I would have to start all over again. I was afraid that if that happened, I would never find the strength to go through the first few days of "Hell."

During my struggle with addiction Ron kept smoking, which did not bother me because he was considerate and did not smoke in the car or in the house. His smoking was not a temptation for me because my resolve to quit smoking came from within me. It had nothing to do with other people. I never asked him to quit. I knew it had to be his choice.

On one of our regular trips to California, we spent the night in a motel and had just checked out. Ron finished smoking his morning cigarette, then got into the car and we were on our way to breakfast. He was driving and I was in the passenger seat. He turned toward me and coughed. The stench coming from his mouth was overwhelming. His lungs smelled like rotten, burned, flesh. I looked at him with horror and told him what I was smelling. His eyes got big, but he did not say anything.

That was the last cigarette he ever smoked. Just like that, without any drama, he quit. Later he said that he missed cigarettes for a couple of weeks, but it was "no big deal."

That horrible smell stayed with me. It made me realize what smoking did to our bodies. I could picture my own burned, and rotten lungs, and the thought of puffing on a cigarette became repulsive. That was the end of my smoking.

Ron did the same thing with alcohol. He had been drinking since he was a teenager. In his seventies, when he had a pancreatitis attack, the doctor told him that he had to stop drinking. Ron stopped immediately without any help, and without any withdrawal symptoms. This just goes to show how differently we react to things. To some people, nicotine, alcohol, or drugs are just a habit, but to others, they can be a powerful addiction. For me, alcohol was a habit. I drank in moderation most of my adult life. When I had to give up my two, and sometimes more, daily glasses of wine because of a medication, I quit alcohol without a problem.

Even though I had given up smoking in my fifties, it caught up with me many years later. My consequence came when I was in my seventies, and diagnosed with COPD. I now depend on two inhalers and pills to help with my breathing, and lessen my cough. Unfortunately, I am told that my lungs will just keep getting worse.

Now I try to live a healthy lifestyle. Even the thought of inhaling cigarette smoke, makes my lungs hurt. I also can't stand the smell of cigarette smoke. It makes me cough and I get a severe headache.

My struggle with smoking addiction made me aware of how difficult it is for some people to quit, and I empathize with them. I wish that I had never started smoking, or at least quit before the cigarettes injured my lungs.

Nine months after I quit smoking, I was diagnosed with Breast Cancer. I was told that if I had continued smoking, my cancer treatment would have been much more radical.

Breast Cancer, 1989

It is not always a lump. It could be a dimple.

In 1980, I had a hysterectomy because of excessive bleeding. Two years later, while we were traveling in Germany my hot flashes started. The problem was that every guest house we stayed in had a feather bed. I had many sleepless nights bathed in perspiration, and I was glad when we got back home.

The doctor put me on hormone replacement therapy, which helped with my hot flashes, but I was still having problems remembering words, so I went back to the doctor. He increased my estrogen and progesterone medication, without checking my hormone levels.

In November of 1989, during a routine physical, my new doctor suggested I get a mammogram, my first one ever. I had an indentation on the underside of my left breast when I raised my arm. I told her that I'd had that for about two years, but since there was no lump, I thought that it was just a muscle pull.

I got suspicious when the technician took seven views of my left breast, and only three on my right. Sure enough, three days later I got a call from the doctor telling me I had a lesion on my left breast. I didn't even know what a lesion was. She suggested that I see a surgeon, and recommended

Dr. Seacat. I made an appointment for the following week. I admit that I was worried about the lesion, and what it really meant, but after talking about it with my friends, I decided that there was no point in worrying. I just had to wait and see what the surgeon said.

Dr. Seacat was an older doctor and was very kind. He showed me the mammogram film. I could see an image, like spread out fingers, on the bottom part of my left breast. He also told me that not all breast cancers consisted of a lump.

A biopsy was scheduled for the following week. Because there was no lump, they inserted a very long thin needle into the middle of the finger-like image, so that the surgeon would have a guide where to cut. Dr. Seacat performed the biopsy, and the lumpectomy at the same time.

While I was in the recovery room, the doctor confirmed that I, indeed, had breast cancer. I took the news calmly because by then I was pretty sure that I had cancer. I was ignorant enough to think that it was no big deal: They could just remove my breast and the cancer would be gone. He asked if I had pain in any part of my body and I told him that my back hurt. So, before I left the hospital, they did a bone scan.

The technician was very talkative. He pointed out numerous light images on the screen and told me it was arthritis. He also said that eventually I would be confined to a wheelchair. He had no business telling me that, and I ignored his remarks.

When they wheeled me out of the hospital to where Ron was waiting with the car, I saw that he had been crying. I was surprised because I was not really afraid, and had not cried up to this point.

Three days later, Dr. Seacat told me that the bone scan showed there was arthritis throughout my body, but no cancer. He explained my options for dealing with my breast cancer. I asked him," What would you recommend if I were your wife?"

He said, "A radical mastectomy."

"What does that mean?"

"I would remove the entire left breast, and all the tissue around it, including the chest muscles."

I told him, "Fine. Just get that cancer out of me." We scheduled the operation for the first week in December.

While I was waiting for the operation, I realized that I didn't mind losing my breast, but did I really want my chest muscles removed? The doctor did say that there were other options. Maybe I should check out those options.

When I did some research, I found out that it was not as simple as, just removing the breast and the cancer was gone. The cancer can return and metastasize to other areas. The material I got from the Breast Cancer Foundation did not recommend radical mastectomies, except in rare cases. Their emphasis was on lumpectomies and follow-ups. After reading that, I got worried. Had I chosen the right procedure? My operation was scheduled in two days. What should I do?

I called my sister Lydia, she worked for the Health Department in Portland, and asked her. She told me that I should get a second opinion. And that she would set up an appointment for me with the Oncology Department at OHSU.

The next day was a Tuesday, the day that all the oncologists scheduled their appointments at OHSU. Surprisingly, Lydia was able to get an appointment for me with all three of the oncology doctors on that day, and I canceled my surgery.

I took all of my records with me, and saw the medical oncologist, the radiation oncologist, and the surgical oncologist. None of them recommended a radical mastectomy.

The surgical oncologist at OHSU said that I did not need another lumpectomy. Dr. Seacat had removed all of the cancerous tissue, and I had good healthy margins.

He told me, "Had you not quit smoking, I would have had no choice but to do a radical mastectomy because your immune system would not have been strong enough for any lesser kind of treatment. However, because you no longer smoke, all I need to do is remove some lymph nodes from under your arm."

A week before Christmas, I had the procedure. The surgical oncologist told me, "I don't believe in cutting into lymph nodes. I pulled out a handful of them from under your arm, and found that all of your lymph nodes are clear of cancer." I was very relieved to hear that.

I was nauseated from the anesthetic and could not stop vomiting for two days. They tried several medications, but none of them worked. Finally, I asked Ron to call Salem Hospital and find out what they had given me for nausea when Dr. Seacat did my lumpectomy. They told Ron they had used Scopolamine. Less than an hour after the nurses gave me that drug, my nausea was gone. The following day, they let me go home. Just in time for Christmas.

Before the doctors could decide whether to give me radiation or chemotherapy, they had to evaluate my cancerous tissue, which would take about two weeks. The waiting was very stressful. Knowing that the cancer could come back at any time, made me anxious and afraid. I sat by the river and cried. I raged at God, "Dear God, how can this be? Have I not suffered enough in my life? Why must I endure this too? What have I done to deserve all of this?" Of course, there was no answer to that question.

When the evaluation results came back, I was told that my estrogen and progesterone levels were way off the chart. It was obvious that my cancer was caused by the doctor having prescribed too large a dose of hormones. This was happening to many women at that time. I remember the gynecologist telling me, "The hormones will keep you young. The more you take, the better." Many of the doctors believed this. For example, after my radiation treatments, the radiation oncologist suggested that I go back on my hormone replacement therapy. I told her, "The surgical oncologist said that I should avoid hormones, and I am afraid of taking them."

She just shrugged and replied, "If the cancer comes back, we can treat it again." I couldn't believe what I was hearing, and just shook my head.

To avoid hormones, I switched to drinking almond milk. Almost immediately my stomach aches disappeared. The doctor had misdiagnosed me. He had been treating me for ulcers, but my problem was dairy intolerance.

I was glad that I did not need to have chemotherapy. I just had to have radiation treatments every day at Salem Hospital for six weeks. I did not have any major side effects from those treatments, other than a bad burn on my left breast, and it was sore to the touch. I stopped sleeping on my left side and that helped a lot. The worst side effect was, I could barely move my left arm. A lot of skin had been removed from my armpit when they pulled out my lymph nodes. I had to stretch the remaining skin, which was very painful. I did my stretching exercises every day by walking my fingers up the wall, moving my arm back and forth, and round and round. I was glad when I regained my full arm movement, several weeks later.

I went to the YWCA Breast Cancer Support Group meetings a few times, but that did not help me. It made me more afraid because there were several women in the group whose cancer had returned, and they were close to dying. Also, I was frustrated because some women in the group who were lucky like me, and whose cancer was discovered early, did most of the talking.

The support group let me borrow some meditation tapes by the author, Louise Hayes. They relaxed me, and reduced my fear and anxiety. I listened to those tapes often, and as I did, I became aware that they were also helping me uncover some of the upsetting memories of my past.

On one of her tapes she had the following suggestion: "Let go of anger and hate, by picturing the person who wronged you. He is a little child, all alone and crying. He is hurt, and there is no one to help him and love him."

The person that immediately came to mind was Papa. He had hurt me many times, seldom physically, but in many other ways. I remembered that his parents had died when he was a small boy. He was raised by his uncle, who did not let him go to school, and worked him hard on the farm. I could picture Papa as that hurt little boy and my heart went out to him.

Since then, I have used that same thought process with other people who hurt me. In this way, I have been able to forgive them, and regain peace of mind.

As I listened to the tapes, little by little my anger and hurt subsided. One day I just knew that, this too, would pass. I had a strong feeling that I would survive this cancer, and with the help of God, and the river, I would become strong again.

I have been a cancer survivor for over 28 years. My cancer has not returned. I am grateful that my sister set up the appointments for me at OHSU. Because of that, I kept most of my breast, and more importantly, all of my chest muscles.

My Friend Marilyn

Marilyn Cady was my best friend and mentor. We were friends for only a few years but from the moment we met, we felt like we had known each other all of our lives.

She was the most compassionate and kind woman I have ever known. She was a spiritual person, but she did not preach or talk about it. She lived and practiced what she believed. She had worked in nursing homes and provided hospice care. When I met her, she was teaching a class on death and dying at Chemeketa College. She was also a voracious reader and an excellent writer.

Marilyn

She had taken a class on, "Healing by Writing," and was teaching me how to mourn the death of my son, and how to live with love and gratitude. And then, by example, she showed me how to die with acceptance and grace.

In October 2014, she was diagnosed with a very aggressive form of Leukemia. When she learned that the chance of a cure was very small, and that she would have to spend a whole month in the hospital, she decided not to go through with the treatment. She told me, "I am ready to go home. After all, I have been preparing for that all of my life."

I was horrified and begged her to get those treatments. I did not want to lose her. But ultimately, I had to support her in her decision. I asked her, "How are you so certain that you will be going home?"

She replied, "I have always known deep in the marrow of my bones, that someday I will be going home. I mean, where else am I going to go, but where I came from?"

She continued, "I used to have times when I was home-sick and I knew it was not for a place here on earth. Now, I don't get that way anymore. I do love my life and I don't want to leave it. Dying is not something I asked for, but I'm comfortable with going home. I'm just sad that I will be hurting the loved ones around me."

I said, "I wish I could be as certain as you. I do believe that death is not the end. And I want to believe that when I die, I will be going to a better place. But I am not as certain as you are. If you get to heaven before I do, promise me that you will send me a sign." She said, "I promise to send it, if I can."

My birthday was eight days before her death. Marilyn was too sick to drive, but on that day, she asked her son Danny to drive her to my house so that she could give me a dozen beautiful mauve roses. That's the kind of friend she was!

February 10, 2015 at 1:30 p.m., Marilyn died peacefully at home, surrounded by her family.

About three weeks after she died, on March 5, 2015, Marilyn came to me in my sleep.

I never remember any of my dreams. However, I do remember this one because this was so much more than a dream: I was standing in Marilyn's living room by her back door. The room was full of many beautiful plants, bushes and trees. They were growing right out of the floor. I was admiring the plants, but there were so many of them. I thought, "There is no room to walk through them."

Then I saw Marilyn standing across the room next to the kitchen. She was smiling and said, "Don't worry, I plan on moving some of those plants so that you can pass through to this side easier."

I told her, "That would be great."

"Well, okay then." (One of her favorite sayings).

I said, "I miss you. I am so glad to see you. You look beautiful."

"I am feeling wonderful, and I am very happy."

Next, I felt Marilyn's husband Rick at my side. He said, "Oh good, you can see Marilyn. I have been seeing her and I wasn't sure if she was real, but now that you see her too, I know that she is really with me."

I did not actually see Rick, but I know it was him. I also know that Marilyn's son Danny, and daughter Darcy were in another part of the house. I could feel that there were other people surrounding Marilyn, but I did not see them. The only person that I actually saw, and still see when I close my eyes, is Marilyn. She looks radiant, standing on the opposite side of a room filled with beautiful plants.

When I awoke and opened my eyes I was confused. Why am I in my bed? Had I been dreaming? This couldn't have been a dream. It was so real. One minute I was standing in Marilyn's living room talking to her, and the next minute I am in my bed. How can this be? I am certain that I saw Marilyn, and that she had fulfilled her promise to me. She did give me a sign! Thank you, Marilyn. And thank you for making a path for me, so that I can pass easier when my time comes to join you.

Four years have gone by, and I still feel like Marilyn's spirit is with me every day.

Marilyn's help with my grieving:
I did not get a chance to say goodbye to my son David when he died. And I did not allow myself to truly mourn him because it hurt too much every time, I thought of him.

As the years passed, the family and I did not talk about David because it was just too painful. After many months, I could go a day or two without thinking about David's death. But the pain did not go away. There was also terrible guilt. The thoughts kept recurring: did David deliberately step in front of the car? Am I to blame? Could I have done something? Shouldn't I have been aware that he was depressed? I had been carrying that pain and guilt for over 30 years.

With my friend Marilyn's help, I learned that I needed to stop thinking about David's death and remember his life. I had to change my attitude and be grateful for the 20 years that David was alive. I must let David "Rest in Peace." Maybe then the pain in my heart will lessen.

I told my children what I had learned, and they agreed that we have to celebrate David's life. Because if we don't talk about David, then it is as though David never lived and our memories are only about his death. Hopefully now the healing will begin for all of us.

Marilyn suggested that I try to find a blessing that came out of David's dying. For a very long time I didn't think that was possible.

Now I can think of one blessing:

My remaining three sons, Barry, Brian and Donny, have become so much more precious to me. I have always loved my sons, there's no question of that. But, did I truly appreciate them? Did I always see them, did I hear them, did I tell them that I valued and love them? Now, I make sure that I do. I tell them that I love them every time I talk to them on the phone or in person. I also tell them often how much they mean to me, and I praise them whenever possible.

I can think of another blessing: I am less afraid of dying, because David has gone before me, and I keep holding onto my belief that I will see him on the other side when my time comes.

Another one of Marilyn's suggestions:
Write a letter to David and tell him how you feel.

"Dear David: I love you. I love you. I am sorry. I am so sorry. I miss you. I miss you. Oh, how I miss you!"

How would David answer that letter?

"Dear Mom: please don't hurt, and please don't cry. I hurt when you hurt, and I can't rest. My death was not your fault. I am in a better place now and I am well. I love you. Please be happy."

Believing that he would say those words if he could, helped me. I want him to be at peace and be happy. Now I try to think of him as being in that better place. I also believe that his spirit is with me every day. And so, I try not to hurt when I think of him.

But I still miss David so much, and I always will.

Mushroom Hunting Adventures

Mushroom hunting is my favorite hobby. It started in Germany when I was 12 years old, and went to visit Mr. and Mrs. Klimush (our travel companions on the wagon train). Mrs. Klimush took me to a forest and showed me which mushrooms were edible, and where to find them.

After we came to America, I thought about wild mushrooms once in a while and remembered the fun I'd had hunting for them. But I was too busy working and raising my four sons. I had no time for hunting mushrooms.

When I was in my forties, Ron and I were building our cabin on the Santiam River. We kept passing a sign on Highway 22 that read: "Mushroom Buyer." One day, we stopped and looked at the mushrooms they were buying. I recognized the Chanterelles and asked where we could find them. The buyer told us to go up Breitenbush Road and look around stumps. After searching all afternoon, we found one mushroom that looked like a Chanterelle. We showed it to the buyer and he confirmed that it was. That's how my American mushroom hunting began.

I went to the forest whenever I could. I would go with Ron, or anyone who wanted to go with me. Once I got into the forest I didn't want to leave, and I started to go alone. That way I could hunt for mushrooms all day. It was such a thrill to spot a yellow patch of Chanterelles. It was like hitting the jackpot. The forest was my 'psychiatrist's couch' because it soothed the wounds from the breakup of my first marriage and the death of my youngest son, David. Later, when I was diagnosed with breast cancer, the forest became my escape from worry. Sometimes I would cry, agonize and pray, or talk to David. Other times, I would just forget about everything, and find peace by concentrating on looking for mushrooms, and trying not to get lost. By doing that, I could forget my grief for a little while. As the days and years went by, I grew stronger mentally and physically.

I joined the Salem Mushroom Society. We went on forages and I learned to identify different types of mushrooms.

I also learned about spores and mycelium. But all I really wanted to know was which mushrooms were safe to eat. For that, the mushroom buyer was my best guide. At first, I only picked mushrooms that the buyers bought. That way I knew for sure that my mushrooms were edible.

I always found more mushrooms than we could use or give away to friends, so I started selling them to that same buyer who had gotten me started. I got a chance to meet some of my fellow 'Professional Mushroom Hunters.' What a motley crew they were. But they accepted me readily as one of their own, and I enjoyed getting to know them. They even invited me to a Pot Party, but I declined.

I met, David Arora, who wrote the book, *Mushrooms Demystified*. David is a very interesting guy, and his book is an excellent guide for anybody who is interested in wild mushrooms.

Getting lost was one of my many adventures. It is a dreadful feeling to be in the middle of a forest, surrounded by trees, and not know the way out. During those times I tried hard not to panic and trust my built-in compass to lead me to my pickup. What a relief and flood of joy when I finally saw my truck. Each time I got lost, I learned what not to do.

I learned not to go into the forest at an angle because I lose my sense of direction that way. I learned when coming out of the forest onto a road, not to assume that it is the same road where my pickup is parked. I also learned to pay attention to my surroundings and always keep in mind the direction where I entered the forest.

Now I put several plastic bags in my pockets. When I walk into a new area, I periodically hang a bag in a tree to mark my way back. I make sure that I remove those bags on my way out. The bags also come in handy when I find more mushrooms than my bucket can hold. Also, they are a good head cover if it starts raining.

I heard a mycologist say, "Since mushrooms do not have roots, you don't have to cut them off. You can just pull them out." He may be right, but there is more to it than roots. I cut the stem off at ground level because sometimes there's another tiny mushroom growing just under the ground. By pulling the bigger mushroom out, the tiny one comes out with it. Also, the leftover stem is good fertilizer. I have seen new mushrooms grow on top of an old stem.

I brush the mushrooms off before putting them into the bucket, which makes cleaning them much easier when I get home. Brushing also spreads the spores around the area. I don't pick the very small mushrooms. By doing that I have preserved several patches, and they have produced mushrooms for more than thirty years.

Wildlife adventures:
I was deep in the forest and walking slowly. I kept hearing noises and thought that maybe another mushroom hunter was nearby. Foolishly I hollered, "Who's there?" Suddenly there was a loud crashing and stomping sound. I had frightened a large herd of elk and they started stampeding all around me. I escaped injury by plastering myself to a big tree until the elk were gone.

Another time I was walking down a path and when I came around the bend, a cougar was standing just a few yards ahead, staring at me. I came to a sudden stop and stared back. I didn't know what to do. I didn't want to confront the cougar, but I also didn't want to turn my back. We stood like that for a few seconds, which seemed like hours. Then I remembered the whistle around my neck. I blew the whistle as loudly as I could and clapped my hands. That scared the cougar. She disappeared into the brush and I got out of there as fast as I could. I assumed that it was a female and that she was just protecting her babies.

I loved watching deer. Sometimes when I was very quiet, they would just stand there and let me admire them for a while. One day when I came into a clearing, I saw a doe and a buck. I stood very still and watched them. Suddenly the buck noticed me. He lowered his huge rack of antlers and started coming toward me. At first, I just stood there not believing what I was seeing. "A deer was going to attack me?" I looked for a large tree where I could hide, but they were too far away. Finally, when he was just a few feet away, I burst out, "What are you doing?" The buck raised his antlers, looked at me again, recognized me as being human, and then turned around and ran off. I was very relieved.

When I told this story to our friend Richard, he was very envious. He and Jim, another friend of ours, had been hunting that same week every day, and never even saw a doe, let alone a buck.

Many times, I was stung by a hornet without having a reaction. But when a hornet got under my shirt, and stung me several times, my heart started beating very fast. All I could think of was getting back to my pickup as quickly as possible. Luckily it was nearby. I sat in the truck and took deep breaths until my heart slowed down and I stopped shivering; then I was able to drive home. The only lasting adverse reaction was a swollen and very itchy back.

Another time, I had been in the forest for about an hour. When I got back to the truck, I couldn't find my keys. I was sure that I had put them into the right-hand pocket of my coat, but they were not there. I knew that if the keys had fallen out of my pocket while I was in the woods, I would never find them. I was near panic because it was a long way back to civilization and the truck was locked, with my phone inside. All I could think to do was search through all of my pockets, over and over.

Finally, when I stuck my hand into my right pocket for the umpteenth time, I noticed a small hole. That explained why my keys were gone, but that did not relieve my panic. Now I was sure that the keys had fallen out and were lost somewhere deep in the woods. I prayed, "Oh please, this can't be. There is no way I can walk back to the main road before nightfall."

I was standing there with my head bowed, trying not to cry, when I noticed that the coat had a lining. I quickly searched again, and sure enough, my keys were caught in the bottom of the lining. I breathed a huge sigh of relief and said a little prayer of thanks. After that, I made sure before I went into the forest to put the keys in a pocket without a hole, and that the zipper was closed.

I always look forward to mushroom season. In the spring we look for Morels and King Boletus. After that, I have to wait until early fall. A week or two after a drenching rain, the Chanterelles start popping out again. Later, the Yellow Foot, Hedgehog and Matsutake mushrooms follow. There are a few other mushrooms we find and sometimes take home, such as: Cauliflower, Fried Chicken, Lobster, Angel Wings, Oyster, Puffballs, various forms of Boletus, Russula, and Shaggy Mane. The season ends after a killing frost. Then it's a long wait until spring when the Morel mushrooms return.

I no longer drive into the woods alone. Ron usually goes with me, and we go to familiar places. I also don't wander too far away from the truck. Sadly, most of those places are no longer productive due to logging, over-picking, and climate change. I still have "secret spots" where I find a few mushrooms, but not enough to give away or sell. I cannot hunt for mushrooms as long as I used to, and I always hate to leave the forest.

Paths in the Forest

There are paths in the forest that only the deer and I know.
There are mushrooms that bloom just for me.
My soul sings in the forest, and I am joyful and free.
Free from worry and despair, free from sorrow and regret.
When I go to the forest, I can forgive and forget.

My last mushroom story:

May 19, 2019. I went mushroom hunting today near Sisters.

As I was walking up a hill, my breath kept getting more labored, I was gulping air, and my throat was burning. My right leg was hurting and kept getting more painful with every step. I started to cry when I realized that I couldn't do my favorite hobby anymore.

As I turned to go back down the hill, I felt a presence. First, my friend Marilyn came to mind. Then I thought of my son David, my mama and my real papa. I felt them all around me, and I started to relax. My breathing slowed, and my lungs filled with air. I also realized that my leg was no longer hurting.

I became aware of how peaceful I was feeling; I felt light, almost as though I was floating. That feeling continued as I slowly walked up that hill and through the forest. I couldn't stop smiling, I felt content and happy. There was a tingling sensation throughout my whole body.

Then my doubtful mind clicked in and I thought, "How can I be sure that the spirits are really surrounding me?"

But my smile got bigger and I told myself, "Just enjoy the feeling, and don't question it. You would be foolish to doubt and dismiss this feeling. You believe in God because you want to believe in him. So why don't you let yourself believe that you have loving spirits surrounding you?"

I ignored my negative self, and continued to smile, feeling light and pain free.

Later that day, I saw a deer running toward me. When it got about 20 feet from me, I saw that she was a mature doe. She stopped and looked at me. I stood still and talked to her softly, assuring her that she was safe. She relaxed and started grazing, but kept glancing at me once in a while. I continued watching and admiring her for several minutes. Then I walked slowly around her, and kept on hunting for mushrooms, while the doe stayed close to me and continued eating. After a while we gave each other one more long look, and parted. She went farther into the forest, and I walked back to the truck were Ron was waiting.

I did not find any mushrooms that day because the soil was still too cold. But this mushroom hunting experience surpassed all of my previous adventures.

Selling Fir Cone House, 2006

The thought of giving up my home on Fir Cone Drive was unbearable. We bought that house when my youngest son David was about seven years old. It was the biggest and nicest home I had ever owned and it was perfect for our large family.

When my husband Don and I divorced, I did not mind splitting the assets, but I did not want to give up or sell Fir

Cone house. It was important to me to preserve the family home. I had been uprooted and had moved so many times in my life, I just couldn't do it again. Also, I hoped that someday one of my sons would make it a home for his own family. I was glad that, with the help of my sons, Don let me keep the house.

After I met Ron, we built a cabin on the Santiam River. Later, after Ron and I married, Barry, my oldest son, and his wife lived in the Fir Cone house. They had two sons, and their house was too small, so we switched houses. I hoped that they would eventually buy Fir Cone, but they had their own dreams and bought a newer house.

By then, the old ghosts were gone, and Ron and I moved back into Fir Cone. We remodeled the house, and made it comfortable for us. The important thing was, Fir Cone house remained in the family.

For the next 15 years or more, Ron and I lived in two houses. Friday to Monday, we lived at the river cabin. During the middle of the week, we lived at Fir Cone house. Ron was not happy with that arrangement because he wanted to live full time in our cabin. I knew that it was a lot of work keeping up two properties, but I just could not make myself give up that house. I loved both homes. At Fir Cone I felt at home, while at the River house I felt at peace.

Donny, my third son, was married to Sondra, who had three children, and my son had a daughter of his own. They needed a big house. So, they moved into Fir Cone on a "Lease, with Option to Buy," and Ron and I moved to our cabin. Two years went by and it became clear that Donny could not afford to buy the big house. Instead, they bought Sondra's parents' home.

After they moved out, I had to make a very difficult decision. Should we move back into the big house, or sell it? I knew that if I moved back, it would be much more difficult for me to sell the house. And of course, I could not sell the cabin. I also knew that we would soon be too old to keep up both houses, and, Ron would be very unhappy living in the big house again. With a heavy heart, I put the Fir Cone house on the market in September, 2006.

The stress on me was tremendous, so we set the price below market value, and in less than a month, we had a full price offer. Then, it took another month to close the sale. During that time, I stayed away from the house as much as I could because it felt like a very dear family member was dying.

One day I realized, that the main reason selling the house was so hard on me was because of my son David. Most of my memories of him were connected with that house. I worked hard on letting go, and tried to remember that David was no longer there. He is in a better place. His spirit surrounds me wherever I go, and so do the memories of him.

That was more than twelve years ago, and even now, when I drive by the house, or think about it, I still feel a little tug at my heart. But I am glad that I made myself move to our cabin full-time. Living here has given me time and inspiration to write my memoir.

Imagine a cozy cabin with a one-mile view of the Santiam River. The loud murmuring of white water. A short path to a sandy beach with rocks to sit on, in front of a large fishing/swimming hole. And all the property is surrounded by huge trees and a variety of bushes.

Is it any wonder that I wake up with gratitude every morning? Watching the river flow by and listening to the whitewater makes it easy for me to have peace of mind, and be grateful for all the blessings I have in my life.

I have a loving family! – I am a citizen of America! – I am financially secure! – Have good friends, and have lived a long and interesting life.

Coming to America was my dream. Living in this little spot of paradise, is far more than I could ever have imagined.

And so, my Journey from Russia to Poland, to Germany, and finally to America, ends here in Oregon; a place I love, and call my home.

Part IV

Journeys

Ron and I traveled all over the world. For me, the most personal and memorable journeys were my return to Germany and Russia.

Germany, 1982

While I lived in Germany, I could not afford to travel, so I saw very little of Europe. With this trip, I decided to make up for that. Ron and I bought a three week return flight, and planned on using a Eurail pass for the first two weeks. The third week, we planned on staying in my old home town, Kitzingen.

We activated our two-week Eurail pass right after we landed in Frankfurt, Germany. We enjoyed traveling by train all over Germany, Austria, and Switzerland. With the Eurail pass, we could get on and off the train any time we wanted and stay as long as we wanted. This worked well because we had no reservations. We stayed in many interesting places, including a castle in Würzburg. We found out that most German people spoke English, but they got a lot friendlier when I spoke German to them. Our two weeks just flew by.

On the third week when we arrived in Kitzingen, I felt uncomfortable from the moment we got off the train. The town felt like a hostile place. I had hoped to see my friend, Ellen, whom I was still in contact with, but she had to go to Spain because her mother was ill. She wanted to arrange a homecoming reception for me with some of my former classmates, but I talked her out of it. Most of those girls wanted nothing to do with me when I went to school with them, and now they were just strangers as far as I was concerned. I would have felt very uncomfortable being around them.

We checked into a small hotel near the Crooked Tower (a landmark in Kitzingen). We had a nice comfortable room with a shower. The first two days, we just walked around town. First, we looked for the house on the river, where I had lived for about three years, but it was no longer there, just an empty lot. Then we went to see *Schützenplatz*, where we had lived for about six years, but that too, was gone. All the barracks had been replaced by neat little houses. We did find my former school and the Lutheran church where I was confirmed. But even Wachter's *Metzgerei* (butcher shop), where I had worked as an apprentice, had been moved to a different location. Frau Wachter had died and her daughter, who was now in charge of the shop, did not remember me.

As the days passed, I became very lethargic and did not want to do anymore sightseeing. I just wanted to fly home. When we checked about changing our flight, it was very expensive, so we stayed in the same hotel, and took the train or bus to nearby villages.

We noticed that the people in Kitzingen were not friendly toward us. It reminded me of the discrimination I felt when we lived there after the war. Then, I was discriminated against because I was Russian. Now, was it because I was American?

One night we went into a neighborhood bar, and I started talking with the bartender. He became friendlier when I spoke German and told him why we were in town. I told him about the cold shoulder treatments we were getting. He explained that it was because Kitzingen had an American military base, and they were having a lot of problems with American soldiers getting drunk and rowdy. There were also problems with the soldiers consorting with German *Fräuleins*. The Germans did not want their daughters to associate with the Americans.

He said, "When I saw you coming into the bar, I just assumed that you were parents of an American soldier. So maybe other people in town are assuming the same thing."

I thanked him for his explanation. It made me feel better to know that the unfriendly attitude had nothing to do with me personally. It was interesting how, even after 30 years, going back to Kitzingen could get me so depressed. And that I could not find any happy memories in that town.

I was very relieved when it was time for us to go back to America.

Germany, 2010

We visited Germany again 28 years later, when military friends of ours, Craig and Deb, were stationed there. They had rented a house in a small village, and offered us their home as a base.

We got a Eurail pass for Ron, Deb and me, Craig was in Afghanistan at that time. We traveled all around Germany, Switzerland, Austria, France, and Italy. We loved Paris and Venice, and really enjoyed this trip. By having a home base, we were able to travel when and where we felt like going. Deb drove us through the streets of my former home, Kitzingen, and through Scheinfeldt where my brother Bill was born.

This time, seeing Kitzingen did not make me feel uncomfortable or resentful; I no longer had strong feelings for the town. While writing my memoir, I had let go of all the hurt and shame I had experienced as a child.

I did not want to stop and linger in Kitzingen. The town just looked and felt like any other little town in Germany. America is now my home; all of my hopes and dreams are here. Germany is just a far memory.

Our Other Travels

Between 1982 and 2010, Ron and I traveled all around Europe, Peru, Brazil, Africa, China, Hong Kong, Mexico, and Costa Rica. We also went on many cruises. I'm so glad that we traveled to all of those places and learned about other cultures and how people lived. It made us more understanding and tolerant of other peoples' rituals and beliefs.

After 2010, traveling became more difficult for me, due to my health, but by then we had seen almost everything that we wanted to see. Now we are content staying at home and enjoying our cabin on the river.

Africa, July 1998

Ron did not want to go to Africa. So, my friend Inge agreed to go with me. We booked the trip with a travel agency called Coco's Travel Group. There were 14 of us altogether.

Inge got sick on the plane to New York. The next morning, she was still nauseated, and couldn't go on a New York city tour with us. That afternoon when our plane was leaving, I didn't want to leave her, but Inge and our tour guide insisted that I go on without her. Inge seemed to be feeling better, and we all assumed that she would catch up with us the following day in Johannesburg. However, her nausea did not stop for two more days, and by then, Inge decided to go back home. I felt terrible leaving my friend. And I was lonely without her in spite of people all around me.

One of my safari photos

We flew out of Johannesburg the next day. When we got close to Nairobi, our plane kept circling the airport for a long time. We wondered what was going on and were getting nervous. But all we were told was that we were waiting for clearance to land.

After we landed, we were told that the American Embassy had been bombed by terrorists twenty minutes earlier. We were shocked and alarmed, but they assured us that we would be safe. We got to our hotel without a problem, and were told to stay there. However, a few of us could not resist, and since we were only a few blocks from the embassy, we decided to go and see what happened. But the area around the embassy was roped off, so there was nothing to see.

The next day we were driven to Karen Blixen's old house. I had read her book *Out of Africa*, and looked forward to seeing her home. It was just an ordinary bungalow, but the interesting thing was the compost toilet. I was surprised that it could be used inside the house, and have no odors.

Later that day, we arrived at our first safari camp. All of our camps and lodges were very comfortable and some even luxurious. The Lodge in Tanzania, which had been built by two American movie stars, was showing signs of wear, but it was still splendid. When I got up in the morning, the weather was clear and I had a breathtaking view of Mount Kilimanjaro right in front of my window. Much of the time, the mountain is covered in clouds, so this was a big treat.

During our two-week stay in Kenya and Tanzania, we went on safari most mornings, in an open-sided van. Of course, we hunted with cameras instead of guns.

July was the middle of the great wildebeest migration season on the Masai Mara. We saw huge herds of wildebeests and zebras. Our guides were very good, and knew where to go. We saw elephants, crocodiles, giraffes, lions and tigers, rhinos, buffalos, several kinds of monkeys, and many kinds of birds. We even saw two leopards (which are hard to find). At Lake Nakuru, we saw hundreds of pink flamingos. It was awesome to be so close to all of those wonderful wild animals, and to see them roaming free all around us. In one of the lodges where we stayed, the staff fed the crocodiles every afternoon, so we could see them up close when they came out of the water to feed.

One day, we passed a big herd of elephants. One large bull elephant remained in front of our van for quite a while, and then reluctantly stepped aside. I watched the elephant as we passed him and saw the moment he decided to attack us. First his head moved from side to side, then his whole body shook, as if to say, "How dare you invade my space, and chase me out of the way. I am the king here, and you don't belong in my kingdom." Then he let out a trumpeting roar and started charging after us.

We had a good driver who kept a close eye on that elephant. He quickly stomped on the gas, drove as fast as he could, and we got away.

Another day, we watched a pair of lions mating. It was interesting to see that the female was the aggressor. The mating was very quick, less than a minute. After which, the male flopped down, panting and resting, but the female kept coming back and nudging him for another performance. We saw that repeated three times. Then our driver decided to go on, and give the lions some privacy.

The buildings in most little towns were made of cement blocks. Some were shacks made up of whatever material they could find. The roads were mostly compressed dirt. Poverty was very obvious everywhere we went.

The African people made a huge impression on me. They had few meager possessions, and yet they were always friendly, smiling, laughing and singing.

One of the highlights of our trip was a visit to a Masai village. The Masai tribe are the tall and regal people of Africa. They are also known to be fast runners. Their wealth is measured by the number of cattle they own. They seldom slaughter their cattle, instead, they drink their blood and milk for protein. The huts are made out of cow manure with a hole in the roof so that the smoke from the open fire pit can escape. The entrance is narrow and low for security reasons. Anybody entering the hut, has to bow down, and could easily be knocked out with a wooden club, which hangs inside the entrance. I bought one of those clubs from an elderly Masai man who had carved it. We have it hanging in our entrance. So, burglars beware.

The village is surrounded by a fence made of briar bushes, which keeps villagers and their cattle safe from the wild predators. Every seven years, the Masai burn down their huts and pastureland, and move to another spot. This is their way of sanitizing the area and making sure that the pasture will grow back.

Our next destination was Cape Town, located at the southernmost tip of Africa. It is a lovely town, nestled between Table Mountain and ocean on one side, and farms and vineyards on the other side. The town, with it's interesting architecture, was originally developed by Dutch settlers.

One day we drove along the ocean on a winding road, to see a penguin colony. It was fascinating to be so close to hundreds of penguins, and watch them go about their business. Another day, we visited an old Dutch farm, a winery, and went up to the top of Table Mountain.

After three days in Cape Town, it was time to fly home. Ron picked me up at Portland airport. He told me how worried he had been, and that he did not want me to travel without him again. I was glad to hear that. I had felt lonely, especially at night. Africa was definitely one of my most memorable trips. I am so glad I went. It was worth the tiring thirty plus hours it took to get back home

Peru, 1996

One of the travel companies sent us a brochure with a picture of Machu Picchu, the ancient ruins of an Incan city. I was drawn to it, so Ron and I decided to go with the group.

We landed in Cusco, which was the capital of the Inca Empire from the early 13th century until 1572, when it was conquered by Span. Cusco's population is now over 435,000. Because Cusco's elevation is over 11,000 feet, we were given coca leaf tea to drink, as we got off the plane to ward off elevation sickness. Then, we were told to rest for half an hour when we got to our hotel. This worked, and nobody in our group had a problem with the elevation.

We stayed in a small, quaint hotel with an enclosed courtyard. It was located in Old Town where the buildings are built of stone, cut with great precision and without the use of mortar. We wandered the narrow alleys, admiring the buildings, and the skill of the ancient builders.

There were lots of small shops and street vendors, wearing colorful clothes. Most of the items they were selling were handmade garments made out of Alpaca wool. I bought a sweater from a street vendor, but after I got home, found out that it was too scratchy to wear. I also bought a vest which I love, and have worn many times.

The following day we traveled by train, on a switchback road, over a mountain and down, as far as the train would go. Then we got on a bus and went up another mountain. We rode up a narrow road with very few pullouts. On one side was a big wall, and the other side, a drop-off that went on forever. I was sitting next to a window and saw that at times the bus was hanging over the edge. I got very uncomfortable, and my heart kept racing too fast; so, I stopped looking to my right. I was glad when we finally arrived safely at the entrance to Machu Picchu.

The city is located in a remote area of the Andes mountains. Some archeologists believe that it was a royal estate for the emperor Pachacuti. It was constructed in 1450, and abandoned one hundred years later; the reason is a mystery. The ruins remained unknown to the outside world until Hiram Bingham discovered them in 1911.

Machu Picchu was built on a mountain peak that is about 8000 ft. high, in very steep terrain, with many different levels of terraces, connected by 3000 stone steps. It once had an advanced irrigation system with water flowing to all of the multiple levels.

The city consists of a farming area, a residential area, a royal district, and a sacred area. There are 150 buildings of polished dry-stone, very tightly fitted without mortar; ranging from baths and houses, to temples and sanctuaries. Two famous structures are The Temple of the Sun and a granite stone that functioned as a solar clock or calendar.

To me, Machu Picchu was a most fascinating and spiritual place. The views of the mountain range below are breathtaking. The clouds were moving, and ever-changing just above us. Wandering among the ruins, I could almost feel the ghosts of the Inca around me.

Next to the ruins was a small hotel. I wish we could have stayed there overnight, so that we could explore the ruins after all the tourists were gone. I hated to leave that spiritual place, but I made myself walk away, hoping that I could return someday.

Our next stop was the city of Lima, Peru. All I can remember of Lima is that it was a very big city with a lot of traffic and crazy drivers. Our hotel was located on a corner, in the middle of town. Ron's entertainment was sitting on the balcony of our hotel and watching the crazy drivers pass each other any way they could, and then fight for who crossed the intersection first. He was amazed that there were no accidents; not even a fender bender.

The next day we flew to Brazil.

Brazil, 1996

One of the reasons I wanted to travel to Brazil was to see the jungle. When I was a child in Germany, we played Tarzan games in a nearby wooded area, and later in America, I loved watching Tarzan movies. I was disappointed that, due to excessive logging, the jungles in Brazil consisted mostly of small trees, with dense underbrush. I thought, "There is no way Tarzan could swing from these trees. We have much larger trees in Oregon." However, while taking a tour through the jungle, we were impressed when our guide pointed out how many of the plants were edible, or had medicinal purposes.

The Amazon River is huge, and looks like an ocean many miles before the river enters the ocean. The natives built their huts on tall stilts to avoid flooding, because the banks of the river changed constantly.

We took a cruise down the Amazon river in a large fishing boat, which had been converted into a cruise ship. It was far from being comfortable. But it had air-conditioning. Without that, it would have been unbearably hot and humid.

There were little children navigating that big river in very small dugout canoes; they came very close to our boat showing off their skills and looking for hand-outs. We were amazed at their skill.

When we saw a three toed sloth swimming across the Amazon, the crew brought it onto the boat so that we could inspect him up close. It was interesting to see how very slow his movements were. His color was green mixed with beige, and his pelt was smooth to the touch. The slow movements and camouflage made him nearly invisible. After we were through inspecting the sloth, the crew released him close to the shore he was trying to reach.

While visiting some of the villages and little huts along the river we saw how little the people owned. They survived with the barest necessities. They ate whatever they could harvest from the jungle and catch in the river. They were very friendly, and seemed carefree, like children.

Rio de Janeiro is in a beautiful location; it sits along the bay and is surrounded on three sides by mountains. However, the bay was polluted and much of the city was dirty. It was cloudy and cold the entire time we were there, so, there were no beautiful girls in string bikinis on the beach. I am sure that Ron was disappointed, although he did not say that. He is a smart husband.

Rio also has a huge slum (favela) area. Most of the huts are built of corrugated metal. There are hundreds of them, built on a hill, practically on top of each other. The people are very poor, but the favelas are alive with the sound of music. The young people practice their dancing all year long, hoping to win a prize for best samba at Carnival.

Christ the Redeemer Statue is 125 feet high and stands on a mountain peak high above Rio de Janeiro. It is an unbelievable sight from far away and up close. Jesus stands with his arms open wide, as though welcoming all the humanity of the world. We drove up a very winding road to get close. I was moved by Christ's face, it looked so peaceful and serene. The statue was constructed between 1922 and 1931 during a time when the Catholic Church noticed a lack of religious faith in the area. Now, it is considered to be one of the Wonders of the World.

Brazil's business center is Sao Paulo. It is a big, modern city with many high-rise buildings. They have a huge, open air market where you can buy almost anything you want. It's a fascinating place.

Another impressive sight and amazing experience were, the magnificent Iguassu Falls. It is the largest waterfall system in the world. Located on the border of Brazil and Argentina, there are: 275 falls, up to 269 ft. high, over 260 ft. long, and 1.7 miles wide. They divide the Iguassu River into two levels. We watched the water from a hotel, then from a platform above the falls, and finally, from a large raft. The sound of the water was very loud from above, but the roar below was deafening. We got soaking wet, but it was a wonderful experience.

This trip was interesting, but also tiring. The travel company was new and the itinerary was not well planned. We spent too many hours in airports. Besides flying from home and back, we also flew on two different small planes within Peru and Brazil. One time leaving Lima at dawn, and another time arriving on the Amazon river boat at midnight. We were glad to get back home and rest. But it was a great adventure.

Spain and Portugal, 1987

On this trip, Ron and I went on our own without making any reservations. When we landed in Madrid, we hailed a taxi and asked the driver to take us to a clean and inexpensive hotel. He took us to a nice little apartment instead, which was very reasonably priced. We stayed in Madrid for two nights, mostly walking around town, and enjoying the sights. We visited the Prada Museum and other points of interest.

We decided to take a train to Lisbon, Portugal. When we got to the station, we found out that there was a train strike, and nobody at the ticket window knew how to speak English. We were glad that we had a Spanish/English dictionary with us, so we managed to get a ticket to Lisbon. Unlike our previous Eurail pass, this ticket was not first class. We traveled with the locals and had a lot of fun. It was like a big party. We had fun watching the people managing their children, their chickens, and other small livestock. They were all very friendly and we enjoyed the ride, even though there was no air-conditioning.

When we arrived in Lisbon, we saw several people at the station advertising rooms for rent. We picked a harmless looking lady, who spoke some English, and she drove us to her home. Our room was comfortable and large, with a bathroom and kitchen. The decor was interesting. We thought that it looked like a brothel we had seen on TV. We were close to the center of town and in a good neighborhood. There were several restaurants nearby that offered good and inexpensive food, so we didn't need to cook.

We loved Portugal and had fun getting to know some of the locals. We stayed for a whole week, walking around town and enjoying the narrow cobblestone alleys.

We rode a ferry to an island, and had lunch in a small restaurant. I ordered a bowl of little snails, still in their shell. They were much smaller and tasted more tender then the escargot I ate in Paris. We took public transportation to nearby picturesque villages. All the people were very friendly. If they were unable to speak English, they would find someone who could. So, we communicated quite well.

On a bus to the South of Spain, we weren't sure where we wanted to go, so we bought a ticket to a town near the ocean. However, we never got to that town. Instead, we got off the bus at Alcazares because it was not only on the ocean, it was close to Morocco and Gibraltar. We met a very friendly, young Portuguese couple on the bus who spoke fluent English. They told us they were getting married in Alcazares and asked us to be their witnesses. Outside the bus station, we shared a cab and asked the driver to take us to a clean and cheap hotel. The rooms were nice and comfortable, and each room cost only $17 a night. That evening, the wedding was very simple. The couple was married by a judge and there were just the four of us. We took them out for a nice dinner and wished them a happy life. They left the next morning and we never saw them again.

The following day, we took a ferry to Tangier, Morocco. We walked through a very large bazaar and marveled at all the things that were on display. We saw all kinds of meat carcasses hanging from hooks and fish lying on tables with flies buzzing all around. There were spices, clothes, rugs, leather goods, vegetables, and many other fascinating items.

We had a Couscous lunch in the Casablanca Café and pretended that we were, "Bogie and Bacall."

As we walked around town, we came across a snake handler. I showed off by letting him drape the snake around my neck, and laughed at Ron's revulsion. A little later I rode a camel, which was an interesting experience. I don't know if I could ride it for a long period of time without getting sea sick. Maybe one just gets used to the rocking motion.

Next day, we took a bus to the Rock of Gibraltar where we wandered around all afternoon. Ron was trying to keep me away from the apes that were running loose on the island. But they were so cute and hard to resist, especially the mamas and babies. I kept telling Ron that I wouldn't get close enough to touch them, but he didn't believe me and kept on nagging.

A few days later, we took the night train back to Madrid and came very close to getting robbed.

When we got on the train, Ron waited by the door with our two large suitcases, while I took the shoulder bags and looked for our reserved compartment. I saw a man at the end of the hallway and wondered why he was staring at me. I found our six-person compartment, but it was already occupied by a family of three. The woman waved me off, telling me that the compartment was full. I told her that we had reservations for that compartment. While I was talking to the woman, the man I had seen earlier came up next to me and asked if I needed assistance. I told him no, but he was persistent. He took one of my shoulder bags and put it on the overhead shelf while I was still arguing with that women. When I heard the sound of a zipper, I grabbed the man by his coat and screamed, "No! Get out of here!" After I managed to push him out of the compartment, I noticed that the man had gotten the zipper open. Thankfully, he did not get what he was looking for. Our passports and money were not in that bag.

The people in the compartment were a husband and wife with their young son. They made room for us, after I showed her my ticket. They could not speak English, but with smiles and gestures, we communicated well enough. We managed to get reasonably comfortable, even though the six seats in the compartment did not recline and we had to sleep while sitting in an upright position.

Back in Madrid, we took a taxi to the Emperador Hotel, that Ron's brother had recommended. It was a very nice old hotel. Our room was small, but beautifully furnished and had a very comfortable bed. That night, we had dinner, and saw a flamenco show. The dinner was expensive, but good, and the show was very enjoyable.

The next day we flew home to America.

China, 1992

A travel agency arranged our China trip. Ron and I flew with ten other people from Portland to Los Angeles, and to Narita Airport in Japan, where we spent the night.

The next day we flew to Beijing, China.

At the Beijing Airport, while waiting outside for a ride to our hotel, Ron got a ticket for littering.

He had finished smoking, and looked around for an ash-tray or a garbage can where he could dispose of his cigarette. When he didn't see anything, he threw the cigarette on the ground and stepped on it. Immediately, the litter patrol lady tapped him on the shoulder, pointed to the cigarette butt, and handed him a ticket. That was a tense moment. People stopped and waited for Ron's reaction.

When I saw what had happened, I started laughing because just before we left home, Ron had gotten a ticket for not wearing his seatbelt. I thought it was hilarious, him getting a ticket in America, and then just a few days later, another ticket in China. Would he never learn to behave? As soon as everybody saw me laughing, the atmosphere changed. People relaxed and started smiling. Ron paid the 25-cent fine. But he pointed out that they needed ashtrays, and the litter patrol lady agreed.

The next day our group went sightseeing. I had read a book and saw a movie featuring the Forbidden City so I was looking forward to seeing it in person. We were told that The City served as the home of emperors and their families, and as political center for 500 years. Since 1925 it has been under management of The Palace Museum. The architecture was very interesting, and I would have liked more time to explore the Forbidden City, but there are 980 buildings and 180 acres of land, so all we could see were some of the highlights.

We were impressed when we saw the Great Wall. It is actually a double wall and a wide, flat area on top with guard stations along the way. It is over 13,000 miles long. Hard to imagine people building that wall by hand, in very rough, steep terrain and in remote locations.

Later that week we traveled to Xian, and saw an unbelievable sight: The 8th Wonder of the World, 2200-year-old

Terra Cotta Warriors. There were over 8,000 full-sized, individual and unique, hand-crafted statues. All true-to-life, each weighing 400 pounds. Plus, horses and chariots that had been restored. They stood in a large pit, which used to be a farmer's field. We were told that there are many more statues like these, still waiting to be uncovered, in an area the size of 10,000 football fields. They are part of the mausoleum of Qin Shi Huang, the first Emperor of China. The army was buried with the emperor to protect him in his after-life.

Our cruise on the Yangtze River was very relaxing. We enjoyed the interesting terrain and rock formations.

We were amazed at the amount of people we saw everywhere. China is definitely overcrowded. Now we understand why they placed a limitation on the number of children allowed to be born.

Everywhere we went, there was construction of one kind or another. During our trip we saw very little heavy equipment, most of the construction was done by hand. When we asked why, we were told that this provided jobs. A noticeable thing was the pollution. The air was so thick we could hardly see anything more than a block away.

In one of the overcrowded areas, a lady in our group had $80 stolen out of her handbag, by a pick-pocket. Our interpreter insisted that she go with him to the police station and make a theft report. She was afraid to go, so I volunteered to go with them. We were led through a very narrow alley, into a small dirty room. That was the police station. We saw an old desk, some chairs, and a sleeping cot, with a dirty pillow and blanket. We could hear terrible sounds coming out of the back room. It was obvious that the police were interrogating a prisoner. The sounds of the blows and the moaning made me sick to my stomach.

It took an hour for the police to get the report written. The translator showed us the form and said, "The police are claiming that $800 was stolen."

The lady told him again that her loss was less than $80, but the interpreter said, "They say it is better if you claim that $800 was stolen."

She and I talked it over and decided that it would be foolish to lie and falsify a document. When she refused to sign the form, they tore it up, and told us to leave. We didn't argue, and the interpreter took us back to our group.

We told our guide what had happened, and he said that we did the right thing. There was a lot of corruption in China and we might have gotten in trouble for signing a false police report. We were sorry that we had wasted so much time at the police station. The lady did not get her money back, and we had missed seeing the Summer Palace, which we were told, was beautiful.

The main tour ended in Shanghai. It was a very busy city, with various European-style architecture and bumper-to-bumper traffic. It took forever to drive to the harbor, just a few blocks away, which was overcrowded with very large cargo ships.

The next day we took a train to Hong Kong, which was still occupied by the English. The following year England returned control back to China.

We marveled at the number of tall buildings in Hong Kong. We could understand why they call it the "Vertical City." There was not enough land to build sideways, so they built up to the sky. When we drove by a small golf course, our tour guide told us that it cost half a million dollars to be a member of that golf club because the price of land is so high. We've heard that it's a lot more expensive now.

We were also amazed at the number of boats, sampans, and junks in the harbor. They were almost touching each other. Many of the boats had people living on them full-time.

The traffic was horrendous. We had a very exciting ride on a Double Decker bus. I sat on the upper deck next to the driver, right behind a huge windshield that went below my knees. Nobody else wanted to sit there. I admit it was a bit scary. Every time the bus stopped, I had to brace myself and hold on tight. There were no seat belts, and at times I was sure that I would fly right through the windshield on top of the cars below. But it was exciting, and I had fun feeling like a kid again.

We saw stores and markets everywhere, and you could buy almost anything your heart desired. A lot of it was knock-off merchandise such as fake Rolex watches for $2, fake jade, illegal copies of American CDs, fake designer-clothing and handbags, and on and on. Everything was very cheap. You could also have a suit tailored to your exact measurements, in an hour's time, for a very reasonable price.

On our last night in Hong Kong, Ron and I decided to go out to dinner on our own. There were several restaurants near our five-star hotel. The menus and prices were in English and posted outside the restaurants. We were reading the menu when a Chinese couple came out of the restaurant. The man said to us, "Good. Go to eat" (this reminded me of the way my mama talked). He was right, the food was very good. Ron and I have repeated, "Go to eat" many times since then.

We enjoyed visiting China and Hong Kong. We saw many wondrous things, the people were very friendly, and the food was delicious. I am glad that we saw China before it became so industrialized.

Cruises

Ron and I liked cruise-ship travel because it was more relaxing than land travel. All we had to do was unpack once. After that, we could either stay on board ship, or take the many excursions that the cruise ships offered. It was also a fast and easy way to see many countries and towns.

We visited Alaska, the east and west Caribbean islands, the Mexican Riviera, and other popular islands. They were all very enjoyable, and we talked about coming back and spending more time on those islands. But there were just too many other places we wanted to see, so we never returned.

One of the most interesting cruises was in 2005 when we saw parts of Italy, Greece, and Turkey.

The highlights were: Pompeii Ruins, Rome, the Coliseum and the Forum. We also visited Athens, the Acropolis, the Temple of Zeus, and the islands Mykonos and Santorini, as well as Istanbul, the Grand Bazaar, Topkapi Palace, and the Blue Mosque.

The most memorable of these, was a large archeological site near Naples. I was fascinated by the Roman city of Pompeii, AD 62, which was once a thriving and sophisticated city. When Mt. Vesuvius erupted in AD 79, the city was buried in tons of volcanic ash. The restoration we saw was excellent. We could walk the streets, inspect the houses and temples, and imagine what it was like to live there long ago. We saw beautiful frescoes and marveled at their baths and places of leisure. But the most powerful sights were the mummified bodies of people caught at the moment of death with horror imprinted on their faces. It reminded me how fleeting life is and how sudden disaster can strike.

Nina, in Turkey, trying to make a pottery vase

In Turkey, the ancient Roman city, Ephesus, was also very interesting. We saw many large private homes with beautiful frescoes. A tall building that was a library, with grand columns, and lovely, carved statues. Ephesus also had an efficient fresh water and sewer system.

I was fascinated by a large "Public Toilet Room" with benches along the walls, and several round holes cut into the benches. That way several people could use the Toilet Room at the same time. I imagined that, while they were sitting and doing their business, they could visit with their neighbors and catch up on the latest gossip. It reminded me of today's neighborhood pubs. Same principle. It was interesting how they acknowledged and took for granted that everyone had certain bodily functions, and that it was a natural thing.

After the cruise ended, we took an extended land trip to Ankara, the capital of Turkey. Then, a bus ride to Cappadocia, which was fascinating. The Landscape consists of ancient volcanic rock. It had eroded over time into spectacular pillars and formations that look like fairy chimneys.

People carved caves, underground cities, houses, and churches from the soft rocks. We walked through a long, narrow, and low, tunnel into an underground city, one of many cities where the early Christians took refuge. Sometimes they lived in those tunnels for many months in darkness, except for a small cooking fire which they lit only when the smoke could not be seen by their enemies. I was amazed at the strong faith of those people and what they were willing to endure for their Christian beliefs. Cave exploration was my favorite hobby when I lived in Germany. I would have loved to stay longer, and explored more caves in Cappadocia

There are more than a thousand cave churches, dating from the earliest days of Christianity to the thirteenth century. Some are carved with domed ceilings and columns. Many are decorated with splendid colorful frescoes and religious paintings. That was an interesting trip.

Before we flew home from Ankara, I foolishly bought a bottle of water from a small boy who was selling water on the street. I checked and made sure that the cap was sealed. However, that little Urchin must have refilled the bottle and re-sealed it.

After drinking the water, I found out that it was contaminated. I was vomiting and had severe diarrhea all at the same time. By the time we got on the plane, I was so sick that I sat on the toilet almost the entire flight. When we landed in Frankfurt, I was taken off the plane on a stretcher. At the infirmary, they started an IV, which made me feel much better. But we had missed our connecting flight and had to stay in Frankfurt overnight.

The next morning, I felt fine and we flew back home. I can't believe I bought water from that boy. Having raised four sons, I should have known better. You can't trust little boys, no matter how cute and innocent they look.

Costa Rica, 2006

Costa Rica was our last overseas trip. We traveled by bus, and enjoyed seeing the rugged terrain and volcanoes. The lush green rainforests were teaming with spider monkeys, a large variety of beautiful birds, and butterflies. Costa Rica has many lovely beaches on two coastlines. On one side is the Pacific Ocean and on the other is the Caribbean Sea.

We traveled from one luxurious resort to another where we had dinner and spent the night. Among the beauty was also poverty. We saw many little huts with corrugated roofs along the roads we traveled. Even though we enjoyed seeing the beautiful countryside, it was a tiring trip. We spent many hours on the bus, riding over very rough roads.

Toward the end of our trip I ate, or drank, something that did not agree with me and I got sick and dehydrated again.

Paramedics came to our hotel and began an IV which made me feel better, but I still needed to stay close to the toilet the next day.

I was disappointed because I missed out seeing the butterfly museum, and a zipline adventure. I had looked forward to trying out the zipline, but I consoled myself with the fact that we did not have to be riding the bus that day, which would have been really awful in my condition.

That was the third time that I had gotten sick while traveling. So, after that trip, we decided we had better stop and stay home for a while.

As we traveled, we saw many wonderful things. But we also saw many poor people, which reminded us of how lucky we are to be living in America. It made me even more grateful for all of my blessings.

We love our home on the river. Living here is like a vacation year-round, and I don't mind staying close to home.

Return to Russia, 1993

Two-year Russian History, 1991–1993

December 26, 1991, the USSR collapses. Mikhail Gorbachev President of the Soviet Union, and last leader of the Communist Party, was ousted by his own party. Gorbachev started Perestroika (reconstruction) and Glazunov (openness). The Russian Federation was formed, and Boris Yeltsin became head of the Russian Federation.

Saturday, July 25, 1993, Russia's Central Bank abruptly announced that all ruble bills, issued before 1993, will not be honored as of Monday, July 27. Everyone had to exchange their old, devalued, rubles for new rubles.

October, 1993, The Constitutional Crisis. A political stand-off between Boris Yeltsin and the Russian Parliament was resolved by using military force. The reported death toll was as high as 2,000.

In July of 1993, two years after the fall of communism, Ron and I decided to visit Russia. Four years before, when I was diagnosed with breast cancer, I had a longing to visit Russia before I died. That longing never went away. Mama and I had talked about going back to Russia for many years. But when I got serious about going, Mama changed her mind. Later, I found out that Papa had forbid her to go.

Papa did not want Ron and me to go either and Mama tried to talk us out of it. I'm not sure why, but I suspect that Papa did not want me to find out too much about their past. However, I already knew that my mama had run away with "new papa," while my real papa was away fighting with the Russian Army. I did not judge them, and I was glad to be living in America.

I told my parents that I had to go, and hoped that eventually they would understand.

We booked our trip with a very new travel group called: "Waterways of the Czars." Our itinerary was to be a 14-day river cruise. For the first seven days we would cruise from St. Petersburg to Moscow. The next seven days we would go from Moscow to Kazan, and then return to Moscow. After the cruise, we planned to spend three days with my two half-sisters, Nina and Raya, and some of my other Ukrainian family.

As the plane approached St. Petersburg, we could see thousands of trees that had been cut down a long time ago and left to rot.

Later, we noticed another oddity: There was scaffolding on many buildings. It was obvious that the scaffolding had been put up many years ago, but the repairs on the buildings had never been completed. When we got off the plane, we saw a beautiful old building which used to be the Terminal, but it was locked. We were led to a shack with an attached open structure, covered with a corrugated metal roof. That's what they were using for a terminal. That was our first impression of St. Petersburg.

Our plane had arrived late, and there was a long wait for our visa and passport check. While we were waiting, I discovered that my wallet was missing! It contained my driver's license, government ID card, credit card, and $200 in cash. Luckily, my passport, my visa, and the rest of my money, were in a pouch around my neck. I was upset, and didn't know what to do. Our plane had already left, so I couldn't go back to see if I had dropped my wallet on the plane. All I could do was go on and hope that someone on the ship could help me.

After we left the terminal area, we were met by two young women from the ship. They could not speak English and were surprised that I spoke Russian. I told them about my missing items, but I was told that they could not do anything about it. We had to wait until we met with our interpreter, Leon, the next day. They said that Leon had gone with another American couple to the ballet, which we had missed because our plane came in too late.

We never did find my wallet, and it took two days before we could finally convince Leon that we had to call our credit card company to report the loss. It seemed to take forever to reach them, and then the connection was so bad that I was not sure if they understood what I said. I worried about that until we got home. Then I called the credit company again. I was glad that I did, because Master Card said that the loss had not been reported. About a month later, the card company called and told me that someone had used my credit card to buy gas somewhere in Russia, but we were not going to be held responsible. That's all I ever heard about it. However, it felt a little uncomfortable to think that someone in Russia had my driver's license, and Government ID card.

Our ride from the airport to the ship was very pleasant. The young ladies were pretty and friendly. They said that my husband looked just like the Marlboro man. I assume it's because he was wearing jeans and a cowboy hat. I think Ron got a big kick out of that.

It was late by the time we boarded our cruise ship. We were led to our cabin and served a snack. Our cabin was small, but comfortable. There was a big window with a couch on each side which made into twin beds, with a nightstand in between. There was also a big wardrobe, plus several shelves. The toilet and sink were inside a shower stall which saved space. Everything was very cleverly designed. We were told that the ship was designed by German engineers.

The next morning at breakfast we met our interpreter, Leon, and the only other Americans on board, an older couple from Kansas. All of the other people on the ship were Russians. That morning, we were supposed to tour St. Petersburg, but my stomach was acting up, so I stayed onboard ship. I insisted that Ron go on the tour.

After about an hour, my stomach was better, so I decided to explore the ship. Everyone was very friendly, and pleased that I spoke Russian. I met our cruise director, Vera, who was a very jolly, round, little woman. When I told her how sorry I was to miss the tour of St. Petersburg, she asked,

"Why don't you just go by yourself? You speak good Russian, and there is no reason why you can't take the subway into town."

She was very sure that there would be no problem. She also told me where to get on and off the subway. She made it sound very easy, and convinced me to go.

When I got on the subway, I sat down next to an old lady and introduced myself. I asked her to tell me about life in Russia. She said, "Things are very bad now and I am so worried about the future. I have a small pension, and during the communist rule, I was getting by all right because my apartment was cheap, and things did not cost so much. But now everything is much more expensive, and I don't know if my pension will continue. The communists promised that if I worked hard, I did not need to worry, and they would take care of me when I got old. But now that the communists are no longer in charge, who will take care of me?"

I felt sad for her, and wanted to continue our conversation, but we arrived at the stop Vera had told me to take, so I had to leave the old lady. Later I found out that many older people in Russia felt that they had been betrayed. They had been told that the communists would provide for them in their old age, but now their future was very uncertain and they were afraid.

I got off the subway in the middle of St. Petersburg. I saw wide streets and beautiful old buildings all around me, and people hurrying along the sidewalks. No one was paying the slightest bit of attention to me, other than an occasional sideways glance because I was walking so slowly.

It was like an out-of-body experience to be walking around all alone in the country of my birth, among Russian people. It was such a strange feeling! I felt disconnected from America and my family. Lonely and lost, and yet, I felt a connection with the people around me that I can't describe.

I heard music and stopped to listen to the street musicians. I dropped a BIC lighter and a dollar bill into their hat, and saw their eyes get big when they saw what I had done. I moved on, smiling to myself.

I wandered around until I got tired. Then I sat down on a bench and watched the people go by. Other than a few ladies wearing "babushkas" on their heads, the people looked pretty much like Americans. I felt very comfortable just sitting there, but I decided I had better start back before I wandered off too far and lost my way.

I noticed that many people were carrying bouquets of flowers. I also saw several flower vendors on the street. On the way back to the subway entrance, I stopped at a flower stand and asked the lady how much the flowers cost. She asked, "What can you pay?"

I gave her one dollar, and before I could give her more, she quickly took the money, and started to hand me flowers. I think she would have given me most of her bucket of daffodils, but I told her that all I wanted were a few stems.

I continued walking and was relieved when I found the right subway entrance, and was able to figure out which train to take back to the ship.

Now, when I look back on that little adventure, I am amazed that I was so brave. I was also careless. I had forgotten to write down the name of our cruise ship. The only identification I had on me was my passport and visa. If anything would have happened to me, and I couldn't talk, no one would have known where my home base was in Russia.

When I got back on the subway, I sat down next to another old lady. Again, I introduced myself and asked her about life in Russia. The answer was the total opposite from the previous old lady. She said, "Life is good. We have our basic needs. We have our *Dacha* and a little piece of land outside the city, which is available to everyone who lives in the apartments. We grow our own vegetables, and preserve them for the winter. I sew all of our clothes, so we are doing just fine."

When I got off at my stop, I shook my head and thought, it's the same in every country; life is hard or easy, depending on your state of mind.

I got back on board the ship in time for lunch. All of our lunches and dinners during the entire trip consisted mostly of potatoes, cabbage, carrots, a little bit of meat or fish, and bread. But there was plenty of food, and we didn't mind, because we knew that they were giving us the best they had.

In the afternoon, Leon took us on another tour of St. Petersburg. This time, we got to see not only part of the city, but also the Palace and the Museum. Both were full of treasures and marvelous things. The city was lovely. No wonder they call it the Venice of Russia. There were canals throughout the city, and the buildings were beautiful with interesting architecture, but many of them needed paint and repair. I enjoyed the guided tour, and wished that we could spend more time in St. Petersburg. But I was also anxious to see more of Russia.

We got back in time for dinner and our nightly entertainment, which was a musical performed by the ship's staff. It was fun and we got to know the crew better. Later that night we strolled along the Volga River, and were amazed that it looked like it was high noon instead of 11 o'clock at night. Now we understood what is meant by "White Nights".

The ship was much smaller than any of the cruise ships we had been on before. I'm guessing there were about a hundred passengers, plus the crew. On the first seven days of our voyage, the passengers were all professional people such as lawyers, doctors, and teachers. Everyone was very friendly and curious about the Americans, because most of them had only seen Americans on TV. The ship had a television and they showed American soap operas. The Russians loved the soap, "Santa Barbara." They were disappointed when I told them that the majority of Americans did not live that kind of life.

Our interpreter, Leon, was a Russian professor who taught English at the Russian University, and spoke very proper English. The Kansas couple, and Ron and I, went on excursions every day and Leon accompanied us. We also had a local guide at every stop. Most of them spoke pretty good English, but they had a problem pronouncing the words, because they had never talked to any Americans. They had learned English from a book.

For instance, the guide in Novgorod kept saying, "There were many beers in this park many years ago." Ron kept nodding like he understood, but I did not understand, and actually neither did he. So, I finally asked her to explain "beers." What she meant to say was "bears." She was very appreciative when I told her how to pronounce the word, and she asked me to correct her if she mispronounced any other words.

After a day of sightseeing and dinner, we always went downstairs to the bar where we got to know a lot of the passengers, especially five Russian women. There was a judge, a lawyer, a business executive, a teacher, and a nurse. They took turns dancing the swing with my husband. The band onboard was very good and played mostly American dance music. I had many conversations with the women. I tried to answer as many of their questions about America as I could, and they told me about their lives in Russia.

I told them, "Our life in America is very good. Yes, when we arrived in America, my parents and I worked hard for many years. We lived frugally and saved our money, but we always had enough food, and what we needed. Now we own our home, have most of what we want, and the freedom to do whatever we want."

They told me that under communist rule, professional people, such as doctors, were not paid any more than laborers. Everybody was supposed to be treated equally. The outcome was that people did not work hard, because there were no incentives and everybody got paid just the same. There was a lot of corruption at the top, and many communist officials got wealthy. Many things were mismanaged and so the Russian economic system fell apart. That is why there is such a shortage of food and everything else. Now, even though Russians are supposedly no longer communists, it is hard for people to change their ways, and it will take a long time before things improve. But they were hopeful that in the end, things will be better.

Our interpreter Leon was very upfront with us and told us everything we wanted to know. He pretty much told us the same things as the ladies. He also said, "Healthcare is free, but very bad. There are not enough doctors and nurses to take care of all the sick people. Hospitals are overcrowded and unsanitary. For instance, the bathrooms are filthy, because nobody wants to clean them. Families have to bring in all the necessary items such as linens and soap for the patients, and stay with them to make sure that they are taken care of. I know this, because my wife was in the hospital recently, and I saw just how bad the conditions really are."

One evening when we were downstairs in the bar, Nadia, one of the ladies that I got to know pretty well, did not show up. The next evening, I asked her, "What happened to you? "

She said, "I spent the night with a man." I was surprised. I had not seen her with a man.

So, I asked something like, "Who . . . what . . . why did you do that?"

She said, "He had fish."

I didn't think that I had heard right, so I asked, "He had what?"

She repeated, "He had fish." She said it in a very matter-of-fact way, like, "Doesn't every woman sleep with a man who gives her fish?"

I looked at the other women, but they just sat there nonchalant. I opened my mouth, but didn't know what to say. So, I closed my mouth, stopped staring, didn't ask any more questions, and quickly changed the subject.

The next day, Nadia gave me a nice-sized perch, all dry and well preserved. I thanked her, but I didn't know what to do with it, so I just wrapped it up, and put it in the bottom of my suitcase. (Several days later, my sister, Nina, was very happy to get that fish).

I was sorry when the first seven days of our trip ended because we really enjoyed being with the Russian people. They had treated us like celebrities, especially at night when we were with them in the bar.

On the last evening, when we entered the bar, everybody stood up and cheered. They were chanting "Nina, Nina. . ." I was overwhelmed with emotion! I will never forget that evening!

At the end of the first seven-day cruise, one of the Russian couples we met asked us to come to lunch at their home so that their son could practice speaking English he had learned at school. The plan was, they would depart the ship very early in the morning, and we would come to their home after we had finished sightseeing. We were interested in seeing how the Russian people lived, so we agreed.

We found out that they lived in Moscow, in one of the many tall apartment buildings that were all over Russia. They had a two-bedroom apartment, which was very clean and nicely decorated. In that short period of time, they had managed to prepare a full meal of fried chicken, potatoes and vegetables; even though someone had stolen their electric meter while they were on the cruise. Each apartment had its own meter outside the door. They put money in the meter for electricity, as needed. Amazingly, before we arrived, they had obtained another meter and had it installed.

They told us that they had a very good life. They had a small Dacha, with a little piece of land, outside of town. That's where they grew their fruits and vegetables. They showed us how they preserved the vegetables by layering them in gallon-sized, glass jars. The woman was a good seamstress, and she sewed and knitted all of their clothes. The man worked for the city, and the woman was a teacher. We were very impressed with them. They seemed to be a happy family. They only had one son who meant the world to them. I did speak English with him and he asked a lot of questions, which I was happy to answer.

When we got back to the ship, all of the Russian passengers had disembarked, and the next, seven-day passengers had gotten on board ship.

While in Moscow, we saw the Kremlin, Red Square, and the fantastic St. Basil's Cathedral, plus other beautiful churches. We also saw, "Gums," a very upscale shopping mall, where only the wealthy people were allowed to enter the shops. There was a guard at most of the store's entrances, and he decided who was allowed to go inside. After Leon talked to the guards, they let us enter. We saw some expensive electronics, watches and jewelry, and we wondered who could afford to buy them.

Throughout that cruise, we saw many quaint little villages, museums and fortresses. We also saw many beautiful churches and monasteries, which were now open. We wondered how the numerous icons and gold altars had survived communism.

We also got to go through the locks on the Volga River. That was the first time for me. It was very interesting how they raised the ship by filling each lock with water, until the ship reached the upper level of the river.

Our next seven-day itinerary, took us from Moscow to Kazan and back. Again, the couple from Kansas, and we, were the only Americans onboard. All of the other passengers were Russians. The new passengers were louder. Their children were not as well-behaved, and kept coming up to us wanting to talk. The grown-ups were friendly, but most of them were only interested in finding out what work we did in America. We felt that they were evaluating us to see if we could be useful to them. Unlike the first group, these passengers were merchants. The fall of communism had opened the doors to capitalism, and these merchants wanted to do business wherever they could.

The atmosphere aboard the ship was different. We noticed that the waitresses were not as friendly toward the new passengers. Most of the men were pretty heavy drinkers. They would buy a bottle of vodka from the bar, uncork it, and place it in the middle of the table. This meant that everybody had to drink until the bottle was empty. We drank with them, but when they got really rowdy, we went back to our room, in spite of their loud objections. The next morning at breakfast, they all looked like they had never had a drop to drink.

Later, when we were with my family, my niece told me that people hated the merchants. They felt that they were parasites and that they took advantage of people to get rich. This was not the way it was supposed to be. Under communism, the people were told that they were all equal, and everyone should share. But now, there were kiosks on every corner, and the parasites were selling stuff at much higher prices than the government-owned stores. I told my niece, "This is very common in America, because that's what Capitalism is all about. From what I had observed, the reason the kiosks made money, was because the government stores were not open in the evenings, or on weekends. Also, there were only a few government stores, and they were not in handy locations. So, in my opinion, there was nothing wrong with the kiosks making a profit." But she was not convinced. To her, Capitalism was selfish.

Our cruise ended when we arrived back in Moscow. It was hard to say good-by to the crew. They had treated us like royalty and we felt like we had become close friends. We disembarked, and were greeted by our "In-tourist" guide and interpreter. Her name was Olga. She was a pretty, blond, young woman who looked like a teenager. Her father was our driver.

I was excited, and looked forward to meeting my family. I had written to them and told them that we had reservations at the Moscow Hotel. That's where my family was supposed to meet us. But when we got to the hotel, we were told that they did not have any rooms for us. They told us we had to go to the Sputnik Hotel. Olga was very shy, so it was up to me to explain that we were supposed to meet my family at this hotel, and if we left, they would not know where to find us. The woman behind the counter just shrugged her shoulders. But another woman said, "When your family comes, I will direct them to the Sputnik Hotel."

I thanked her and wrote down our names, and my sister's name. That's all we could do, and we hoped for the best.

When we arrived at the modernistic Sputnik Hotel, we were not allowed to go up to our room, because we did not have an "entry stamp" in our passport. The travel company we had gone through was new and inexperienced, and did not know that we needed an entry stamp once we got off the ship.

Olga's father drove us to the nearest police station to get our passports stamped. We stood in line for about an hour. When we finally got to the counter, we were told that the passport department was closed, and we would have to come back the next day. This time I was not brave enough to argue, because of the hostile looks we got from the people behind the counter. Olga explained that we really needed the "entry stamp," because, without it, we could not get into our hotel room. The man just sneered at her and turned away. We probably should have given him a bribe, but we did not know that, and Olga was too young and inexperienced to figure it out.

By the time we got back to the hotel, my sister, Nina, and her daughter, Lena, were waiting for us. We were very happy to see them. Lena told me that they saw my note in the wastebasket at the Moscow Hotel, and that's how they knew where to find us.

Olga told us to leave our passports with her and she would get them stamped the next day. She told Ron and me to go on to my sister's house, and she would meet us back at the hotel in three days.

We had to leave some of our luggage at the hotel because my sister Nina lived outside of Moscow. We had to take a crowded bus, change to a train, and finally walk several blocks to get to her home. Nina lived in a typical, large apartment complex. Her apartment had a living room, a small kitchen, a bathroom, and one bedroom. It was shared by three people: Nina, her husband, Nikolai, and their grown daughter, Lena.

Lena slept in the bedroom, while her parents slept in the living room on a fold-out sofa. Lena gave up her bedroom for us and slept at a friend's house. I felt bad about that, and was glad that we would not be inconveniencing them for more than three days. My other sister, Raya, and my Aunt Froysa (my mother's oldest sister) also came to see us and stayed for three nights. They slept on the floor. It was a very crowded apartment.

That night I could not sleep. I kept thinking about our day. Suddenly, I realized that we had done a very stupid thing. How could we have given up our passports to someone we did not know? We only knew what Olga had told us, and we didn't really know anything about that travel company, other than they were based in St. Petersburg. The longer I thought about it, the worse I felt. What if Olga got into an accident, or lost our passports? Add to this the fact that I had lost all of my other identification papers. So now, with my passport gone, I was in Russia with absolutely no identification papers. I was near panic when I woke Ron. He tried to calm me down by reminding me that he still had his identification papers, and that we had copies of our passports and other documents. His assurance helped a little and it stopped my panic attack, but I could not stop thinking about all the bad things that could happen to us.

Also, the fact that my passport showed that I was born in Russia, added to my anxiety. "What if they won't let me go home to America?" I was sure that I would lose my mind if that happened. The sad part was that my anxiety about the passports kept me from enjoying my visit with my sisters and my Aunt.

My two sisters were very different. Nina became a Christian as soon as communism ended, but Raya was convinced that communism was still the best, even though she lived in a small, one-room house in Ukraine with only one light bulb and no plumbing. She had to get her water from a well in the middle of town. Still, she defended the communist way of life. It was interesting, listening to Nina and Raya argue. Nina pointed out how corrupt the communist system was, and that many of the communist leaders were not living the ideal of "share and share alike,"

L to R: sister Nina, Nina, sister Raya

Raya replied, "They deserve to have better homes and more things, because they have worked hard for our country."

Nina could not convince her otherwise. I just kept quiet because it was obvious that Raya had made up her mind. The other differences between the two sisters were: Nina was a lovely blonde with a kind face and soft voice. Raya had a pretty face, she was heavier, had black hair, red skin from the sun, and calloused hands from hard work. I could tell that Raya did not like me from the minute she saw me. I thought, maybe it's because I was a Capitalist and "too American." Nina later told me, "Raya is mad because your mama left without divorcing our papa, so Papa could not marry our mother, and she is taking it out on you. I know that's crazy, so just don't worry about it."

I was glad that Ron, and Nina's husband Nikolai, got along well. Even though they didn't speak each other's

L to R: Nikolai, Lena, sister Raya, Ron, Froysa, sister Nina

language, they enjoyed being with each other. They had fun drinking beer and playing cards on a little enclosed veranda, away from all the noise of the excited women.

Nina and Froysa

We brought a good amount of money with us, but there was very little to buy in the stores. One store had just a few cans of food on the shelf, and the only items in the cooler were, one fish that was oozing a yellow liquid, and one very yellow-looking chicken. We were told that, whenever there was a rumor that a store was getting any kind of food, such as cabbage or eggs, a line began to form in front of that store, several hours ahead. Most of the time, there was not enough food for everyone who had waited in line.

While we were in the store, I saw a man fall to the floor and have an epileptic seizure. All of the people ignored him and just walked around the man. When I tried to help him, Lena took my arm and told me to leave him alone. She said that people did not touch or help a person who was ill, unless they were nurses or physicians, because they could make the situation worse. Here again is a lesson, when traveling in a foreign country: do as the natives do.

Most of the people we met looked unhappy. One day on the way back from the store, we saw a woman with a basket full of mushrooms. Since my favorite hobby is mushroom-hunting, I thought this would be a good way to connect with the woman, so I asked her if she had picked them. She snapped, "Well, what do you think?" and just walked away.

When we got back to the apartment, Nikolai, who had left early that morning, was back from picking mushrooms. He had a large variety, but I only recognized a couple of the mushrooms. Nina put them all in a pot, boiled them, and then fried them. I wasn't sure if we should eat those mushrooms, but she assured me that they had been eating them for many years and had never gotten sick. I had read in one of my books that boiling the mushrooms before frying took out most of the toxins. So, we went ahead and ate them. I must admit, they were delicious, and we did not get ill.

My family and I talked about many things, but the main theme was how poor they were, and how hard life was for them. I was glad I had brought a whole suitcase full of clothes, material, and other gifts to leave with them. I also gave them most of the money we had brought with us. Still, I wish that we could have given them more because our life in America is so much richer. We had not exchanged many of our dollars for Russian money because we noticed most of the people preferred American dollars.

On a Saturday morning, when we boarded the bus to go into town, the bus driver would not take Lena's Russian money. A woman on the bus gave us the money for the bus fare and Lena gave her a couple of American dollars I had given her.

We were told that the Russian government had announced early that morning, that the old rubles were no longer valid. On the following Monday, the Russian people could exchange up to 30,000 old rubles (about $35) for new rubles. The rest of their old rubles were worthless. The people were very upset about the money situation. There were mobs waiting in front of the banks all weekend. Later, we found out the reason for the money exchange was that inflation had gotten much too high. Also, there was so much counterfeit money in circulation that the old rubles had become worthless.

Our visit was not the joyful reunion that I had hoped for because my family was worried about their money and I was worried about our passports. All of the time I was with my family I was tense and nervous because I kept thinking about our prearranged meeting with Olga. Would she be there? Would we get our passports back? Later I was glad that we had taken many pictures and recorded a video. Otherwise, my visit with my family would have mostly been a blur.

Finally, the day arrived, and we got back to the hotel at the appointed time.

However, Olga was not there!

I could feel the panic coming on again, but I tried to stay calm. I told the woman behind the counter our name, and asked her, "Did Olga come back with our passports?"

She said, "I do not know Olga".

"Do we have rooms?"

She shrugged and said, "I do not know."

As my panic began to rise, so did my voice. I said, "Let me talk to your supervisor."

"Supervisor don't know."

"Let me call our travel company."

"You have to call St. Petersburg. It will take many hours before calls go through. By then everything is closed. You will have no answer until tomorrow."

(By the way, nobody there spoke English. I had to rely on my somewhat-limited Russian. My sister, Nina, and my niece, Lena, were too intimidated to argue with the hotel woman).

I asked, "But, where are we going to sleep?"

Same answer, "I do not know." And obviously, she did not care.

Now, I'd had enough!

I yelled, "Listen to me. Somebody paid our hotel bill. You give me the name and telephone number of that person. Right Now."

Reluctantly, she gave me a name and a phone number, and pointed to a telephone on the wall. My fingers were shaking, as I dialed the number. I was glad when a man answered. I gave him my name, and asked, "Do you know a woman named Olga?"

He said, "Yes." What a relief! My knees almost buckled!

I said, "But, where is she? She was supposed to meet us at 3 o'clock, and she is not here. She has our passports, and nobody here at the hotel knows her. I have been very worried about our passports. Besides that, they won't let us into our rooms."

The man said, "Olga got held up. She is helping other people with their passports, and she will meet you tomorrow morning."

I said, "Oh, NO! I want her here, NOW! I want our passports, NOW! I have been worried about losing our passports for three days, and I don't want to wait until tomorrow morning."

He said, "If you want her to come this evening, it will cost you $20."

"Fine. I don't care. Just make sure she comes here this evening. But, what about our room? How can we get in? "

He said, "Let me talk to the woman at the desk."

When the woman got off the phone, she handed me the key, and told us that we could go up to our room.

We were all very relieved.

Our room was nice. It had a big, comfortable bed, a small table, two chairs, a wardrobe, and an adjoining bathroom with a shower. The only thing odd was, instead of a roll of toilet paper, there was a stack of very slick, onion-skin paper squares. (We had to learn the art of wiping again).

Shortly after we got unpacked, we had a surprise.

There was a knock on the door. When we opened it, three of my cousins from Ukraine, were standing there. I was amazed that they had found us. They said they had been waiting for us in Moscow for two days. I was so glad to see them, but I felt bad that they had come all the way from Ukraine, and we only had a short time to visit. There was a large area just outside our room, with a big table and plenty of chairs. We managed to get some food and drink and had a very nice visit. They told us that they were glad we were meeting at the hotel because they would be embarrassed for us to see their homes.

One of my cousins said, "We live in a small village and our homes are old and very small. We have no running water and have to use an outhouse."

I told them, "Don't be embarrassed about that, because that's how I had lived in Germany. Your homes would be fine and we hope that someday we can come to you for a visit."

Olga arrived after ten o'clock that evening. I was very relieved to see her, I gave her the $20, and she gave us our passports. She still did not have the required stamps. We were leaving the country the next afternoon, so I couldn't understand why we still needed that stamp. She said, "You will need it at the airport."

The next morning Olga took us to a private residence, where we paid a woman to type up a statement. We were told to present that statement at the airport, along with our visas and passports, and there would be no problem. I hoped that she was right because I was anxious to get out of Russia. When we got to the airport, the man at the customs counter just glanced at the statement and our visas, then he tore them up, threw them away and let us pass through. I could not believe that we had gone through all of that trouble for nothing. All that fuss and worry about a stamp that, in the end, nobody cared about. The people in charge did not care; they seemed very disorganized. It was obvious, they didn't know what they were doing.

While we were standing in line, I overheard two young men behind the counter talking in Russian. It sounded like they were looking for an American sugar mama. One of the men pointed at me and said to the other, "Hey look at her, she is a good one."

The other man said, "Yes, she looks good, but I like them thinner. She is too fat for me."

I couldn't believe what I was hearing. I was standing right in front of them. Apparently, they thought that I couldn't understand them. I wanted to call them all kinds of nasty names, but I didn't know any cuss words in Russian, so I just looked away, shaking my head. Later I thought, "I should have at least let them know that I understood them, and told them that they were acting like little boys, and should be ashamed of themselves."

Another, similar incident happened about ten days earlier.

We had just visited a very old ornate church that was built entirely without nails. On our way back to the ship, we saw a group of rowdy American tourists coming up the hill. As they were passing us, one of the women saw my sweatshirt, which had a San Francisco logo in front. The woman laughed shrilly and very loudly said, "Look at that Russian, wearing a San Francisco sweatshirt, I bet she has no idea where San Francisco is, and has never been there." The others all laughed in agreement. I was speechless. I couldn't believe that the stupid woman was saying such a thing, without knowing anything about me. She just assumed that I was Russian. I should have told her what a fool she was, but what good would that do? She was proving it by just opening her mouth. She was a perfect example of an "ugly American abroad".

We were relieved that we had passed all of the checkpoints at the airport. We would be boarding Lufthansa, a German plane, and soon be on our way back home.

But our adventure was not over yet. When we entered the waiting area, we saw a room full of Americans in a very agitated state. One of the ladies told us that they were supposed to get back to their cruise ship early that morning, but the Russian airplane, Aeroflot, had a mechanical problem, and nobody would tell them when it would be fixed. They had been waiting for many hours. They could not leave the airport because their visas had been destroyed when they checked in. They were worried about how they would meet up with their cruise ship. I could understand their frustration and felt sorry for them.

I told her, "Well, we are flying out on Lufthansa, not Aeroflot, so I don't think that we will have any delays."

She said, "Don't be too sure."

Our plane arrived on time. However, shortly after that, we saw smoke pouring out of our airplane. I could not believe what I was seeing. Now what?

The American woman said, "Told you so."

We spent many anxious minutes wondering what would happen to us. But before long, we were told that there was a problem with the air-conditioning unit and that we would be delayed for a couple of hours. Once we knew what the problem was, we relaxed. The plane was fixed in less than two hours and we were on our way. The other Americans were still waiting and they still did not know when the Aeroflot plane would be repaired.

We were surprised to find many Russian people on our flight who were immigrating to America. Most of them had families in America and the Russian government had allowed them to leave Russia. They were all very excited. They had a lot of questions and concerns, but I assured them that everything would be wonderful in America.

There was also an American businessman on our flight whom we talked to. He told us that he had come to Russia to open a mining business, but changed his mind. He said, "The Russians are so ignorant about business, and their equipment is so old and dilapidated, that I decided against doing business with them." We were not surprised.

When we arrived in Frankfurt, we found out that we had missed our connecting flight. However, Lufthansa put us up in a very comfortable hotel room at the airport. The next morning, we saw a very generous breakfast buffet. There was bacon and sausage, eggs any style, all kinds of fruit, waffles and pancakes, and on and on. We could not believe what we were seeing. After 18 days of sparse Russian food, all this wonderful food in front of us looked like a great feast. We enjoyed that breakfast very much!

Shortly after, we boarded a direct flight to Portland, Oregon. We had a comfortable and uneventful flight.

On our many excursions from the ship, I bought several souvenirs, Marushka dolls, lacquered boxes, decorated eggs, and a *Samovar* (a Russian tea maker). I also bought a small, gilded icon of the mother Mary and baby Jesus at one of the churches we visited.

Years later, when our good friend Anna Frank was dying, I went to visit her to say goodbye, and to tell her how grateful we were for finding a sponsor for us, which allowed us to come to America. To show my gratitude I gave her the icon of Mary and Jesus. She was so happy to know that it came from a Russian church. At Anna's funeral, her daughter told me, "Our Mom held onto the icon after you left, and would not let it go. She asked to be buried with that icon in her hands."

I was happy to know that I had given Anna something meaningful. She had done so much for us. Without her help, we may never have been able to immigrate to America.

I am glad that we visited Russia and my family. My curiosity was satisfied. And my longing, to see the country of my birth is gone.

I returned with a renewed appreciation for America. We have so much more, not only material things, but freedoms and possibilities.

Our Declaration of Independence states that all men are created equal and that we have a fundamental right to life, liberty, and the pursuit of happiness. We have the right to live life in a way that makes us happy as long as we don't do anything illegal or violate the rights of others.

But we need to remember that all people are created equal, and have the same rights. We must not take those rights and our freedom for granted. We should ask ourselves what we can do to help keep our country peaceful and comfortable.

I am so very grateful that America is my home. All of my travel proved to me just how special America is, and reminded me that I do not want to live anywhere else in the world.

Flashbacks, 2016

A while back, I was watching "Gray's Anatomy," a popular television show. One of the doctors on that show was a veteran of the Iraq war. A patient of his was in the last stages of terminal cancer, and was asking the doctor to help him die.

This caused the doctor to have a flashback: He was back in Iraq. There were very graphic pictures of scattered body parts and burning corpses. A wounded soldier, in great pain, was begging to be killed.

As I was staring at this horrible scene, I noticed a tightening in my chest, and my breathing became labored. Gasping for air, I started sobbing and moaning.

I was having a flashback of my own:

I am back to World War II. The bombs are falling, and I am five years old again. I am holding my Mama's hand and we are running. There is fire and smoke. I see dead and dying people all around me. I hear loud booming noises, and the roar of airplanes. People are screaming and moaning. A man is lying in a pool of blood. His leg is blown off, and he keeps yelling," Somebody, please kill me, please kill me..." I stop and stare at him until Mama pulls me away.

The scene fades, slowly my sobbing stops. I take deep breaths and start yawning.

I was not surprised that I reacted so strongly to that bombing scene on television. All my life, I have not been able to watch war movies. To me, there is nothing entertaining about them. They are the worst kind of horror movies. The revulsion to war is, and will always be part of me.

Sometimes I wonder how all of the horrors I experienced have affected my life? How different would I be had I not lived through the war? Of course, I'll never know.

I do know how very grateful I am for all the blessings I have now—I not only sympathize, but empathize with people who are living in war zones, and I cry for them.

And this I know for sure; *War is the greatest evil of all.* It is a license to mass murder innocent people. *We must find other ways to resolve conflict*!

Acknowledgements

I have many people to thank: Beginning with my grandson, Matt Carmichael, who started it all by asking me to tell my story. My husband, Ron, who patiently read my drafts and kept encouraging me to continue. My three sons, Barry, Brian, and Donny Carmichael, who read the first draft and gave me permission to, "Tell it all the way it was."

A big thank you to my dear friend Marilyn Cady, who encouraged me to write down my feelings about losing my son David, which helped me heal.

Thank you to all of the people in my writing group, especially Ruth McWayne, who was the first to edit my book, and Bonnie Stere, who told me that she was a big fan of mine. Also, Dick Lewis, Lana Schindler, David DeLapp, Bob Williams, Herb and Sachiko Bastuscheck, Larry Crompton, and Robin Humelbaugh. They all listened patiently as I practiced writing my stories, and then, reading them again and again. They made helpful suggestions, and in the end, encouraged me to publish my memoir.

Recently I joined another Writing Group, and those members helped me 'polish' my writing. I am grateful to, Doug Sweet, Don Robinson, Leane Cornwell, Suzanne Watson, Deborah Kassmeier, and the rest of the group.

Cretia Benolken, Cynthia Wilcox, Ron Parker, Jane Hansen, Tom and Norma Mack, and Lillian Halseth Taylor have read and edited my drafts, and encouraged me to keep writing. Pamela Parker, deleted about a thousand unnecessary commas.

Jean Moule, who read the 'almost finished story' and encouraged me to publish it.

Thank you, Vito Pileggi and Carol Dunlap, for editing, and giving me the courage to submit my book to publisher

Hinrich Muller. Thank You to Carole Kelsch and Bonnie Stere for editing the final proof.

My special Thank You, goes to Michael Miller, Director and Bibliographer for the *Germans from Russia Heritage Collection*, for giving me permission to use material from that Collection. Reading the stories of *The Long Trek*, and about the horrors that went on in the town of Litzmannstadt, Poland, a ghetto and people sorting place, was illuminating. I was too young at that time to fully understand the world around me, and too traumatized to remember all that happened. I learned a lot from reading the stories in the Russian Heritage Collection.

I am very grateful to *all* of my family and friends who have helped and encouraged me along the way. Without them my story would never have been written.

Epilogue

Now I realize that the old feelings and fears can no longer hurt me.

Writing my memoir was one of the most difficult things I have ever done, but it is also one of the most rewarding. I learned so much about myself. Writing brought the buried feelings of pain, fear, guilt, and insecurities to the surface and let me examine them.

During the last ten years as I wrote my story, I hurt and cried, but kept on writing. I have mourned and agonized over the death of my son, and I know that I will continue to mourn his death for the rest of my life. But now I can talk about him, most of the time, without crying. I also know that in between my tears there is laughter.

As I embraced the little girl I used to be, frightened and unloved, in a world gone mad, I began to feel less sad and the heavy burden of guilt became lighter. I felt guilty because of the mistakes I made in my life, especially while raising my children. As I wrote, I started to accept that I had done the best I could, considering the circumstances of my life, and the knowledge that I had at the time.

I have realized that, although my ex-husband Don, was not the right life partner for me, he was the man I needed in the beginning. He made me feel loved and valued. He also helped me to transform myself from a young and insecure teenager into a confident woman. Don died in 2013. Now when I think of him, I choose to remember the good times we had during our 24+year marriage.

Writing has also changed me in other ways. I have become a more compassionate and generous person. There was a time when I listened to people complain about minor problems, and I thought, "You really have nothing to complain about." Now, I am aware that everyone has problems and pain, big or small, those problems are real to them and worthy of compassion.

As most of my sadness and guilt left me, so did my depression. It was replaced with positive feelings. Now my days are filled with gratitude, in spite of my abused and deteriorating old body there are still many blessings.

I had a wonderful 80th birthday, surrounded by my loving family. There were many gifts. Also, a dozen roses from Ron, and Rick Cady (Marilyn's husband). Plus, two men wrote poems just for me. I thought the days of poems and roses were long gone, but amazingly just for a little, the years disappeared and I was young again.

I am experiencing a new feeling once in a while. Can that feeling be joy? It comes unbidden, while I am in the pool exercising, watching the river flow by, or looking around our cozy cabin full of items that bring back lovely memories.

I am thankful that I was able to overcome the adversities in my life, but I know that I did not do it alone. Call it God, Guardian Angels, or a Greater Power. Someone walked with me and helped me to survive bombs, hunger, hate, sorrow, death, and cancer. That Power helped, and saved me, time and time again.

My American dream turned out to be so much more than I ever thought it could be. I am a happy woman.

Our Stayton Writing Group (aka, *Marilyn's Writing Group*) monitor, Dick Lewis—a gifted poet, wrote the following poem for my 80th Birthday surprise party:

Shashka
(A Russian Sword)
02/05/2018

I sing a song of happiness
I sing a song of praise
Nina's birthday
Twenty-Nine Thousand
Two Hundred days

Eighty years beyond
Born in the fertile fields of the Ukraine
Like metal from the earth
Forged through ravages of war
And Hammered on the Anvil of Hunger

Tempered by hardships
Only those that endured them can know
Honed by inner strength
Tempered by generosity and kindness
Of those brought into her life

Stature has become her pommel
Elegance her haft
Intelligence and laughter
Compose her blade

A strong elegance sword
Polished by the seasons of life.

Dick Lewis

ADDENDUM

Mama's Recipes

Following are four of my mama's recipes that the family love. She made a very simple version of these recipes while we lived in Germany because most of the time we could not afford to buy meat, cheese, and butter. However, after we came to America and could afford to buy those foods, Mama made these dishes, with the following ingredients, whenever she felt like it. Mama was a great cook, but all of her recipes were in her head. She never wrote them down. Sometimes I helped her cook, and saw how she made these foods, but she never used measuring cups or spoons, so I never learned the exact amounts.

After Mama died, I improvised and kept trying, until I got the food to taste as close to Mama's as I could. My recipes are also approximate, I add or subtract the ingredients as I cook. I also often substitute items with what I have on hand, like Mama did.

Perishky

Filling
1 1/2 lb. Hamburger meat (lean)
1 lb. Pork sausage (Jimmy Dean)
Fry both in large fry pan, and set aside in bowl
1 large Onion   Chop fine and sauté
1 – 2 teaspoons Garlic
1/2 quart Sauerkraut   Rinse and drain
Salt & Pepper (to taste)
Add all above ingredients together and cook for 5 to 10 minutes
2 large Eggs   Beat, add to mixture after it's cooled down

Dough
Keep all ingredients warm.
Mama did everything by hand. She dissolved yeast in a small amount of warm water with some sugar – let it stand 5 to 10 minutes – beat the eggs. Then combined all ingredients listed below. She kneaded the dough thoroughly – let it rise in a warm area – and kneaded it again, adding more flour, as needed.

Bread Machine style
2 large Eggs   Beat well
7 oz. Milk   warm
2 teaspoons Sugar   1 teaspoon Salt
Mix all above ingredients together, and put into Bread Machine
3 1/2 cups Flour – packed   Add to Bread Machine
4 tablespoons Butter   Put in corners of Bread Machine.
2 pkg. Yeast   Put in middle of Bread Machine (not into liquid)
Program machine for dough and start. After final beep, (make sure dough has risen, if not, put in warm oven to rise) remove dough.
Place risen dough on floured board, and knead. Add flour as needed, until no longer sticky.
Divide dough in two. Form into two long rolls, about 2″ thick. Cut each roll into about 15 pieces, about 1/2″ thick. Form into round balls and flatten. On floured board roll out each piece into large pancake rounds.
Place 1+ large tablespoon of **Filling** in middle of each round. Wet the ends, pinch closed, and mold into oblong pockets. Place pinched side down on two large, buttered cookie sheets. Brush with melted butter. Let rise in pre-warmed oven 20 to 30 minutes.
Bake at 375 degrees for 25 minutes, or in convection oven 325 degrees for 30 minutes, until golden brown (rotate cookie sheets half way through).
After baked, brush Perishky with melted butter, top and bottom
Yields about 30 Perishky. Serve with Sour Cream.
(Other Filling Option: Potatoes, mashed with sour cream, sautéed chopped onions, and grated cheese)

Holuptsi (Cabbage Rolls)

FILLING
2 LB. HAMBURGER MEAT (lean)
1 LB. PORK SAUSAGE (Jimmy Dean).
Fry both in large fry pan until done. Remove and set aside in bowl.
In the same fry pan mix in the following:
1 LARGE ONION   Chop fine and sauté
1 TABLESPOON GARLIC
1 1/2 – 2 CUPS COOKED RICE
1 – 8OZ. CAN TOMATO SAUCE
SALT & PEPPER (to taste)
1 TEASPOON DILL
3 BAY LEAVES (crushed)
Sauté all above ingredients. Add back Hamburger mix to fry pan and
continue to sauté for 5 more minutes.
2 LARGE EGGS   Beat; add after above ingredients cool down

CABBAGE PREPARATION
2 LARGE HEADS OF CABBAGE   Remove the core and torn
leaves. Place one head at a time, core side down, into large pot of 4
cups of boiling water. Parboil cabbage about 5 minutes.
As cabbage is boiling, keep removing outer leaves, with wooden
spoon (careful not to tear), and place in colander. Pare down thick
part of leaves at core end.
In Heavy Roaster, place: **4 CARROTS, 2 RIBS CELERY**, and the
small **LEFTOVER CABBAGE LEAVES.**
Fill leaves with **1 – 2 TABLESPOONS FILLING**. Then, starting at
core end, roll up while tucking sides in, until roll is firm. Place rolls
close together in roaster on top of carrots and celery.
Add **1 CUP BEEF BROTH** (or **ONE 8 OZ. CAN OF TOMATO
SAUCE**). Pour on top of cabbage.
Spray tops of cabbage rolls with oil. Cover Roaster.
Bake at 325 degrees for approx. 1 hour.
Remove cabbage rolls and place in large casserole dish.
Cook down the remaining sauce, and pour on top of cabbage rolls.

Boiled Varenyky – Filled Pasta Pockets

Dough
3 cups Flour
1 Potato   boiled and mashed
1 cup Milk   (approximately)
Salt & Pepper (to taste)
2 tablespoons Butter (melted)
Combine above ingredients. Knead until smooth and elastic, and no longer sticky. Add more flour if needed. Form into ball, cover with bowl and let rest for 10 minutes. Roll out on floured board until thin. Cut into 3″ circles. (Use lg. water glass). Fill each circle with **1–2 tablespoons Filling**. Fold, and pinch together tightly.

Cheese filling
Mix together:
1 lb. dry Cottage Cheese   (drain well)
1 egg (beaten)
Salt and Sugar
Sour Cream   or cream cheese
Drop filled Varenyky into a large pot of boiling, salted water. (Don't crowd). Stir. Continue to stir occasionally while boiling. After Varenyky rise to the top, cook for 5 more minutes.
Remove to colander, let drain. Place in large bowl, gently stir in **1/2 cube (or more) melted butter**, and large dollop of **Sour Cream**, or **Sautéed Onions**.
Serve with additional Sour Cream.

Optional Fillings:
Potato filling
8 or 9 cooked Potatoes. Mash with **Butter, Sour Cream, and 1/2 lb. of American Cheese, Salt & Pepper, 1 Chopped Onion** (browned in butter).
Fruit filling
Fresh **Cherries** (pitted) or **other Fresh Fruit.** Sprinkle with **Sugar.** Add **Cornstarch** (if fruit is juicy).

Red Cabbage – Sweet and Sour

1 LG. HEAD RED CABBAGE   Cut into quarters.
Remove damaged cabbage leaves. Remove core. Slice cabbage into thin, short strips.

SAUTÉ IN LARGE, COVERED FRY PAN:
5 TABLESPOONS BUTTER (OR BACON FAT)
1 LG. ONION (chopped fine)
1 TEASPOON. GARLIC
1/4 + CUP APPLE– OR WINE VINEGAR
2 BAY LEAVES (crushed)
1/2 TEASPOON DILL
1 – 2 TABLESPOONS SUGAR, plus
2 TABLESPOONS of **JELLY OR JAM**
SALT & PEPPER (to taste)
1 LG. GREEN APPLE (cored and chopped)
Add part of sliced cabbage to mixture, and continue adding as mixture shrinks.
Slow cook (stir often), about 1 hour.
NOTE: Add more or less vinegar, or sugar, as preferred. Vinegar keeps cabbage from turning dark when cooked.
Cabbage tastes great reheated.

About the Author

Nina Carmichael Treece was born in Ukraine. She escaped with her mother and Stepfather during World War II.

She started school in Poland, and continued her education in Germany, where she lived for over nine years.

As a "Displaced Person" living in Germany, her options were very limited.

She came to America in 1954 and worked as a domestic for her sponsors. She became a nurse's aide at St. Vincent's hospital, where she met her first husband, Don Carmichael. By the time she was 25 years old, she had given birth to four sons.

She was a successful Real Estate Broker for over 35 years, and wrote her memoir after retiring.

Now, Nina lives happily with her second husband, Ron Treece, in a cabin they built by the Santiam River in Oregon.

Made in the USA
Monee, IL
19 January 2020